History is the depository of great actions,
the witness of what is past,
the example and instructor of the present,
and the monitor to the future.

—Miguel de Cervantes

Gasparilla, Pirate Genius

Gasparilla, Pirate Genius

James F. Kaserman

Pirate Publishing International

Manufactured in the United States of America
Library of Congress Catalog Card Number: 99-75882
ISBN: 0-9674081-0-5
Book design and production by Tabby House
Cover design: Pearl and Associates

Gasparilla Sarsaparilla is a trademarked product of
Pirate Publishing International.

Pirate Publishing International
6323 St. Andrews Circle
Fort Myers, FL 33919-1719

Acknowledgments

I would like to thank and acknowledge the many people who have contributed to the quality and direction of this book. The book took two years to complete and would not have been possible without the help of the following people, and many others to whom I apologize for not naming.

Shirley Albers, Renee Schmitt, my two sons, Jim and Rick, for reading the original chapter manuscripts critically and making the many positive suggestions to make the book better and consistent with actual historical events. Your thoughtful comments and insights caused me to dig deeper into my characters and actions and improve the book as a result.

To all my dear friends whom I have known and loved over the past fifty-seven years, especially Betsy, Robert, Shari, Barb, Karen, Susan, and others with whom I have been honored to work and who gave life and insight to many of the characters in this novel.

To the many librarians, charter boat captains, local historians, and others in Charlotte, Collier, Dade, Hillsborough, Lee, Manatee, and Monroe counties in Florida, who provided me with many versions of the stories of Gasparilla and other pirates, and who gave me obscure paperwork on the local histories of pirates, wreckers, and their relationship to Gasparilla. I appreciate their diligence in answering my many questions as well as volunteering additional information to make this book possible.

To those Internet Web sites, both domestic as well as international, and those representatives who responded via E-mail in obtaining the critical historical information used in many parts of this book.

A special thanks to my wife, Sarah Jane, who supported and encouraged me to write and finish this novel, and who also patiently corrected the many grammatical errors evident in the original draft. She has been a true editor and "will always be the star on my Christmas tree."

To my parents, brother, and our families for their support and encouragement of my efforts. No one could be blessed with a better family.

I would like to especially acknowledge my grandsons, James Hunter and Reed Samuel, who were the inspiration to finally sit down and write the adult historical novel that has been in my head the past twenty years. Recognizing one's own mortality can become a great motivator.

Contents

Introduction

"Genius is timeless. If we would only take the time to understand the past we could better understand our present and our future."
—José Gaspar, alias Gasparilla, December 1817

Pirates fulfilled a fantasy prohibited to the rest of us. They lived freely, took what they wanted, and feared no man. Pirates were a part of some of the only true democracies known to man.

The history of piracy dates back thousands of years before the birth of Jesus Christ, as noted in many historical and literary documents. The history of mankind has been used to either chronicle or destroy evidence of man's attempt to rise above the human frailties of the corruption of government, man's inhumanity to mankind, and the seeking of power, sex, fame and fortune at the expense of others. Such may have been the circumstance with the story of Gasparilla, the pirate genius. José Gaspar, also known as Gasparilla, is a fictional character who represents one of the most tragic pirate leaders of the last decades of pirate supremacy in the waters of the Gulf of Mexico.

History has recorded the seizure of Julius Caesar with his eventual release after payment. The literature points out that Caesar later pursued and captured these pirates from the north coast of Africa. However, a precedent was established and the capture of prisoners to be held for valuable ransom or the unlawful seizure of goods or money was a primary source of income for the pirate, a custom that is true to this day.

The Vikings captured and plundered the ships of both France and England. The Barbary pirates were the scourge of the Mediterranean Sea. Abraham Lincoln, later to become president of the United States, was a victim of river pirates.

The very act of piracy caused the construction and design of ships to be improved. Piracy directly altered many tactics utilized by mariners, which in turn changed the course of history. Additionally, the pirates and privateers employed by warring nations forever altered the makeup and context of the world in which we live.

Spain's utilization of more pirates, privateers, and buccaneers than any other nation in the history of the world conjured up fear and hatred for that country in other countries and lands.

For more than three hundred years, Spain persecuted, looted, and attacked almost every country or territory it explored or in which it established colonies. In addition to taking the resources, the Spanish either enslaved the native population or brought in outside slaves to plunder or work in these lands in order to take treasure or goods of great value back to Spain. To transport the treasures from what was referred to as the Spanish Main back to Spain, the enlistment of illiterate and unscrupulous individuals, in many instances felons, to the Spanish enlisted navy corps was common. An intelligent and capable cadre of commissioned naval officers was often offset by the poor quality of regular sailors in the Spanish Navy.

Governments of the eighteenth century often reduced the size of their navies to save tax monies. When discharged, the common sailors became pirates and privateers rather than returning to poor neighborhoods at home. The smaller navies of these nations actually gave greater freedom to the pirates to plunder and steal from all countries trading in the region.

It comes as no surprise in our fictional story that the corrupt Spanish monarchy accused Adm. José Gaspar, a young Spanish naval hero, of theft and caused the tragic loss of his beloved mother, wife, and daughter. José Gaspar, in exile, was forced to turn his efforts to developing an empire based upon a true democracy, including rules and discipline, meanwhile gaining wealth for all in the enterprise. Gaspar, then calling himself Gasparilla, chose a Confederation form of government that became more successful, in providing for its members, than other traditional forms of governments of the period. The Confederation I have described is based on accounts of pirate governments established by strict codes and rules.

As you read this book, please enjoy the historical depiction of Gasparilla, the man who wanted to be a pirate king but who also accepted the need for democracy. I also hope you derive from his genius that which may enhance your understanding of life during any age.

As Gasparilla once said, "All the genius you might have lies in this statement: When you have a worthy subject at hand, study it profoundly."

In writing this novel, it has been difficult to find a great amount of written documentation. It would be fair to say that written accounts of the early history of Florida are sparse. Pirates did not employ historians nor want to record written histories of their adventures in a diary or ship's log for fear these could be used against them in trials. During the peak of piracy, Florida was a haven for immigrants, runaway slaves, Indians, and others who might not be literate. Therefore I have been forced to rely upon a combination of stories and myths, knowing that storytellers are not famous for their reliance upon facts.

I have contemplated and theorized on the events and occurrences that form the history of *Gasparilla: Pirate Genius*. I have tried to be accurate in my incorporation of historic events, and other matters of fact that provide the backdrop for the fictional Gasparilla's adventures. Gasparilla's fleet would have shared the seas with slave ships, mercantile ships, battleships from several nations, other pirates, privateers and buccaneers. The times are rough: murders are savage; sex can be raw; revenge vicious, and treatment of women, crude. And yet, even among pirates, there is a code of honor, a measure of gallantry, and the love of a beautiful woman.

So, enjoy the exotic excursion, but take from it some of the profound thinking of Gasparilla, the pirate genius. Genius is timeless. And remember that there is always some pirate in all of us.

JAMES F. KASERMAN

CHAPTER 1

End of The Dream

"If you want your dreams to come true don't age, don't let greed consume you, and never compromise your youthful beliefs!"
—José Gaspar, alias Gasparilla, November 4, 1821

Sixty-five years old, Gasparilla, the pirate, also known as José Gaspar—a victim of the idealistic democratic process that he had insisted upon when he initially organized the Confederation or Brotherhood of Pirates in September 1784—undertook what would be his last voyage.

November 4th in 1821 was an unusually hot day that dulled the senses of Gasparilla and his fellow pirates, the remnants of what had once been a magnificent example of democracy. The sweat dripped off their bodies with their frenzied activity as the heavy blanket of humidity pressed down unrelentingly upon them.

The preceding days had seen Gasparilla urging the older and most trusted Confederation brothers and their families onto the sleek, and well-maintained, two-masted schooners that had been designed and built in Mystic, Connecticut.

The recent sale of Florida to the youthful United States of America, the increased American naval presence harassing the Confederation's ships, Gen. Andrew Jackson's eight years of attacks on the friendly Indian allies throughout Florida, and the loss of corrupt merchant outlets in Havana and New Orleans had influenced the Confederation's decision to leave Florida and move the entire enterprise to Venezuela. Gasparilla, himself, intended to retire as a gentleman after establishing a new viable colony there for his younger pirate brothers.

The few who remained on Gasparilla Island were an assorted group—youthful and inexperienced new recruits and Gasparilla, with a few of his old and trusted friends. They remained only to dig up the last of the buried treasures and load them on the creaky old flagship of Gaspar's pirate navy, the *Doña Rosalita*, the former Spanish naval ship, *Florida Blanca*. The men had been laboring for four days in the sweltering subtropical heat to unearth caches of treasure that so far amounted to more than seventeen million dollars. The sheer weight of the eleven million dollars of silver and gold already on board had the *Doña Rosalita* riding exceptionally low in the water. Additionally, more than six million dollars had been brought to the dock but could not be loaded on the overweight ship. Gasparilla had determined that all remaining treasure buried throughout the many small islands surrounding Gasparilla Island would be left and reclaimed the following summer. To hide the treasure left on the dock, Gaspar ordered twenty of his men to dig a long slit-trench near the northeast end of the island beneath a row of coconut palms that the Brothers of the Confederacy had planted eight years earlier. Into this trench were carefully being deposited twenty-three casks and chests containing the six million dollars in the form of pieces of eight, Mexican jewelry, and gold. They had carved extensive markings into both the palms and the nearby hardwoods, which were then referenced to the map that Gasparilla had drawn for the following year's recovery expedition. Gasparilla, with a smile on his bearded and sweat-streaked face, now carefully folded this treasure map and placed it in a tattered pouch next to the soiled and yellowing glove of his beloved Rosalita. He replaced the pouch around his leathery neck.

As lunch was served, including the mandatory citrus juices and the Gasparilla Sarsaparilla that Gasparilla insisted be consumed to prevent scurvy, the talk centered on the desire of all to celebrate Christmas in South America. "The country that we are going to will be new to us, but the ways of the Spanish in Venezuela will be like they were here in the old days," Gasparilla laughed.

"Yes, it will be good to be able to bribe the politicians again and deal directly with those merchants who worry only about what wealth we can earn for them," added Miguel Rodriquez, who had been a colleague of Gaspar since the 1770s.

The younger men listened intently to these two shaggy-haired weathered pirates who had reached their sixth decade, a feat in itself for members of a profession in which most suffered youthful death. Within moments, however, their respect for the aged wisdom of these leaders would be drowned in personal greed and the ambition of acquiring even more wealth without regard to potential risk.

"Yo, a brigantine is approaching near Cayo Costa!" came the excited shout of the youthful lookout who had been posted in a clump of hardwoods on a mound west of the encampment. "She is two-masted and is riding low in the water. She must be carrying a heavy cargo, flies no flag, and is not armed."

The younger men were quick to awake from their daydreams of South America. Immediately, Santos Veslasquez, a stocky, well-built brother, leaped to his feet and yelled to the lookout, "Are you sure the trader is not armed or with escort?"

Cayo Costa's land-based pirate fortifications, which had been built years before by Gasparilla's Confederation, had twenty-four- and thirty-two-pound cannon that prohibited any uninvited ships from entering Charlotte Harbor. This massive, earthen fort was in stark contrast to the white sand and azure waters that made this island one of the most breathtakingly beautiful in the world.

"She is absolutely alone! She bobs like a cork so close to the shore we could take her with a longboat," came the reply from above. "Wait, she is turning west-northwest and heading into the gulf. What shall we do?"

Santos looked at Gasparilla quizzically. Gasparilla immediately said, "We have only the *Doña Rosalita* and she is overloaded, overbarnacled, and years beyond her days of battle. Were it not for the fact it is our largest ship, it would be a ship more worthy of scuttling with honor than sailing anywhere."

The *Doña Rosalita* rose and fell gently in the water behind the growing crowd of men as if listening, and its aging timbers creaked as if attempting to protest.

"But, sir, it appears this merchant could be taken by a longboat. I believe that we can raise our red flag of battle and cause the brigantine to surrender without a fight," Santos disputed. The other lads, largely inexperienced, listened intently with mounting enthusiasm in the anticipation of one more battle.

José, without his core of experienced friends and comrades, argued, "Remember, dying is one of the few things that can be done as easily as lying down. I suggest that rather than risk death and the treasure we have, that we lie down, take a siesta, and dream of Christmas in South America. This is not a good day to do battle. Besides, the Americans are not to be trusted. I fear the flagless brigantine may well be one of their ships. I do not understand why an American naval fleet chooses to avoid us and then a lone intruder comes into our territory. I submit to you that this is either a trap or the most ignorant captain to ever command a ship."

Santos spoke for the young brigands when he asked for a vote to be taken. According to Gasparilla's Confederation compact, a democratic vote by all brothers present was to be taken prior to any action that could affect the whole group. These citizens of the Confederation would constitute a quorum, in spite of the small number casting a vote.

Gasparilla knew before the vote was taken that it would be based upon the greed of the majority rather than the experience of the minority. In a last futile effort, he beseeched, "The weakness of our time is our inability to distinguish our needs from our greed. We have more treasure here than we can possibly carry. This is not logical, but there is no armor around logic. Let's take the vote!"

The actual vote was closer than Gasparilla and his older mates had anticipated. There were thirty-one yea votes to attack the seemingly helpless brigantine, and fourteen nay. Those members voting against the attack wished to continue packing the ship in order to leave the next day as planned. Forty-five men constituted less than one third of the crew necessary to man the *Doña Rosalita* for battle. This small, skeleton crew was the minimum number of sailors necessary to sail the former man-of-war. Gasparilla had kept only a minimal number of sailors so that he could transport more weight in gold and silver.

If Gasparilla had decided to keep his seven schooners and their crews together at Gasparilla Island earlier that week, rather than sending them ahead in pairs, his dream of becoming a gentleman farmer and establishing another empire in South America would most certainly have been realized. Not only would the majority have voted with him, but even if they had not, one or two of the sleek schooners, now absent, could have sailed out to confront the lone brigantine, almost assuring another prize victory.

The pirates joined hands in a circle to reinforce the feelings of brotherhood. Gasparilla, one of the most literate and intelligent men of his time, spoke to the group. "Cato the Elder, said in 150 B.C., 'After I'm dead I would rather have people ask why I have no monument than why I have one.' This is the question that many who will follow us to this land will ask if we foolishly attack the brigantine."

It was now early afternoon and the enthusiasm of youth was sustained as the men prepared to put the *Doña Rosalita* to sea. José walked with his three most trusted friends: his cousin León Gaspar, who had watched over José since his boyhood; Juan Gomez, one of his most trusted subordinates on Gasparilla Island, and Miguel Rodriquez, his best friend and ship's captain. José placed his hands on Juan's shoulder and whispered,

"It is important that you stay behind and finish preparations for our departure tomorrow." Then he paused and said loudly, "Remember that tomorrow is the most important thing in our lives. Tomorrow hopes we've learned something from yesterday!" It was now time for him to board and take command of his ship. As he hugged his compatriots remaining on shore he added, "When you have duties to perform, always do the most disagreeable first. This is the most disagreeable since it is madness to go to sea at this time. The sea is a cursed mistress who demands everything and seldom gives back anything. We're off!"

The aged timbers of the *Doña Rosalita* moaned, as the light southwest breeze caught her sails. To a man, the crew could feel the burden weighing on their veteran flagship. The ship's lookout, a slight teen named Paquito Fernandez, doubted his eyes. The target brigantine appeared to be having difficulty catching the same wind. Within the first hour, the Confederation pirate ship was bearing down upon the stern of the unflagged merchant vessel.

Gasparilla, seeking confirmation that they were indeed closing on the prize, yelled back and forth between the helmsman and the lookout. The helmsman was a giant African ex-slave, Moses St. George, who had served Gasparilla for more than two decades. Moses had aided José in designing and developing the schooners that had given Gasparilla's Confederation dominance in the area from Elliott Key on the East Coast to Pensacola, on the West Coast of Florida from 1800 through 1816.

"Cap'n, this old girl is sure hard to steer," Moses complained. "If we make it through this day, I suggest we unload some of our gold to lighten our ship for the journey south."

"I agree. This may be the biggest mistake we have made," Gasparilla concurred. "I do not understand how our overburdened vessel is gaining on the merchantman. The crew could not be that incompetent, else how did they get this far? I believe, Moses, that though good judgment comes from experience, experience may also come from bad judgment. I pray that we are not victims of bad judgment."

"We're within the hour of reaching our target," the lookout called.

As Gasparilla glanced over the black perspiration-drenched shoulder of Moses back to Gasparilla Island, José recalled the first day he had seen the utopian isle with its canopy of trees, whispering sea oats, and phosphorescent water under the sunny skies nearly always present in this part of La Florida. It had been in the late fall of 1779.

Gasparilla's mind flashed back to memories of himself: first as José Gaspar, son of a well-to-do family; then as a successful admiral in the

Spanish Navy; later as husband to his cherished wife and father to two precious children, and lastly as a respected and democratic Confederation leader.

Thanks to his mother, Dulcie, Gasparilla was a true polyglot with a repertoire of five languages, having read the Bible and all the classics many times over. His mother's best friend had taught him to be appreciative, caring, and understanding with women. He had been taught by both to be true to his beliefs and to maintain the highest personal character.

With the breeze blowing over his sweating brow, his retrospection carried him back to his childhood in Spain.

C_{HAPTE} R 2

A Mother's Love, a Father's Influence

*"Opportunity is not luck or chance. Our environment does not cause it.
The golden opportunity we all seek is within ourselves; at times it may come from
the help of others, but the fact remains, the golden opportunities
we seek must be found from within."*
—Señora Dulcie Gaspar, José's Mother, 1762

As Gasparilla squinted into the brilliant Florida sky, he recalled the blue sky of his early childhood on the banks of the Guadalquivir River in Spain. He could still smell the scent of the nocturnal Spanish flower called Lady of the Night.

José Gaspar was born in 1756 to Ramón and Dulcie Gonzalvo Gaspar on an estate outside Seville, the mysterious port city on the Iberian Peninsula. Seville, a city with a mosaic of unlikely alliances, was confusing to those who were strangers. As a child, José often went to the plaza where there stood an eleventh century synagogue, a twelfth century mosque, and a fifteenth century cathedral, all facing each other peacefully. Seville was an uncommon city of intense loves and hatreds with differing languages.

His obese father, Ramón, had extensive land holdings, which his wife had inherited from her aristocratic father, Don Pedro Gonzalvo, who had been one of Spain's naval heroes. Ramón was a wine merchant who was not known for honesty in his business dealings, but he was a smart businessman and consistently profited from his successful, if devious, business ventures. José often worked in his father's wine warehouses.

José's mother, Dulcie, was a beautiful raven-haired woman, who valued reading and education above almost everything else. She was well educated, was an insatiable reader, and spoke five languages. Dulcie also had a strong theatrical gift, passing on to José an appreciation and a flair for the unusual. Everyone who met Dulcie felt an attraction to her and felt comfortable in her presence.

This parental combination would help to develop a caring, intelligent, ambitious, as well as cunning, child. From his mother José gained a voracious appetite for learning as well as a great respect for women, and from his father he formed a ruthless understanding of business dealing and building wealth, regardless from what source it was acquired. His parents gave him a solid upper-class existence, and the love of his mother and the influence of his father would mold José's later life.

José's mother read her Bible and other literature to him daily, often speaking in different languages. At a time when the majority of the population was illiterate, Dulcie taught José Castillian Spanish, the parlance of the upper class in Spain; Portuguese, the language of navigation; Latin, the language of scholars; French, the language of the arts, and English, the language of law.

Dulcie and young José went for long walks into the country, enjoying the sunshine and fresh air. Dulcie enjoyed exposing José to nature and its marvels and used nature in developing parables to help her young son learn of life. She often pointed to the mountains and exclaimed to José, "Always live your life as you would climb that mountain. When you look to the top, it gives you a goal to attain. Then carefully learn to enjoy each step you must take on the climb. Reaching the top will make the effort worthwhile. Often you will find the journey more rewarding than reaching your ultimate goal. Always look high when planning your goals."

The days of José's youth seemed to pass quickly. In spite of his small stature and spindly frame, José learned that a quick mind, common sense, and possession of superior knowledge served him well in gaining the trust and leadership of his larger and physically stronger peers. He was always the leader in school, whether it was in a positive endeavor or a youthful prank.

As he grew into puberty, José also learned that his intellect and sincere appreciation of women gained the trust and confidence of many giggling, adoring, young schoolgirls. The wall that divided the girls' school from the boys' school was often crowded with more than one female fan of José. The girls enjoyed watching José organize games for the boys to play in the school yard. His attraction to the opposite sex would have great impact on the many directions José's life would take throughout his sixty-five years.

José was fourteen years old in November of 1769 when he had his first romantic and sexual contact. As he was going home from school, he was joined by Josalin Díaz, whose development was more advanced than was that of the other girls her age.

"José, will you walk me home? The boys that hang around near your father's warehouse often threaten and scare me," she said pleadingly. "I know they will leave me alone if I am with someone as strong as you."

With his mother's inculcation of duty towards women, José agreed to walk her home upon the condition she would stop and allow him time to sweep the floor and loading area of his father's warehouse—one of his necessary after-school chores.

Josalin went inside the warehouse with José and jumped up to sit on a railing that separated the office area from the shipping area of the building. José noticed that she had kicked off her shoes, and that her skirt was showing a good deal more leg than he was accustomed to seeing. Being a gentleman, José lowered his head and went about his work, but he could not keep from glancing in the direction of the slim but well-developed Josalin. It wasn't only the late afternoon heat that warmed him; he felt inexplicably different than any time before in his young life.

When he was finished, José approached Josalin, who was still sitting on the railing. As he came closer, she stretched out her leg with her long, bare toes extended as befitting a world-class ballerina and gently pushed her right foot into José's crotch. He slowly reached down and gently grabbed the soft underside of her sole. After she giggled and asked him if he found her attractive, José attempted to reply. However, with his hand around her warm foot and an unknown sensation between his legs commanding all of his brain's attention, he simply nodded sheepishly.

As he looked up into her intent eyes, she asked José if he would like to see her naked.

"I guess so; other than my mother's breasts and the time I saw a neighbor's servant taking a bath, I have never seen a girl without clothes," José nervously replied.

With that Josalin removed her blouse and revealed her small, but well-sculptured, breasts.

"What is it like to have breasts?" José asked, "Do they feel funny?"

"No, they don't feel like anything. Sometimes they even get in the way," she laughed.

"Can I touch them?"

"Go ahead, José, but please be gentle. No one has ever touched them before."

The excited José reached forward with both hands to cup these soft and tender assets of womanhood.

"Please kiss them. It feels so tingly, I want to know what it feels like to have your mouth kiss them," she sighed.

For an instant, José worried that he was hurting her; but her reassuring smile and the look in her eyes allayed that fear and he lightly licked her left breast. He was surprised to feel the nipple harden under his tongue as if a cold winter's wind had blown upon it from the snow-covered peak of Montserrat. She moaned and stretched back to present her entire bosom to his mouth.

José surrounded Josalin's torso with his arms and lifted her down to the floor with him. She was soft and yielding, willing to allow his caresses. As they enveloped one another's body in the youthful, wondrous, natural dance of pure joy, their joining together was suddenly broken by the blinding sunlight of late afternoon. It came from the open doorway of the large warehouse door that had been thrust open by the huge silhouette standing in the doorway.

"What in God's name is going on!" exclaimed a bellowing voice of disbelief. In the doorway stood the man whom José had come to fear, but not respect, his father, Ramón.

"You young wench, cover yourself up and I will see you home! If you are lucky, I will not tell your mother and father what I witnessed," he boomed at Josalin.

"As for you, he continued, turning to José with an angry glint in his eyes, "I want you to go directly home and to your room. Tell your mother nothing or you will surely break her heart. I will deal with you after I take this young lady, whom you sought to disgrace this day, home."

As shame coursed through him, José could not understand how something that felt so wonderful could be wrong.

End of Childhood

"I believe it was easier for my parents to suppress my first desire than it was for me to satisfy the many that followed in my life."
—José Gaspar, July 1818

Upon José's return home, he forewarned his mother that he had committed an act that was most surely disappointing to her and the honorable Gaspar family name. Without telling her any details, José sat sullenly awaiting his father's predicted dictatorial return home. Ignoring his mother's questioning, he picked the Gaspar family album from his mother's library and read again, as he had done so many times, about the courage and bravery of his decorated grandfather, Don Pedro Gonzalvo, and his actions on behalf of the Spanish crown in 1733. He enjoyed reading about how Captain Gonzalvo had become an admiral.

On 13 July 1733, a Spanish fleet composed of three armed galleons, eighteen merchant vessels, and numerous smaller ships carrying a variety of products from Mexico, left the Spanish port in Havana, Cuba, bound for Spain. This treasure-laden convoy was under the command of Captain-General Rodrigo de Torres. Captain Don Pedro Gonzalvo was in command of one of the Spanish Navy galleon escort vessels.

An experienced naval veteran, Rodrigo de Torres, only twenty hours after leaving Havana, sensed that a hurricane or severe tropical storm was imminent. Just off the Florida Keys, he ordered his armada of ships to return to Havana immediately. Although his hunch was correct, by nightfall the convoy was consumed by a terrible hurricane. As the swift-moving storm subsided, most of the ships were scattered over nearly eighty miles of shoreline up and down the Florida Keys. Only one ship had managed to return to Havana immediately following the storm.

The largest of the ships ran aground or were partially sunk in an area called "Head of the Martyrs." The remainder were sunk, swamped, or run aground for miles on either side of this point.

Capt. Don Pedro Gonzalvo, commanding one of the Spanish galleons still operational, immediately rallied those around him. Meeting with the surviving ships' captains, Don Pedro dispatched one of the smaller ships to Havana to request that the admiralty send back a salvage operation.

Meanwhile, Captain Gonzalvo organized and dispatched various groups to mark the locations of the wrecks and to place them on the maps for future salvage efforts.

As a result of his quick thinking, nine salvage vessels loaded heavily with food, supplies, soldiers, divers, and equipment arrived within two days of the sinkings to begin a series of successful salvage operations.

The loss of the 1733 fleet would have been a major financial disaster for the Spanish Crown had not the salvers recovered losses. In fact, as indicated in the recognition of Don Pedro Gonzalvo's heroics, more gold and silver were actually recovered than appeared in the original ship's manifests. This was because contraband was inevitably a part of ships of the Spanish Main. Smuggling by underpaid sailors was a common occurrence.

For his leadership, bravery, quick thinking, and actions in saving the Spanish Government from this major financial loss, Don Pedro Gonzalvo was promoted to the rank of admiral and honored in the King's Court back in Madrid, Spain.

A firm hand gripped José on the shoulder. A look at the unsmiling face of his father encouraged his full attention to the present.

"So, my young José, I am sure you have not told your mother of your deeds with Josalin Díaz this afternoon?" came the stern voice awakening José from his deep thoughts concerning his hero grandfather. His father had finally arrived home, much later than José had anticipated.

José's first thought was that perhaps his father was trying to replicate with Josalin's mother his own earlier actions in the warehouse. After all, each time Josalin's parents visited Ramón's business or stopped by his home, José suspected that his father harbored sexual thoughts towards Josalin's beautiful, voluptuous mother. In José's opinion, what he had done with Josalin was no worse than his father's afternoon affairs, which were common knowledge among the employees. José decided that his bit of sexual activity was probably minor in comparison to his father's. *After all,* he wondered, *aren't boys supposed to be sexually aggressive?*

José dreaded having to look into his mother's brown eyes and face her disappointment. The bond between his mother and him was one of trust and understanding and he knew that it had been broken and would never again be the same.

Although José did not trust his father, he understood the "business comes before all else" teachings that Ramón had instilled in José's training. He was glad that his father had taken control of the uncomfortable situation and would be treating it like a business decision instead of the emotional confrontation that he had envisioned earlier in the evening.

"Dulcie, when I returned to the warehouse this evening I found José and Josalin Díaz in a sexual situation. We know such things happen, but we hope that we never have to deal with these issues," Ramón stated matter-of-factly. "I sent José home and then escorted the young lady to her family."

Dulcie simply lowered her head as if in prayer that this were not true. Beneath her bowed head, José could see tears moistening her cheeks. Ramón continued his judicial recitation.

"After apologizing to the Díaz family, I promised them that this would never happen again. I told them I was going home to discuss with you the possibility of using your father's legacy to have José attend the Naval Academy at Cadiz."

José's mother was weeping as she begged her husband to give José another chance as he was so young and had much to offer the family and Ramón's business. Dulcie moved from her chair to kneel at Ramón's feet pleading for her son, but to no avail.

Ramón surprised José with his calm businesslike handling of this family crisis. "José needs to be taught life's most important lesson," Ramón began. "When you betray someone, you also betray yourself and your family."

Ramón gently placed his hand on Dulcie's head and continued. "The academy will be good for him. It will give him the self-discipline that he needs," continued Ramón. "He is a most intelligent young man, but until he learns to control his desires, he has much to learn about life."

"But, he is so small and young to be in a military setting," pleaded Dulcie, rising and going to José's side.

José sat silently reflecting on his options. He knew that if he were to say anything at this point it would only make a terrible situation worse.

"The academy does not entertain another class for nine months. What will he do until then?" José's mother asked expectantly, hoping that José could atone for his transgressions in Seville.

"We will allow José to spend next month and Christmas with us. In the meantime, we will write your good friend, the widow María Gonzalez, who lives near Cadiz to ask that José be allowed to stay with her on her ranch, working to earn his keep," Ramón responded firmly. "I will also give her a sizable amount of money for her time and trouble."

José looked towards his weeping mother and saw the sorrow in her eyes. He felt he had burdened his mother terribly and recognized, for the first time, the problems that mothers must endure in maintaining the family unit.

She smiled sadly at José and said in a reassuring voice, "It will be fine my son. María is a lively and intelligent woman. She has raised five outstanding children and was married to one of Spain's most dashing cavalry officers until he was killed saving the life of a lieutenant. Like your grandfather, María's husband was a true hero and a pinnacle of Spain's pride."

"María will teach you much about life before you enter the Naval Academy next fall, my son. This I promise you and you can be sure I will ask her in the name of our lifelong friendship."

José hugged his mother's waist tightly, as tears stung his eyes, knowing he would seldom have that opportunity in the future. He looked into her eyes with thankfulness. "I will never do anything stupid again," José cried with his head in her chest.

"No, José, always dare to be naïve, for then you will always be inquisitive," Dulcie replied, patting José's head.

Dulcie added, with a kiss to José's head and a whisper in his ear, "Never be inferior to any man, nor think you are superior. Remember that every man and woman is your equal. And, don't ever feel that you should carry the guilt of the world alone upon your shoulders."

With this motherly advice, José's innocent childhood came to a close.

CHAPTER 4

Learning To Love

"Patience is the most necessary qualification for success, be it in business, love, or war. One moment of patience can prevent disaster; a moment of impatience may guarantee it!"
—María Gonzalez, January 21, 1770

José had never been to Southern Spain and he was immediately impressed with both the beauty of the area and of the widow María Gonzalez, who lived on a large ranch outside of Cadiz. In fact, José felt that she was the most beautiful woman he had ever seen, with her lively dancing eyes and her face glowing with a warm smile. María was as limber and lithe as a girl one-third her age. She had maintained a shapely body with long arms and legs and a tiny waist topped with firm breasts. José found it incredible that she was old enough to have five grown children.

He quickly decided that physical exercise must be one of the secrets to María's youthful beauty. Before breakfast, she would insist that José either join her for a fast jaunt around the ranch or race with her between the main house and outbuildings. "One who does not take the time for exercise now may need to set aside time for illness later," María would often say during these early morning outings. José could have chosen no better physical preparation for the Naval Academy.

After breakfast, María and José would go out to the pastures on horseback to maintain the property. José doubted that there could be any better horseback rider than his hostess. He begged her to teach him the skills she so easily exhibited. "In order to become great at anything, one must take risks," María proclaimed, "but I will teach you."

It was not only an appreciation of exercise and the skills of horsemanship that José would learn from María; these seven months would teach José much about caring, patience, and the equality of men and women.

After the long mornings of exercise and working the estate, María spent the afternoons teaching José not only horseback skills but also fencing skills. In an era when most women knew little, José had been blessed to have two women who knew so much. His mother and María were willing to teach him not only the skills but also the mental toughness to deal with any situation. María turned out to be one of the finest fencers José would ever face, and José became well prepared to become one of the best fencers to ever enter the Spanish Naval Academy.

"José, in fencing and other things you will learn at the academy, you must realize the importance of strategy," María said breathlessly after a particularly hard workout with the teen. "You must not only be able to plan strategy but also be able to change that strategy decisively. Those who can plan and then adapt to change are nearly always victorious."

The evenings were spent in long hours of discussion, sometimes walking, oft times simply sitting outside the main house. As his mentor, María taught José the importance of integrity and a strong character. "Those who maintain their integrity are seldom shaken by the storms of daily life," María said with conviction. "Your character and integrity are the roots of your strength."

"I believe that in order to truly believe in something, it is necessary for that belief to come from your convictions," José agreed. "You must stand firm in your convictions."

By the time José had been on the ranch for two months these evening discourses were often preceded by their bathing in the hot springs located in a small building near the main house. At first, after soaking in the warm therapeutic water, both María and José would get fully clothed again for their discussion. As the weeks went on and they became more comfortable with each other, they simply went to the patio in night robes.

One night, María invited José to place his bare feet in her lap and she, in turn, placed hers on his lap. "My husband brought back a great secret from China years ago. The art of foot massage is believed to control or affect all of one's body. Let me show you," María continued, as she began to rub the bottom of his feet, "the toes can help the sinuses; the eyes, the breathing. The ball of the foot deals with the stomach, the back of the head, the ears, and the lungs. The arch affects the spine and the kidneys, while the outside of the foot, just below the ball, helps soothe the heart. The heel aids the intestines, colon, lower back, and knees." All the while she rubbed each area of José's feet and in turn instructed him as he rubbed hers. As she spoke, her voice took on a more sensual tone while José became strangely quiet.

This massaging of María's feet awoke again in José the same feelings within that he had felt in the Seville warehouse. He again felt the tingling sensation in his lower abdomen and knew he was losing control of his emotions.

María, sensing the arousal, spoke quietly to José, "You should not hide your feelings. When that happens, you apologize for the truth. Show me what you want . . . with patience."

CHAPTER 5

Naval Academy Years

"The purpose of an education is to learn how we might best serve the world."
—José Gaspar, June 6, 1776

The seven months José spent with María were a great preparation for understanding life and the importance of becoming a leader. Their closeness had turned into an intimacy that resulted in hours of lovemaking, teaching young José the importance of patience, caring, and concern for women. And, the hours of discussing many topics convinced him that those who are born with the ability to lead must seize upon leadership.

María led the entourage that took young José to the Academia Real de Navegacíon at Cadiz. The academy was located in an old fortress across the harbor from the seaport city. It was an impressive structure and would make a lasting impact on José in the coming years.

The evening prior to José's admittance to the academy, he and María visited Capt. Antonio Narvarro, who was an instructor and expert fencer at the Naval Academy. Navarro and his wife had been good friends of María and her late husband.

"I believe, sir, that a teacher can never know what influence they may have on their students," José stated with a new maturity. "A teacher influences eternity."

"I agree, young man," Captain Narvarro nodded. "If a student has confidence in what is being taught and incorporates what is learned, it will become a part of him. We should not only use all the brain we have, but also use all the brains around us to learn."

After a leisurely meal, with stimulating stories regarding Captain Narvarro and the time he served in the King's Guard of the Spanish Army with María's husband, the host and hostess finally retired.

As María and José stood looking across the bay, viewing the dark, red-tinged sky of an endless sunset in the west, María placed her arm under José's loose shirt and began rubbing his back. The soft stroking relaxed José, who was nervously thinking about the academy. He turned to María and placed both his hands on her sides next to the firm breasts that reflected the moonlight of the late evening sky. He gently kissed her forehead, the tip of her nose, and her cheeks. Then he nuzzled her left ear and the scent of her hair.

In the meantime, María's hands had massaged José's chest and moved downward to unhook his pants. She whispered in his ear and in unison they moved to a nearby bedroom. With no further words spoken, María cleared José's mind of his concerns for the next morning.

After breakfast, José set out with Captain Narvarro to begin training to become one of the finest sea captains ever to graduate from the academy. José and María had tears in their eyes as they said good-bye at the iron gate of the Narvarro's home.

On the carriage ride to the academy, Navarro and young José discussed many topics. Navarro told José that one of the most important things a good military leader learns is that, "a wise man learns many things from his enemies."

"One thing María taught me was to always know what I don't know and then learn that," José smiled. "She also taught me that the man who knows the least often thinks he knows the most. Leadership and learning are one and the same. Good leaders have an appetite to learn."

Although smaller than most of the other midshipmen, José gained the respect and admiration of his fellow students with his intelligence and skills in navigation, tactics, and battle strategies. Not only did José become an expert in the rigging of the sailing ships, but he actually modified the sailing sloop hulls of the academy ships, making them maneuver and turn quicker as well as slice through the water faster.

An irony of commanding a sailing ship of the late 1700s was that often a battle was decided by the crew's hand-to-hand combat training and which crew could use the cutlass and small fire arms more efficiently. Understanding this, José dedicated himself to learning gunnery, hand-to-hand fighting, and particularly to swordplay, not only for his own benefit, but also to aid in training a crew. These skills would elevate his stature with all whom he served and fought in the coming years.

During vacation periods, José alternated visits on leave between his parents' home and María's villa estate. The former visits allowed him to get closer to his mother and better understand the mercantile mind of his father, while the visits with María filled his days with the stimulation of his intellect and his evenings with stimulation of his body.

During his third year at the academy, José was put in charge of overseeing the incoming students. His role quickly became one of protecting the youngsters from the hazing and harassment of the seniors.

"When we see the younger generations, we tend not to like them," José often said. "The true glory is that these youngsters set their own precedents."

José gave a memorable speech on leadership, including the statement, "Leadership is like playing a musical instrument in public. You learn as you go on performing." Just prior to releasing the new class to those in their final year, he cautioned the first-year students, "Expect everything to happen, then nothing will ever surprise you."

José had a very successful third year and was ranked first in his class. He was recognized as one of the top leaders in the entire academy and he was, by far, the most daring and skillful sailor as the academy ships plied the waters of the bay.

José's daring often brought a variety of reactions from the merchant ships and naval ships that navigated the waters of Cadiz. José laughed often when describing the 'English salute' given him by other ships' captains trying to avoid colliding with him.

"What is an English salute?" María asked him during the vacation time between his third and fourth year. They were lying on a blanket at María's ranch after a midday lovemaking session. "I keep hearing you telling others about it."

"I am embarrassed to tell you, but if you must know," José grinned as his face reddened, "before the Battle of Agincourt in 1415, the French, anticipating victory over the English, proposed cutting off the middle finger of all captured English soldiers. Without their middle finger, it would be impossible for them to draw the renowned English longbow and they would therefore be incapable of fighting in the future. Much to the bewilderment of the French, the English won a major upset and began mocking the French by waving their middle fingers at the defeated French. Since then it has taken on an even greater meaning, I guess."

They both laughed, understanding the meaning of the universal international signal of derision.

As he entered his final year at the academy, he would gain a fuller understanding of leadership, power, and sex.

CHAPTER 6

Sex and Leadership

*"I think men often use their power to gain sex
and women often use sex to gain power!"*
—José Gaspar, midshipman, Naval Academy, 1778

"As I prepare for a command position in the military where everyone will look to me for leadership," José commented to his roommate at the academy, "I am becoming more serious about the subjects of my studies."

José's favorite instructor was Capt. Pedro Sanibel, a famous Spanish sea captain, who was teaching while awaiting the assignment of a new ship, a large man-of-war to be named *FloridaBlanca* for the minister of the Spanish Navy. José spent hours talking with the straight-shouldered erect and gentle Sanibel who introduced the young midshipman to stories of the Spanish Main.

At Jose's request, Sanibel told of his heroism while on escort duty in the late fall of 1770. Not only did José learn a great deal about leadership, but also he discovered how dangerous the clear waters of the Florida Keys could be to Spanish shipping.

Sanibel was captain of the *San Fernando*, a 712-ton Spanish naval vessel carrying fifty guns, which was on escort duty between Cadiz, Spain and Vera Cruz, Mexico. On November 3, 1770, the *San Fernando* escorted eight merchant vessels bound from Cadiz for Vera Cruz. One of the ships, *El Nauva Victoriosa*, under the command of Capt. Joséph Varan, hit a reef in ten feet of water at the head of the Florida Keys. Captain Sanibel guided his ship next to the grounded ship. Most of the treasure on board, the small cannon and small arms, and most of the crew were saved by the *San Fernando*. The next day, Sanibel attempted to tow the stricken vessel off the reef. However, due to the damage, the *El Nauva Victoriosa* settled into twenty-five feet of water just southeast of Caesar's Creek. Sanibel completed the journey with the remaining ships and received a commendation, an appointment as aide to the secretary of the Navy, and an appearance in Madrid before King Charles III.

José idolized and respected the experienced Captain Sanibel, as well as Captain Narvarro who had taught him swordsmanship and hand-to-hand combat skills. They influenced much of José's thinking on leadership.

José relished these discussions in the dark, dank halls of the Moorish castle that had been converted into the Naval Academy. The midshipmen often joked that the reason they studied so hard was to escape this harsh environment.

Captain Sanibel and Captain Narvarro had both experienced the King's Court and the struggle for power that was constant in Madrid. King Charles III had created an administrative class, which was displacing the old bureaucracies and influence of the church and universities. The ministers and civil servants under King Charles III, men such as FloridaBlanca, Jovellanos and Compomanes, were determined to reassert the crown against encroachments by the church. This administration saw the colonies and possessions in America as key to a Spanish revival in Europe. They believed in liberalizing commercial regulations and providing government protection to increase revenue in the period known as European Enlightenment. This was indeed a prosperous period in Spain due in large part to its population growth, from about eight million people at the beginning of the century, to eleven million during the time José was at the academy. All in all, the economy of Spain and its drive to become more European had most citizens feeling good about their nation's leadership.

These Spanish leaders, as well as other monarchies throughout history, worked in glorious surroundings. Their workplace was a golden, gilded palace where artwork, sculpture, and architecture rivaled the King's Court, and where it was commonplace for women to seek power and influence.

It was this elegant royal environment in Madrid that caused José and the two wise captains to discuss the vagaries of power, leadership, and sex that seemed to be essential in becoming a great leader, in Madrid or anywhere else.

José was surprised at the two captains' primary premise that no great leader in all of history was lacking in sex drive, but all three agreed that sex has to be the creative energy of all geniuses. Sanibel remarked, "Sex and power are more intertwined than people like to believe or admit."

36

"All people need sex. Leaders just seem to need it more," Navarro laughed. "People who are drawn into political life tend to be aggressive and ambitious with large sexual appetites."

"I agree!" Sanibel smiled while leaning forward toward José. "Sex is essential. It makes most of us feel alive and brings out the vitality in us. A strong sex life lets us feel that everything else in the world can be dealt with in its proper perspective."

"But isn't our religious faith opposed to this?" José asked quite seriously and then with an attempt at humor murmured, "I have been made to believe that excessive copulation is a sin."

"The problem with people who have no vices is that they often have some annoying virtues," Sanibel grinned as he lit a cigar. "I believe that morality is moral only when it comes from within a person."

Captain Navarro, more directly answering José's concern, explained, "There are many religious traditions that incorporated sexual imagery into their fables and dogma. The ancient Greeks and Romans, for example, believed that the sexual exploits of their gods were rituals that, like other religious rites, tried to make present the spirit that makes all human endeavors effective. During their time, sex was no great separation from their spiritual beliefs."

"But, today, our Catholic Church has so many . . .," José began before being cut off.

"The church today feels that sex has become exaggerated and gratuitous," Sanibel interrupted. "Unlike the Greeks, whose culture permitted a more holistic view of their body and a more sensual, spiritual approach to their sexuality, the people who followed them made sex an obsession and the act of sex almost pornographic. This is the reason our church has encouraged our society to repress sex unless it is to produce offspring. By making things sinful, the church gains greater control. This is one reason why King Charles is instituting so many changes in our country."

"Another reason might be to justify the many affairs and indiscretions going on among the leaders in Madrid," Navarro laughed as he poured another glass of wine.

As a future officer, José also expressed his concern with the way that both his church and his government dealt with the issue of homosexuality. He had learned during his first two years of education in the academy that a high percentage of seamen on merchant vessels as well as enlisted sailors on naval vessels were indeed homosexual.

"I think it is because women are prohibited on most ships," a wine-mellowed Navarro chuckled.

"He is partly right again, as usual," Captain Sanibel agreed. "So many young boys serve on board ships as cabin boys and powder monkeys, where there are no women present and there are months of boredom at sea, that the older sailors sexually abuse them. Someday, everyone will understand that sexually abused boys may become abusers themselves when they grow older. With the violence of shipboard life, we have an ongoing problem, not only on merchant ships, but among our sailors as well."

"Do you believe homosexual sailors are created and not born that way?" José asked frankly.

"I really don't know the answer, my son." Sanibel answered with a troubled look on his face. "What I do know is that as a ship's captain, it is important to recognize a person's strengths and build upon them, not focus on their weaknesses. The church and society have their public opinions on the subject, but we need to draw our own conclusions."

"As long as the church and society put homosexuals in the same class as robbers and murderers, we will never recognize sexual equality," Navarro nodded in agreement. "And, anyone who condemns homosexuals but does not condemn adultery among heterosexuals is a hypocrite."

"That brings up another problem, Captain," Sanibel remarked while picking up the wine flask from his friend and pouring both another glass, "a problem nearly all of us have been guilty of sometime."

"What do you mean?" Navarro asked.

"We often go from our fantasies regarding women to action," Sanibel answered. "Men, especially, are constantly thinking about sex and are ready to act. Women, on the other hand, seek males they consider to have admirable qualities to create offspring. This reduces the chances for fidelity to only one mate. In reality, we are like the other animals. What do you think the chances are of birds or mammals staying faithful to only one partner?"

José pondered these two elders' thoughts and asked many questions. He enjoyed these open discussions. When he pressed the issue of fidelity with Sanibel with regard to sex, he relished the answer Sanibel gave him.

"Sex can be so intense for men, that many suffer from temporary amnesia afterward," the wise old captain said, smiling, "the physical exertion required by the man causes all the blood to run from the brain to the penis. This causes a lack of blood in the central part of one's brain and allows us to be gallant the following morning. We can simply say, 'Last night? I forgot already, my dear.' It allows for greater latitude for men. While the woman may be making love, we can simply be enjoying sex."

One afternoon, during José's final year at the academy, the three gathered after a day of classes to discuss some of the up-and-comers currently in waiting at the King's Court in Madrid. The post-class meeting was sparked by a lively academic classroom presentation as to whether a great leader can possess ethics, integrity, and morals.

Captain Narvarro, who had been reassigned to the Naval Academy from the King's Court because of the jealousy of one of the ladies of the court, spoke first. "Leadership is a highly competitive arena. A strong libido with sexual energy, is one of the reasons men make it to the top. And, nymphomania is common among those women who seek power. Let's be honest. Sexual energy goes with creative genius. Both of these, I believe, are essential to leadership."

"Yes, my friend, but women are truly different from men, "interrupted Sanibel. "Men are constantly in search of seduction and of physical release. Women, on the other hand, seek a powerful and strong male to father their offspring. The female seeks an emotional release, whereas the male, why hell, he seeks conquests, and the more forbidden the more exciting." Sanibel chuckled at his analysis.

"You believe that men who have great creativity, harbor a competitive drive, and enjoy high risk, also have an insatiable sex drive?" José questioned his favorite mentor.

"Listen to yourself José, within your question is already the answer. Without those traits you mention, what we have left would be simple mediocrity!" Sanibel answered.

"I agree. Why in Madrid today we have a member of the Spanish Army in the court who, I tell you, will use his ambition, competitive drive and sexual libido to surpass the indolent, ignorant King Charles IV, waiting to take over for his father," Captain Narvarro exclaimed.

"Who do you mean? José questioned. "How could this happen?"

"Manuel Godoy. He is head of the household guard. Stories and rumors abound of how he has seduced or allowed himself to be seduced by every woman who can help him rise in power," Narvarro continued. "I can assure you that Godoy has allowed his manhood to penetrate valleys where normal men would fear to enter."

This statement brought roars of laughter from the three officers.

"José, if you ever go to Madrid you will be quickly involved in the libido game of get and give. Every man and woman there is a player in this perverted climb to power," Sanibel cautioned.

"Is there no one in our government bureaucracy with moral leadership?" José earnestly inquired.

"Never during times of growth or good economy will you find leaders who are totally moral. Perhaps, if things get bad enough, people will seek the leadership of a person with ethics. But, most people will tolerate corruption and immoral leadership in the capital as long as their lifestyle is good," Sanibel concluded. Then he added, "When times are bad economically, people return to the church and its teachings, but for now, finding someone in Madrid with the character you admire is not an easy task."

"José, there is some hope for you. I met a beautiful woman, the Doña Rosalita Santiago, a widow, who lives outside Madrid. She has access to the court and audience with the king. She is beyond reproach," Navarro continued, "and should you ever go to Madrid, she would be one woman you could respect."

"I am sure that I will only serve my corrupt and immoral king with risk of life and limb out at sea, alone with my loyal crew. I will never go to Madrid," José added.

"But, José, the same drive that propels people like Godoy is necessary for you, also in order to become a great officer. Men who are adventurous and take risks have a need to seduce as well." Sanibel smiled at José, "Don't ever repress your natural feelings. If you repress one part of yourself, the other parts will become repressed as well."

"I fear that men will always use their power to gain sex while women will do the same to gain more power," José said, then added thoughtfully, "Generally we forget that women can do everything men can do. My question for the future would be, could true equality cheapen life itself?"

CHAPTER 7

Hero of the Barbary Coast

"A person who is hailed a hero is often destined to lead a tragic life thereafter!"
—Captain Pedro Sanibel, October 5, 1778

As José Gaspar ended his career at the Naval Academy in the spring of 1778 he was the top midshipman in his class and the icon of all Spanish manhood, although shorter and slimmer than most. He had a dashing appearance with his handsome face, dark penetrating eyes, and his shining black hair slicked back, emphasizing a stubborn and determined jaw. He was well built and muscular with his uniform exhibiting his body to perfection.

The consummate leader, Gaspar embodied what the Frenchman Marquis de Sade professed, "Egotism is the primary law of nature." Perhaps, young José possessed too much of the egotism and impulsiveness of youth. During the last week of his final year at the academy, José conspired with the commandant's housemaids to arrange a tryst with the commandant's oldest niece. Unfortunately, the affair was discovered, and the red-faced, obviously enraged commandant turned his back on José during the awarding of his official commission, and after the ceremony, accosted him with a knife. The kindly Captain Sanibel intervened and, in return for letting José graduate alive, agreed to get the young man out of town immediately after the ceremony. José was assigned to Sanibel's new ship to patrol the dangerous Barbary Coast. José now understood why sexual desires are often strongest toward those who seem unattainable.

Were it not for the carriage ride graciously offered by Captain Sanibel, young José would have been forced to walk the dirt roads to the Navy quay with his heavy locker on his shoulder. The fuming commandant refused to allow Gaspar to ride in the academy carriages that took his

41

classmates to the docks—quite a rebuke for the top-ranking graduate in the class!

During the ride, Sanibel and José reflected on their new assignment— the crew they would command and the state of their readiness. Sanibel would be commanding a new ship of the line. It was especially designed for warfare against the pirates of the Barbary Coast known as Corsairs.

Sanibel commented sadly, "Lieutenant Gaspar, I fail to understand how the Spanish Crown can spend so much money building new ships and weapons and pay so little attention to the crews who will man them. We are expected to educate and train a crew made up of ex-convicts, illiterates, and other dregs of our society so that we can serve and protect the rising Spanish merchant class and the rich men it creates."

"I fear that as business and merchants like my father grow more powerful than government, we will see an even greater income inequality and fewer educated people to make up our already diverse citizenry," Gaspar stated thoughtfully. "As this happens, it is unrealistic to expect government to reverse this trend. The government will become rich from the taxes levied. Government will speak of diversity rather than educating people to the highest level possible."

"My young friend, I do not envy you. I am fortunate enough to be old and near the end of my career. I will stick to my job until it is finished. I have lived long enough to be able to witness injustice without feeling the need to get even," the weary Sanibel replied.

"It seems to be a timeless problem. The rich want to live apart from the poor such as those who make up our crew. They do this in part because they fear the poor and in part because they feel they deserve such a life and, at least in their minds, are superior to those with less," Gaspar answered wistfully.

As the old salt and the newest Spanish naval officer sat quietly, the carriage rumbled on upon the newly laid cobblestone road to the Navy quay. Looking out the side curtain, an excited José saw the bowsprit of his first ship, the *Margarita*.

The *Margarita* was a small two-masted vessel of 100 tons, with light cannon and falconets used to fire small grapeshot and scrap iron. The ketch was sleek and built low to the water, causing her to appear even smaller to Gaspar. The new ship, with her maneuverability, would be difficult to ram by the sea-raiding Corsairs. She was a ship designed to operate in the relatively calm waters of the Mediterranean.

Gaspar's first assignment, to serve on the Barbary Coast of Africa, seemed a formidable responsibility as this task could either advance or destroy his career. José was certain the Naval Academy commandant had pulled strings to give him this worst of all possible assignments.

Spanish cargo ships had been the targets of pirates since 600 B.C. In those early days, ships were not able to handle rough seas and they stayed close to shore, making them an easy prey for pirates who simply darted out from shore to attack, plunder, and quickly return to their encampments. The Corsairs resided just outside the well-traveled sea lanes and spent little time actually at sea. Corsairs were well fed, strong, and well rested and could easily overtake and overpower their prey who spent many consecutive months at sea. Their hit-and-run strategy was quickly noted by José Gaspar.

Another Corsair tactic that he would take from his service in the Mediterranean was that of capturing people for ransom as well as capturing cargo. Rather than risk life and limb in attacking convoys of protected gold and other prized loot, the Corsairs took hostages. Living captives with money or position were worth much to those who would buy their freedom. Persons without monetary value could either choose to join the enterprise or be put to work for the brotherhood. If they were uncooperative, they could easily become slaves. As a last resort, it was easy to kill them and feed them to the sharks. José would remember these strategies that the Corsairs had used successfully for centuries and use them later in his life when he formed his Confederation.

Captain Sanibel and José spent most of July and August of 1778 training their inexperienced crew. The *Margarita* sailed with Spanish naval ships as well as Christian privateers loyal to Spain.

No naval engagements took place during this time period although the *Margarita* was successful in pursuing a ship of pirate Corsairs. The Corsairs were chased from the coast of Algiers into a trap set by a trio of Christian privateers. The privateers however were not inclined to thank or celebrate with an official Spanish naval vessel and, in fact, the *Margarita* was actually threatened by them. After insuring that Sanibel's ship would not interfere, the Christian privateers headed towards Spain with their prize.

In September, the *Margarita* joined a Spanish fleet holding siege to the port of Tripoli. On the night of their arrival, José and Captain Sanibel took the longboat to the admiral's flagship to officially report for duty with the fleet. This would be a fateful meeting.

After the initial exchange of pleasantries and a fine meal, Captain Sanibel, José, the admiral, his attendants, and an intense Capt. Miguel Rodriguez of the supply brigantine, *La Esclavitud,* retired to the admiral's quarters in the stern.

José immediately took a liking to the smiling Miguel Rodriguez—a highly decorated naval combat veteran who had made the mistake of befriending Pablo de Olavide. Olavide was the reforming intendant of Seville, who disappeared into a cell during the Spanish Inquisition of 1776. Rodriguez was not sentenced to a cell, but given command of the *La Esclavitud*. Rodriquez was disappointed with this lowly assignment, as the hot-blooded warrior would rather lay siege than haul supplies.

From this initial meeting, Miguel and José developed a lifelong attachment. Decades later, these two Spanish sea captains might have ruled the world around Florida were it not for the United States of America.

The two older captains were content to sit and sip rum and reminisce of conquests of old, real and imagined. Conversely, young and eager, José and Miguel studied the charts of the harbor at Tripoli and plotted how to steal back from the Corsairs the legendary old galleon, *Trinity*. The *Trinity*, which was blatantly anchored at the mouth of the harbor, had significant historical value to the Spanish.

Obviously, the crafty Corsairs knew the Spanish would do anything to get back a useless relic of the past while ignoring the hundreds of Spanish prisoners being held in the bagnio. This pleased the Corsairs because, by anchoring the *Trinity* in plain sight, they knew they could tie up much of the Spanish naval fleet. This strategy allowed other Corsairs to roam freely up and down the sea lanes while the Spanish anchored off Tripoli attempting to recapture the relic.

Late that night, Gaspar and Rodriguez went on deck and commandeered the pinnace, a small boat found on man-of-wars. They rowed the pinnace to the anchored *Trinity* under cover of the moonless night. They knew one weakness of the Corsairs was that they were men of action and when not engaged in piracy were usually drinking, fighting, chasing women, and enjoying the fruits of their labors. This meant that not many would volunteer for the mundane duty of guarding the *Trinity*.

Shortly after they quietly slipped over the side of the captured Spanish ship, José and Miguel knew they were right. Only five Corsairs were on the ship and it appeared that their sexual orientation was not one of chasing women through the streets and quays of Tripoli. Gaspar and Rodriguez quietly left the ship and rowed ashore to scout out the bagnio, the fortress prison city, where the Spanish sailors were imprisoned.

The bagnio was like an enclosed city with shops and other amenities instead of a prison. The unfortunate prisoners there faced a life sentence of hard work and possible sale into slavery anywhere in the world. Some prisoners were lucky enough to be from countries that had treaties with the Corsairs, which meant it was possible they could be ransomed. However, this was not true of the Spanish captives as they and other Christian prisoners had as their only option that of "turning Turk" and adopting the Muslim religion, which might gain them an easier sentence or eventual freedom.

As Gaspar and Rodriguez climbed into this danger, it was José's goal to find a person who had become a Turk but to whom José could offer freedom in exchange for his help inside the prison. Fate was on their side as they soon discovered just such a man. Ironically, he had taken the name Dragut Reis, a famous Corsair of the 1500s known for his daring and courage. With Reis, they arranged for the escape of the *Trinity* crew from the bagnio the following night.

The following evening, in spite of negative feelings of the high command within the Spanish fleet, one longboat with José, and another with Miguel, were lowered into the water, along with six other marine volunteers. The longboat was chosen since it could carry twenty men. If successful, José and Miguel would not only rescue the prized ship but save the crew from the bagnio as well.

At 3:00 A.M., the two longboats silently slid ashore. José, Miguel, and the six marines quietly sneaked to the south wall of the bagnio, for it was the least guarded. José crept up behind one of the guards, grabbed his mouth and with a slash of his stiletto, decapitated the hapless Corsair. It was the first time José had used a blade to kill another human being. It would not be his last.

Meanwhile Miguel and two of the marines killed the guards at the south gate. They went inside the prison and found the convert Reis at the prearranged spot. Reis guided them to the enclosed area where the Spanish officers and crew were quartered, locked in chains. Gaspar and Rodriguez boldly walked into the guardhouse, waking the soon-to-be headless Corsair in charge of the keys. After taking the bloodied keys, Gaspar freed the *Trinity* officers and crew. He was saddened that he could not take all the pleading prisoners with him, but his duty was to rescue the Spanish ship, not start a revolution within the bagnio.

José took half the men and went around the western side of the bagnio, while Miguel took the other half and went around the eastern wall. That way, if one of the groups were to be captured, the remaining sailors could still take the *Trinity* and sail off. José would use this tactic many times later in his career.

Both groups met at the longboats and quietly began rowing towards the black outline of the *Trinity*. Again, the two groups split up, each going to an opposite side of the anchored ship. No one was on deck, so the groups went below and sought out the five Corsairs guarding the ship. The *Trinity* officers wanted to slay the pirates, but Gaspar convinced them to use the tactic he had recently learned from the Corsairs, and hold them for ransom. Gaspar calmed the vengeful group with the statement, "Those who fly off into rages seldom like where they land."

Upon the taking of the *Trinity*, José and Miguel insisted upon manning the windlass, and they quietly cranked up the anchor while the crew climbed over the rigging. A fortunate breeze caught the sails and the *Trinity* slipped silently out of the harbor at Tripoli.

When the bright morning sun woke the Corsairs in Tripoli the next morning the Spanish fleet was gone, along with the prize they had formerly held in the harbor. At the south gate of the bagnio a note was attached to the three heads of the murdered Corsairs, directing their stunned comrades as to where they might send gold in return for the hostages now chained below the deck of the *Trinity*. José Gaspar, of the Spanish Navy, had signed the note.

"We have won this war!" the Spanish admiral in command shouted to all the ships and crews the next day. "Another glorious victory for Spain."

"I sometimes question the whole concept of war," Gaspar softly confided to Captain Sanibel. "It seems to me that war doesn't decide who was right; war simply determines who is left."

"You will learn that often boastful leaders are privately cowards," Sanibel replied. "Any coward can fight a war that he knows he can win. Unfortunately, Spain uses its overwhelming power often. Perhaps countries become more cowardly as they grow older and have much to lose."

With his aggressive actions, José Gaspar became a hero during his first official confrontation with an enemy. It was unusual for a Spanish naval officer to be a hero in a land engagement, and his fame would not endear him to the highest-ranking Army officer, Manuel Godoy, back at the King's Court.

"You will be rewarded for your achievement," Sanibel smiled with a wink at Gaspar. "In a bureaucracy, everyone above someone who achieves benefits by that person's deeds. In your case you deserve a reward."

"I believe that if a person doesn't try something beyond what he has already learned, he will never grow," José offered in reply. "And, in reality, I think that if he tries something spectacular and it fails miserably, he might still gain immortality."

CHAPTER 8

Unfair Politics

"Justice I can deal with; what hurts is dealing with injustice!"
—José Gaspar, September 1778

Upon their return to Spain with the *Trinity* and its crew as a prize, Captain Sanibel, Lieutenant Gaspar and the crew were hailed as conquering heroes and ordered to appear before King Charles III in the capital city of Madrid. Captain Sanibel praised José to the admiral as well as those crew members who were a part of the welcoming party. The king, like all politicians, was always alert to gaining political advantage, especially during this period when he was promoting mercantilism over all other issues.

Captain Rodriguez and the crew of the *La Esclavitud* were given a cursory reception with the other ships of the returning fleet. They were then discreetly directed to the warehouse docks, away from the Navy quay, by the harbor pilot under orders from the crown. It was obvious that the bureaucracy in Madrid was in no mood to give equal, or any, credit to Captain Rodriguez and his crew. Miguel Rodriguez was certainly paying the political price for his support of the minority position during the Inquisition of 1776. Grudgingly, the crown agreed to give the captain and crew of *La Esclavitud* a thirty-day shore leave so the sailors could visit their hometowns throughout Spain. Shortly before the leave began, Captain Rodriguez and crew received orders to report to the Spanish Main on their return. Apparently, having the *La Esclavitud* sailing between Havana, Cuba, and St. Augustine, Florida, would conveniently put these heroes out of sight and out of mind of the Spanish citizens and focus all the attention on Gaspar and his ship's crew.

José was livid at the official snub that was given to his friend, Miguel. As José was about to turn to the naval attaché now boarding the *Margarita* to voice his displeasure, Captain Sanibel discreetly stepped between them and murmured, "The Bible tells us that a wise man restrains his anger and overlooks insults."

"But, sir, a man who is good enough to risk his life for his country is certainly good enough to be honored afterward," José retorted, "I don't understand how anyone could ignore Captain Rodriguez's bravery!"

"You will learn, my young friend, that the world and Spain feel that they are always right on many issues," Sanibel quietly answered while grasping José's forearm. "Because they feel they are right, they feel no need to be consistent."

"By simply silencing a man or isolating him, you have not converted him or made him loyal," José protested.

"That issue is above and beyond our power in this matter," Sanibel sternly replied. "I order you to remain civil throughout these ceremonies. Damn it, Gaspar! Forget what is past. No one can be successful focusing on what happened in the past. You must learn one of life's hardest lessons. We each must adjust to an always changing world, while remaining loyal to our own unchanging personal value system."

"But, I. . . ." José never finished his statement since he found himself coming to attention, saluting, and shaking hands with more officers wearing gold braids than he had ever imagined. During the ceremony on both the *Margarita* and the dock of the Navy quay, Lieutenant Gaspar was quite busy with organizing the crew, accepting congratulations, and insuring the decorum of the moment.

After the ceremony, at which Captain Sanibel, José, and the rest of the crew were also given a month's leave, José left the Navy quay. With his footlocker thrown over his left shoulder, he walked alone through the hot late afternoon heat toward the warehouse district, seeking the lonely wharf where the Spanish politicos had determined the *La Esclavitud* would be berthed. As long shadows engulfed the dirty and dingy dock, José brightened considerably when he saw his heroic friend, Miguel, doing pull-ups on the wooden spar of the mainsail.

"Permission to board, Captain," José hollered.

Miguel ran to the gangplank with a broad smile. "Come aboard for, with no other officers on board, I am all alone."

"I heard from the naval officers that you and your crew were also given leave," José replied. "Are you not going to take advantage of this vacation?"

"My two junior officers are both married and family men and will spend this time with their families. Of course I cannot take leave with my enlisted crew, so my plans are uncertain," Miguel stated. "It is true, my friend, that a lonely sailor is often like a fish out of water when he goes ashore."

"Where are you from? Perhaps, you should visit your home."

"I grew up in Granada, probably the greatest city in all of Spain! I tell you, there is no city more beautiful and exciting, " Miguel said with pride, "and how about you?"

"I may try to visit my good friend, Señora María Gonzalez, although I really would rather have a true vacation. Being away from the Spanish Navy for one day will seem like a month in the country, no matter what I do," José added.

"Why don't we both go to Granada? We could enjoy my family, my brothers and sisters, and if we get bored, we can always go over to the gypsy camps to drink and enjoy the sensuous flamenco dancing. I can assure you, my friend, that these dancers will enchant you, if they don't move you in another manly way," Miguel laughed.

Whether it was because José felt sorry for his friend or somehow felt responsible, it was as if Atlas had removed a world of worry from his shoulders. He was relieved when he heard Miguel give one of the most profound statements he had ever heard.

"In serving Spain there are always two tragedies, one is not getting credit for its actions, the other is in getting the credit. I am the lucky one, for I don't have to live up to the expectations the crown will now place upon your head and your career," Miguel calmly stated, "but for the next month, we can be ourselves and enrich our friendship."

"The king of Spain uses those who help him maintain or build his power and seeks to destroy or isolate those who would reduce his power," José said. Then he added, "The king, in Madrid, thinks he can influence the world with power. If he wants to do that, the best way would be for him to learn to control the world's weather. Now that would be true natural power!"

"José, learn from my mistakes," Miguel nodded. "You are a hero now. Take advantage of the possibilities this role presents you to encourage the changes you believe in."

"But, I don't want to be a hero," José protested. "I don't want to be a public figure. This just seemed to happen and I guess I will just have to make the best of it."

"Yes, our lives are often not determined by what happens to us, but how we react to what happens," Miguel smiled as he put an understanding arm around José's shoulders.

José waited for Miguel to arrange for the overseeing of his ship with the harbor master. In the interim, he contacted the Navy quay and they agreed to post a guard on the merchant wharf to protect the *La Esclavitud* while they were away.

Three weeks in learning about the beautiful city of Granada, with its Moorish history and arches, capped off with a week in the arms of beautiful María, should prepare José for the politics of Madrid, which he mentally compared to the world's oldest profession.

When Miguel returned, José quietly told his friend, "Miguel, I am so upset that you did not get the credit you earned equally with me at Tripoli. I can deal with justice, but I cannot deal with the injustice our government is doing to you."

"I know and you know what happened. My concern is that you will soon be going to the seat of power. Power intoxicates and corrupts men. Beware of both the men and the women in Madrid. Always be true to the person whose reflection you see in a mirror," Miguel answered. " I shall not have that problem in the Caribbean."

C HAPTE R 9

Love At First Sight!

*"When you meet the woman who is the love of your life,
you will know it the first time you see her."*
—José Gaspar, reflecting on meeting Doña Rosalita, September 1778

*The two most difficult times during a vacation are the last days leading up
to it and the first days coming back from it,* thought José. He stared at the
countryside as his carriage bounced along the rutted roadway leading
towards Madrid. *Worse yet,* he thought, *I am going to a place that I have
neither been to nor desired to go to, ever in my life.* At that instant, he was
envious that his friend Miguel was returning to his own ship and ship-
mates, in spite of the fact the *La Esclavitud* was being banished to a boring duty in the turbulent region surrounding La Florida.

As the carriage rocked to and fro en route to Madrid, José reflected
upon his visit to Granada and mused over the old Spanish saying, "A man
has seen nothing until he has seen Granada." Granada had cast a spell on
José from its setting in the foothills of the Sierra Nevada mountains with
the backdrop of snow-covered mountain peaks. He had enjoyed his visit
to Alhambra, the castle fortress built for Moorish kings and a true expression of Moorish architecture and design. It was last castle abandoned by
the Moors in 1492. José smiled as he fondly recalled entering the Alhambra
through the Port of Justice to its many courtyards. He and Miguel were
both impressed with the "Room of Secrets." They then went out into the
Court of Lions with its reflective pools and gardens, surrounded by columns and a beautiful fountain held up by twelve alabaster lions.

José agreed with Miguel that leaving the Alhambra and the adjoining
castles would have been quite difficult for the defeated Moors nearly three
centuries earlier. To the Moors, desert people from Africa, Granada must

have been a vision of heaven with its flowing waters, numerous shade and fruit trees, colorful flowers, and the many fountains singing and dancing in the bright sunshine.

He remembered the moment of parting with his courageous friend Miguel outside the Moorish walls of Alhambra as María's carriage waited for José.

"You never told me the reason you were leaving Granada a week early was to spend it with not only a beautiful, but obviously rich, woman," Miguel laughed.

"You must believe me, Miguel, when I tell you these past weeks have been the most enjoyable I could have experienced. If only we could serve on the same ship. Perhaps when I go to Madrid, I could. . . ."

Miguel interrupted, "You know that I shall always be your loyal friend and if you are my friend, you will realize that loyalty sometimes demands keeping one's mouth shut. Remember, I believe it is more important to be faithful to a friend than famous."

"Perhaps someday we can join one another in Florida and create our own country free of the corruption that happens when so many people each try to dictate their own desires. Together we could create the only true democracy the world," José enthusiastically speculated. "In studying maps of Florida, I noticed that no part of that land is further than sixty-five miles from a coast. That geographical fact would make us the strongest country in the world. Our Navy could control all the shipping lanes into and out of the rich Spanish Main."

"Get out of here, my dreaming friend. You are becoming jealous of my assignment involving the extremely difficult task of sailing into clear blue waters, covering my eyes from the glistening white beaches, and partaking in the joys of the beautiful native women. Go quickly to your María. If you don't, I fear you will become a stowaway on my ship!" With that, Miguel gave his slight friend a giant hug.

The next week with María was nearly as spectacular as his first two weeks in Granada.

Dejected because his vacation was drawing to a close, José now rode in a military carriage en route to Madrid. He was startled to alertness by the sliding stop of his carriage. He jerked open the door and jumped out of the carriage, ready to battle the thieves who controlled many of the roads into Madrid. With one hand on his sword and the other up to shield his eyes from the sun, he found he was looking into a pair of expressive brown eyes. As his eyes focused further, they took in a pert nose, high cheekbones, a gamine smile, and dark hair with reddish glints cascading down the shoulders of what seemed to be the body of Venus. *The only exception,* José thought, *is that this Venus has beautiful long arms and legs*.

"Might I ask your assistance, sir," came a soft, clear, voice and in that instant he knew what it must feel like to be inside an exploding bomb. Dulcie Gaspar had taught her son early that to be loved, one must be lovable. So, with a boyish smile and a giant bow from the waist, José found himself saying, "I shall gladly service you. . .," After realizing his faux pas, he felt the color flooding his face as he corrected the statement. "I shall gladly be of service to you."

With a kind smile and lowering of her beautiful eyes, the lady allowed this embarrassing moment to pass. She took the lead in introducing herself. "I am Doña Rosalita Santiago. I am a widow. . . ." She stopped short, realizing that her remark to a handsome stranger was indiscreet.

It was now José's turn to relieve an awkward moment by simply projecting the conversation to the problem at hand. "What can I do to help you?"

Doña Rosalita walked with José to the side of the road where her carriage was stopped in front of a smaller, two-wheeled, peddler's cart. The obviously old cart had some rotting boards, and one of the wheels had come off and was lying in a water-filled ditch. As he surveyed the situation he could see that the majority of the travelers using the road must have concluded that simply allowing this cart to rot away would be the best solution. From a tactical standpoint he was in full agreement. However, as he turned to give his opinion to the beautiful lady, his eyes met hers and seeing the hope and anticipation there, knew that he must attempt to help her repair the worthless antique.

In his freshly pressed and immaculate uniform, he slid down the side of the ditch to retrieve the errant wheel. Knee-deep in water, José called to his escort to throw him a rope, which he attached to the wheel. He then ordered the wheel hauled up the bank. He slid and slipped on the muddy bank as he scrambled up the slope after it and, still in complete charge, José ordered the coachman and his attaché to lift the side of the peddler's cart so that he and Doña Rosalita could replace the wheel.

They picked up the wheel together and as he leaned close to her, José could smell the fresh scent of her hair. He looked over her head to her bare, slightly freckled shoulders. The wheel proved to be stubborn and heavier than it appeared, but finally it slid onto the old axle. Just as it did, José caught a glimpse of Doña Rosalita's breasts beneath the peasant blouse she wore. He felt a rush of adrenaline that gave him the added strength to shove home the axle. But it needed grease, so José took some from around the hubs of his carriage. After smearing the lubrication on the axle and wheel, his hands were filthy. As he tried to wipe them on the grass Rosalita took one of her white gloves and offered it to him. José finished wiping his hands on his uniform pants, but took her offering to mop his sweating brow.

With the wheel secured, José made a gallant bow. Rosalita extended her hand. José, instead of shaking it, bent down to gently kiss it. Impulsively, she bent over and kissed his brow. Looking flustered, she then retreated to her carriage.

With her remembered thanks ringing in his ears, the two carriages and the cart headed up the road towards Madrid. José could not get Shakespeare's thoughts on love out of his mind. "Love sought is good, but given unsought is better." José was sure of one thing, only, the remainder of the trip; he had met the love of his life and the woman he intended to marry.

He took the soiled glove she had given him, smelled the fragrance of her perfume on it, and gently folded it, placing it in the pocket over his left breast. Reflecting on his passionate feelings for the beauty of Granada, he realized that there are many beautiful things that catch your eye, but very few things capture your heart. This beautiful woman had captured his heart and he was determined to pursue her.

Love and Politics

"Love is something that raises man to noble heights,
politics on the other hand causes man to reach his most dishonorable depth."
—José Gaspar, September 7, 1778

José's carriage entered the walled city of Madrid. It had been Spain's capital since 1561 when King Phillip the II, who was residing with his court in nearby Toledo, sent a letter to Madrid's town administrators. In that letter, Phillip II had informed the administrators of Madrid that he and his entourage would be coming to stay for awhile. However, they never left, literally moving the seat of Spanish government there.

José was immediately impressed with the spacious boulevards and roads; he was used to the narrow streets and structures of his native southern Spain. As he entered the Puerto del Sol, the square from which all roads in Madrid radiate, he was delighted with the bustle and activity of a great city.

The carriage moved on to the Plaza Mayor, through a nine-arched gateway, and José was in the midst of the Great Square. He sensed it was the hub of life for all of Madrid. Nowhere else could be gathered so many attractive women and so many men busying themselves with boundless activity, although José was not sure that it was productive activity.

He observed the various balconies that surrounded Plaza Mayor as his attaché explained that in the days of old, royalty and other notables had stood upon these balconies to witness men on horseback fighting bulls, which were released into the square. When he asked if bull fighting was the sport of the powerful of Spain, the aide responded, "Yes, Madrid is the mecca of the Fiesta Brava!" José remarked that he was glad that a coliseum had since been constructed for such a purpose.

As the carriage continued on the wide boulevard, he noted the fountains and the park areas for the common citizens of Madrid. "The Moors must have loved Madrid as much as Granada," Gaspar mused as he traveled through the heart of the medieval quarter, with its vast windowless walls stretching away on both sides of his carriage.

The carriage approached the Royal Palaces built over the old fortress of Alcazar. José noticed how new and plush they were. Constructed in a neoclassical style, they covered more than three hundred and fifty acres with beautiful parks and flowering gardens. "Politics may smell at times, but the gardens always smell wonderful," José remarked to his aide.

As José exited the carriage and entered a darkened foyer, ten degrees cooler than the street, he was shocked to see Manuel Godoy and Princess María Louisa in the shadows. Manual Godoy was nuzzling her naked breasts. José wanted to retreat quickly, but it was too late; they looked up and saw him.

Greatly embarrassed, José called his aide and coachmen to attention. Not only abashed with catching the loving pair in a compromising position, José was also ashamed as he remembered he was still wearing his muddied boots and soiled uniform pants—the result of his gallant rescue of Doña Rosalita's wheel. "Sir, I apologize for my appearance. I am Capt. José Gaspar of the Spanish Navy and I have been assigned to the palace."

Struggling for a proper appearance, Manuel Godoy tried to straighten his disheveled clothes. María Louisa meanwhile pulled her dress up to cover her bare bosom. After what seemed an interminable length of time, Godoy finally replied imperiously, returning José's salute, "Yes, Captain Gaspar, everyone here at the palace knows of you and wants to meet you. I have heard of your pursuit of excellence, which is gratifying."

"I am glad to see that you are not obsessive in your pursuit of uniform perfection," Godoy added as he focused on José's soiled uniform.

"I jumped into a ditch to retrieve the wheel of a cart belonging to a distressed lady just a few hours ago," José explained apologetically.

"Ah, the man of action I have been told about," Godoy responded coldly. "I assumed you could walk on the water rather than sinking like the rest of us."

"Manuel, this is our honored guest. Enough of your displeasing comments," María Louisa interrupted, now properly attired. Of course, María's royal position dictated that the antagonistic discussion come to an immediate halt.

José introduced himself to her and was indeed thankful for her intervention. He noted that Manuel Godoy was a handsome army officer, a bit on the paunchy side, with cold gray eyes. He obviously did not possess an engaging personality.

María Louisa appeared to lack the characteristics normally associated with women of her station. She was overweight and had a complexion problem that she sought to cover with makeup. Her only redeeming physical quality, in José's masculine opinion, was her very large breasts and well-exposed cleavage exhibited by her low-cut dress. José saw that her stare was as steely as that of her companion.

"Manuel is dealing with many of the issues in the Americas, María said, "You see, the *criollos* are constantly challenging our authority. I simply do not understand how these criollos, who are like you and me except for being born and bred in the Americas, want to populate and infiltrate all levels of our government with their wild ideas and changes to our system."

"Be assured that our king will replace these criollos with trusted bureaucrats from peninsular Spain," Godoy responded, "but now, my dear, I suggest we leave Captain Gaspar to freshen up and change into more suitable, or at least cleaner, clothes."

With that, Manuel Godoy offered his arm to her and they left José to go to his quarters, as he pondered what he believed to be the basic problem with Spanish government in regard to the colonies in America.

"Autonomy or authority, the Hispanic world has shown a pattern of either dictatorial centralism or liberal regionalism throughout history. Without any discipline ourselves, how can we expect our subjects to possess any?" José stated to no one in particular.

José's next meeting also was a surprise. Before he had reached his quarters, he noticed that he was following a solidly built man whose rolling gait seemed familiar. As the figure turned toward him and attempted a salute, José impulsively ran to him and threw his arms around him. It was his cousin, León Gaspar, who had lived briefly with José's parents just a few years before José left for the academy in Cadiz. An excellent seaman, León Gaspar was a ship's carpenter and had sailed the world. José was thrilled to finally meet someone inside Madrid whom he knew and could trust!

"I am thrilled to see you are alive," José exclaimed as the two men stepped back to look at one another, "I heard that you were on board the *Nuestra Señora del Carmen* when it wrecked on Anastasia Island, near Florida, earlier this year."

"Yes, José, that is true. We were bound from New Orleans to the Canary Islands in very rough seas when it happened," León confirmed. "If it weren't for the dysentery and my need to spend a great deal of time sitting in the head, I might not be here!"

"It's good your behind was on the head," José grinned with boyish devilment. José visualized his poor cousin below the wave lashed decks, sitting on the latrine and hoping the ship wouldn't sink.

"Were I not full of it, I might have drowned and not be here to welcome you to Madrid," León laughed along with José and glad that problem was over.

"Here Captain Gaspar, let me show you to your quarters," the now official-sounding León continued as he picked up José's footlocker and sea bag.

When they reached José's quarters, the two men caught up with news. At twilight, León suggested that José might want to freshen up and perhaps change his muddied uniform. Fortunately, the laundry room was located near León's room, and on the way to his young cousin's.

José laughed, "León, I can tell you that, during this busy day, I have met the most exquisite woman in Spain, and perhaps, in Godoy and María Louisa, two of the worst people in Spain. What a day this has been!"

In responding to the question of how he met Doña Rosalita Santiago José explained in detail the story of how he rescued the peddler's cart and was smitten by a pair of wondrous brown eyes.

León told him what he knew of Doña Rosalita. Her parents were of royal lineage; however, they had accrued great debts to the crown, beyond even Spanish standards of excess. Upon their untimely, and some felt suspicious, death in a carriage accident, the orphaned daughter, Rosalita, was given her parents' estate, Although she was only twelve, King Charles III had arranged for her to marry one of his oldest advisors in the court and his trusted civil servant, Philip Santiago, who was nearing his seventh decade. This arranged marriage would eventually be of benefit to the crown since drafted into the nuptial agreement was the clause that the family estate would return to the crown of Spain upon the death of both parties in the marriage. There was no right of ownership to be passed on to any children born of this union, nor to a subsequent spouse of the eventual widow or widower. "Of course," León laughed, "everyone knew the marriage was never consummated. Old Philip they say was 'soft as seaweed' in a manly sense."

"Are you telling me that Doña Rosalita is a virgin?" José asked.

"Yes, and it drives all the males in Madrid out of their senses when they are near her. You will not meet a man in this city who does not cherish daydreams of what he would do with Doña Rosalita," León continued.

"I must warn you that the king-in-waiting, Charles IV, and his wife's lover, Manuel Godoy, have sought Doña Rosalita's affection at every chance. Perhaps, it would be wise for you to simply change your pants and put both your pants and your thoughts concerning Doña Rosalita in the clothes hamper," León added with a sound of warning in his voice. "When a man stalks an unattainable woman and doesn't admit it, he becomes quite angry toward anyone else who might seek his prize."

"My mind knows you are probably correct; however, my heart is telling me to take a chance with Doña Rosalita," José added. "Life seems to be made up of desires, both big and vital as well as small and absurd. Our desires change from hour to hour."

"People who fall in love are often blind," León quipped and then dramatically falling to his knees continued, "At times like these a friend closes his eyes and prays."

"In any case, I am glad to see you and with regard to whom we are talking about, I will seek your professional advice on carpentry, since I am considering the rebuilding and repair of a peddler's cart belonging to someone I want to know," José laughingly stated.

"It must wait until tomorrow, though, for I have made enough mistakes for one day."

León quietly excused himself as shadows fell across the palace room.

CHAPTER 11

Love-Building, a Project At a Time

"One of the most important things about love is the anticipation it provides."
—José Gaspar, September 8, 1778

José awoke early on his first morning in Madrid, eagerly waiting for the sunrise to arrive so he could get out of bed, meet with Cousin León, and go to the estate of Doña Rosalita Santiago. Through the open French doors that led to a balcony, José could see the burgundy red-and-gold stripes in the east gradually change into vivid coral cloud puffs surrounded by a startling blue background. He could smell the sweet fragrances of the flowers from the extensive gardens of the palace. Even the birds sounded happy as they chirped and whistled outside his window. *While out to sea, one takes for granted the silence and forgets the myriad pleasant landside sounds*, he thought.

At last the sun shone into the stark white room and an eager José decided that he could finally begin the day. On the way to the lavatory, he whistled in unison with the birds. When he got there, looking at the marble and other enhancements built into the most elaborate "head" he had ever utilized, he decided that the monarchy definitely lived a lifestyle different from anyone else's on the Iberian Peninsula. When he finished, he admired his reflection in one of the many ornate mirrors located in the bathhouse and bragged aloud, "Ah, Doña Rosalita, since I cannot win your hand by convincing your parents of all that I can be, then I must convince you that I am a competent man in many ways. Today, we will resurrect the pitiful peddler's cart and make it a thing of beauty! I will show you that I can use my hands as well as my mind!"

"The Bible teaches us that there is one thing worse than a fool, and that is a man who is conceited," a loud voice bellowed from behind the startled José. José turned to see the smiling face of his cousin, León Gas-

60

par, "the Bible also tells us that a conceited man who considers himself wise is worse off than a fool."

Both cousins laughed, and León asked why José had chosen to wear common clothes rather than his majestic naval dress uniform. "I see you must be planning upon actually working today rather than supervising my effort?"

"To impress those who might observe, it is important that I do more than is required of me," José pompously stated to his cousin with a joking smile. "Did you gather the materials we might need and bring along your tool chest?"

"Yes, José, I have a work wagon with a full team of horses out in the palace plaza," León indicated. "Perhaps we can stop at the Plaza Mayor bakery for some fresh-baked goods and coffee shipped from the Spanish Main?"

"Of course, it shall be my treat. I have heard great things about the bakery on the plaza," José replied as the two went through one of the Moorish arches of the palace and passed the small shops and bright awnings that enlivened Madrid's busy streetscape.

After breakfast outside the bakery, José and León mounted the wagon for the drive. Again José was taken with the beauty and breadth of the roadways within the city as well as the parks, flowers, and fountains that were everywhere. And, again, José was impressed with the robust bustle of the citizens of Madrid. He smiled as he watched tarot card readers, street musicians, and mimes interacting with the bureaucrats hurrying to work.

"Look how all these government workers scurry around with a look of great importance on their faces. Everyone outside of the government knows that bureaucrats are the defenders of the status quo, even if they aren't sure what that is," José laughingly stated. "No wonder all these people need a siesta in the middle of the afternoon."

"Yes, José, tomorrow night when we attend the recognition ball in the palace, always remember that the longer the title of the person to whom you are introduced, the less important his job actually is," León chuckled.

"You are so right," José added, "and I know that tomorrow night all the government employees will be expert at saying nothing and meaning it! No one in government can agree or disagree on what nothing is or where to find it. However, the search for it keeps them looking very busy."

Their wagon was halted momentarily by a mounted army patrol of Asturias Infantry Regiment just before the arched gateway from the city. The eight cavalrymen were under the command of Lt. Rolando Gomez, a large, arrogant man with dark hair and black piercing eyes. Astride a large white horse, Gomez was a striking figure in a tricorn hat, knee-length coat, and riding boots. He had a sword, made of the finest steel in Toledo, which hung from a baldric across his chest. Gomez' attitude matched his appearance as he intentionally hovered over the paunchy older driver of the wagon and his slight, mustached, handsome passenger.

"Where are you taking this lumber and other material?" Gomez inquired.

"What business is that of yours?" José retorted impatiently, for he had already determined a personal dislike for this overbearing Army officer. He prided himself in being able to instantly judge the character of those he met.

Sensing immediately that this could be an explosive situation, León quickly announced that he was a member of the Spanish Naval Ministry in Madrid. He also introduced José as his cousin, Capt. José Gaspar of the Royal Navy, who was in town to be recognized and honored by King Charles the following night.

"If this is true, then you won't mind showing me some identification?" Gomez asked impatiently, obviously disgusted and noting that this high ranking naval officer was dressed like the peasants he enjoyed harassing on these forays outside the palace.

Without a word, but continuing to glare at Gomez, José handed the lieutenant his military identification. León also complied, with a watchful eye upon his angry cousin. There was no doubt that these two officers had instantly disliked one another.

"Let these two sailors attempt to navigate their wagon through the gate," Gomez sneered disdainfully, looking even meaner than a few minutes earlier.

As León drove the wagon through the gates and into the country, José spoke so that the Army patrol could hear, "León, never get into a fight with an ugly man because he has nothing to lose."

"Gaspar, there are times it is wise to keep one's mouth shut," Gomez shouted, as the wagon slowly moved through the massive gate and passed one of the ornate buildings embellished with a tile facade.

"The soldier is right, José," León scolded, "while saving your face you sometimes risk losing your ass! That officer is a confidant of Manuel Godoy and is almost always at his side."

"I expect nothing of any Army officer; that way I am never disappointed," José retorted. "But, this is going to be a great day and I'll be damned if I'll let someone like that overstuffed bastard spoil it."

As the two rode silently through the screne countryside, both men's anxieties began to subside. "Spain is a beautiful country. The shame is that nature in every country on earth must tolerate mankind's constant attempt to rape it," Gaspar thought to himself.

The stone walls surrounding Doña Rosalita's estate loomed over a small rise in the road. José could see the two-story main house through the enormous black steel gate as León brought the wagon to a halt. He noticed a red tiled roof above the wooden balconies that surrounded the entire second floor. Below was a flagstone terrace surrounded by poinsettia plants still with bright green leaves this early in the fall. The portion of the courtyard through the gate was shaded by some large trees and, in the middle of a rock garden, filled with hibiscus and other flowering plants was the princess herself, working on the peddler's cart.

José's heart beat faster when he saw her. "Good morning!" he shouted, "I thought you might appreciate some help on your project. I see you are already attending to it."

"Why, Captain Gaspar, what a surprise and what a wonderful offer," the smiling Doña Rosalita offered as she came forward to unlatch the gate, allowing the wagon to pass into the courtyard. "Would you care for some wine or other refreshment?"

"The road is quite dusty," León quickly responded.

"Come, join me in the back of the house for a glass of wine." Doña Rosalita graciously led the two men into the house and down a long wood paneled hallway to another open courtyard. José was almost blinded by the sunlit brilliance of the bougainvillea as he came out of the door and said, "Dear princess, only your beauty could compete with all of this natural beauty!"

Blushing slightly, she called for a servant to bring three glasses of the best sangria and some bread with olive oil for her guests. She removed her hat, shook out her hair, and turned her eyes to José. For a moment, neither spoke, content upon looking at one another and both feeling a little off guard. Doña Rosalita slowly unfastened her gardening apron and let it casually drop to the floor, and then she turned to León and beckoned him to please sit down.

"What do you have in your wagon?" she asked inquisitively.

"When I last saw your cart, it was obvious that repairs were needed," José explained, "so, when I met with my Cousin León, no finer carpenter in all the Spanish Navy, we decided to offer to help you with your project."

"How thoughtful. I enjoy restoring antiques and creating unique things," Doña Rosalita replied. "This old table, for example, dates back to the year 900 and was stored in a dairy barn stable. Farmers had set pails and buckets upon it for years."

As Doña Rosalita leaned forward, her bosom brushed against the table, and José noted that her breasts shifted softly under the lace that touched her lustrous skin. He attempted not to stare at this most-appealing sight.

After nearly an hour of conversation, with León doing little talking, it was León who suggested that perhaps it would be wise to begin work on the cart project. He was sure that if the joy and laughter of both José and Doña Rosalita during the past hour were any indication, the work would not be burdensome for them.

As the afternoon progressed, the cart was completely disassembled and Doña Rosalita, José, and León worked under the scorching sun cutting and nailing together a new frame and base. José, in spite of struggling to do so, could not keep his eyes off Doña Rosalita. In this setting of hard work, the contradictory image of femininity and grimy carpenter's apprentice brought a broad smile from deep within his heart.

Doña Rosalita's face was the prettiest he had ever seen, with her expressive dark brown eyes, the natural color of her skin, her shapely features, and the thick wavy hair that peeked beneath her hat and flowed over her shoulders. She had a shapely figure with tight breasts outlined beneath her blouse and firm legs and buttocks outlined beneath her tight riding trousers and boots. *This woman would give a man joy all of his life,* José thought.

As José and León measured and sawed the various pieces of lumber, Doña exhibited great expertise with hammer and nail, and on this magical day in José's young life, the cart again began to take shape by mid-afternoon. Doña Rosalita suggested they break for some lunch and disappeared into the house.

Within minutes she reappeared and suggested that, with the help of the servants, they could picnic beside the small creek near the house beneath the limbs of hundred-year-old oaks. With the enthusiasm of a true military officer, she removed her cap and pointed the way.

As José and León enjoyed a tasty repast of Andalusian rice, salad, tortilla de patas, and sweet flan, Rosalita spoke of the many things she enjoyed and how they gave her enthusiasm for life. José agreed that enthusiasm and hard work were the two ingredients that every great man had and cherished. Doña Rosalita amended that with, "and, all great women as well."

Her understandable desire to prolong the restful moment may have caused Doña Rosalita to approach the edge of the creekbed. As she attempted to sit down on the ground, José jumped to his feet and grabbed León's jacket, placing it beneath her and causing her to sit upon both the jacket and his hands. That action and the closeness of their faces caused José to flush, and she gave him a forgiving smile as he backed away. She took off her boots and hat and slid her legs into the cool creek water, delighting in the feeling of the sand between her toes. Then, leaning over, she cupped her hands, and took a drink of the clear, springfed creek water, allowing the overflow to cascade over her chest. The water soaked her blouse so that it clung to her body.

As José helped her up the creek bank, Rosalita slipped and their bodies became intertwined as he held her tight, their faces close. José felt a tingling envelope his body and sensed correctly that she did also. Her eyes were wide and her lips were parted. With his right hand he could feel her heart beating. His head was irresistibly drawn to hers as he kissed her mouth and she responded. As their hands touched each other, the moment was shattered by a third party's cough!

"Ahem," León interrupted, " I think if we are to finish the carpentry on the cart, it would be wise to return to it immediately. If you will excuse me, I will get started."

"You are right, León," an embarrassed José replied as he let go of Rosalita.

Startled by the spontaneous and passionate encounter, she excused herself to call the servants to clean up after the picnic lunch.

When the two men returned to the courtyard, they worked the rest of the afternoon, completing the repairs to the cart while Rosalita remained in the main house. Occasionally, she emerged on the balcony to observe their efforts and to bid them thanks and farewell as the afternoon ended.

Whether by chance or with intent, José was pleased to see Rosalita watching from above. His eyes traveled from her head to her feet to commit her image to memory. He could not control the emotions of love and desire that he was feeling inside and understood at that moment how a man is governed by both his brain and his loins and how they have an ongoing conflict from puberty to death.

With his brain taking charge in this situation, José calmly described the workmanship of the cart to Rosalita and told her how it should be completed. Of course, he offered to finish it the day after next since he had to attend the recognition dinner and ball the next night at the palace.

"I'll be there also," Rosalita replied excitedly. "I'll look forward to seeing you honored by the king and the members of the court. If you can, perhaps you will give me a wave?"

"I will look forward not only to a wave, but also to kissing the hand of the fairest woman in all of Spain," José dramatically stated going to one knee. She laughed at his gallantry and gave a final wave before going into the house.

The two men quickly loaded the tools into the wagon and attached the horses for the return to the city. The sun was beginning its daily descent when the wagon rolled through the black gate of Doña Rosalita's estate.

"León, I have never felt this way in my life. I have such great expectations for this relationship," José exclaimed. "I often judge things the first time I see them and that can be dangerous, but I know I will dream of Doña Rosalita!"

"Dreams are important. However, if your dreams fail to materialize, you will still be here," León counseled as he guided the noisy wagon through the Madrid city gate.

"That may be true, my friend, but when you cease to dream, you have ceased to live," José stated openly as they passed crowds of happy Madrilenos who were visiting the various tapas bars. The fourteen bars corresponded to the number of the Stations of the Cross according to Madrilenos' tradition.

"Look, the Madrilenos have an excuse to claim drinking as a religious experience," León chuckled. "Of course, even without the religious connotation, I understand their need to drink after they consume spicy sausages, potatoes in hot pepper sauce, octopus, sardines in garlic oil, and hundreds of other equally hot foods."

"Tomorrow, I shall dream about this very night," José smiled, oblivious to León's chatter.

"Is it possible that getting my coat cleaned of creekbank stains might also be a part of your dreams, José?" León replied.

They laughed loudly as the wagon bounced along the cobblestone street. "Love demands less than friendship," José said while clapping his hand on León's shoulder, "but I will gladly pay for cleaning your jacket."

CHAPTER 12

The Challenge of Success and Politics

"A person, when challenged, must put forth his best abilities
to rise to the occasion and grow in character."
—José Gaspar, September 9, 1778

The morning was cloudy, but José still felt warmth within as remembrance of the previous day dawned in him. This day, however, was to be full of scheduled meetings with various military officers and bureaucrats. In the early afternoon, there would be another meeting with Manuel Godoy and other ministers and, in the evening, the recognition dinner and ball where José would again see the lovely Doña Rosalita. He believed in dealing with the difficult jobs first and the anticipation of being near the beautiful princess dispelled any initial concern José had for the series of meetings.

After breakfast at Monasterio Corpus Christi in the heart of Madrid's medieval quarter, José rode back to the palace and walked through the gardens to the Navy minister's office and his first meeting with the Spanish naval officials.

Foremost on José's agenda was his attempt to convince the ministers and assembled admirals to improve the quality of the enlisted crews who manned the Spanish ships and to improve the construction and drastically change the type of ships to be employed by the Navy in the future.

José was awed by the presence of Minister FloridaBlanca. Also present were a variety of other admirals and attachés who were much less impressive or memorable. With *such a collection of brilliant naval minds, I can hope to create a model for the future of the Spanish Navy*, José thought, with youthful enthusiasm.

Following formal introductions and some brief social banter, the first meeting began. Minister FloridaBlanca was sincere in hearing the opinions of this young Navy officer, a recent Naval Academy graduate who was tops in his class, and currently a hero and the talk of Madrid. The other naval officers present were obviously less enthusiastic and sincere in their questioning and the discussions that followed.

"You indicate dissatisfaction with the current level of sailors serving on Spanish Crown naval ships?" FloridaBlanca somewhat sternly inquired of José before the group.

"Well, sir, we currently conscript men out of prison, pick men off the street, accept application from anyone regardless of any sea experience, and generally have no requirements of those sailing the ships of the king," José replied. "With the exception of the topsail seamen, we seldom have able-bodied crews on board when we leave port. The officers have to spend a great deal of their time training crews in the hopes of creating able seaman."

"What alternative have we?" inquired Capt. Pedro Colón, a former sea captain of some repute. "We have crewed our ships in the same manner for at least two hundred years."

"Exactly my point," José excitedly replied, "We might well learn a great deal from the American colonists currently in revolt against England. They have been able to attract the brightest, strongest, and most able men to be sailors in their navy by making their wages the highest in the world. Conversely, England has the same problem as Spain when it comes to staffing ships. You get from a crew only what you are willing to invest."

"But, Captain Gaspar, you must admit that the American colonists have a navy that is estimated to have only thirty-four vessels," Colón laughed derisively. "With so few ships, we could staff them with our brightest and best as well. No, I think the British will soon defeat these American revolutionaries, and your argument for recruiting better seaman, as they do, will die as well."

"I disagree, sir, I believe the American Revolution is a beginning of a new and different world for all of us. With their employment of privateers or pirates they will be able to hold their own against the English," Gaspar replied. "In fact, the American colonists have enlisted over four hundred privateers to help in their fight against the English."

"What you are suggesting then, Captain Gaspar, is that we consider paying a higher wage and raise the educational standards in order to attract quality men to crew our ships?" FloridaBlanca interrupted leaning forward, his arms on the large table.

"Yes, I believe that the idea of patriotic service should be replaced by individual financial success," Gaspar continued. "In other words, if we train our sailors and pay them for their success in meeting our high standards, we can have outstanding crews who seek to remain in the navy for a career and can successfully defeat Spain's enemies in the future."

"It is an interesting concept Gaspar; but, I fear one that the crown will not readily entertain," FloridaBlanca contemplated. "However, aren't you a prime example of the excellent officer corps we graduate annually from the Naval Academy?"

"I would hope that I am indicative of an academy graduate," Gaspar smiled at FloridaBlanca, "but I must respectfully suggest that we might also improve upon the instruction given at the academy in Cadiz."

"Oh, you find fault there as well?" Colón interjected sarcastically, leaning back in his ornate gold-leaf chair.

"The overall concept of the academy is fine, as are the goals," Gaspar responded, "the problem is that we are trained in outdated methods while the world is changing so fast. It is not that Spain does not pay attention to what is happening in the rest of the world. Naval warfare is changing dramatically. I sincerely believe that many of the instructors at the academy would continue a lecture on navigation while their ship was actually sinking. They do not see things outside their individual classrooms."

"So, you suggest that we raise the pay of our seaman, change the curriculum at the academy to teach unproved possibilities, and increase the number of privateers employed by King Charles to solve our manpower needs in the Navy?" Adm. Luis Castellanos coldly interrupted, "I must suggest to you, young man, that we cannot ask the crown for additional money at this time. In theory, these things might work, but we must be practical."

"I predict the American upstarts will teach all of us a great deal more than any of the other countries on earth," José answered. "Their tenacity, youth, and resourcefulness will serve as a light to which we should all navigate."

The men laughed at what they interpreted as Gaspar's attempt at humor in suggesting that the American colonists of the two-year-old rebellion could challenge or teach the powerful English Navy or Spain anything about naval tactics.

"So, Captain Gaspar, have you any suggestions on how we might save money in building our ships so that we might pay a professional crew of seamen handsomely?" FloridaBlanca asked sarcastically, attempting to withhold his obvious impatience.

Not noting the minister's sarcasm, José responded in yet another direction, "The building of frigates, patterned after the British and French, instead of the forty-four gun, two-deck, convoy vessels we are currently constructing. Our forty-four gun ships are slow and cranky and suited only for convoy or coastal defense duty. Spain needs ships with speed, maneuverability, and power."

An eerie silence enveloped the room, as a strain of annoyance and a cold sense of dislike grew within the group for this young, overconfident upstart. They all turned their heads to look at a reddening Admiral Castellanos as José continued.

"We need to construct a ship, the length of our current ships of the line, but lower in the hull to increase speed in the water. We could accomplish this with our current sail plan. We could arm her with twenty-eight or thirty-six eighteen-pound cannon as the English do, with fourteen or eighteen ports on each side. Above the main deck we could extend the quarterdeck from the main mast to the stern and the forecastle from the main mast to the bow. We could mount nine-pounders on the quarterdeck portion and two twenty-four pounders on the forecastle. We could add even more firepower to the quarterdeck. These ships could carry six months of provisions on board. That way they could choose to simply remain out of range of large battleships or convoys with their speed and maneuverability or attack and fight anything afloat with a speed and fury second to none," Gaspar concluded.

"Anything more you might add to your dreamship's construction, Captain Gaspar?" Admiral Castellanos sternly inquired of the young captain who, for the first time, sensed the negative feelings building within the room.

"Well, gentlemen, there is one thing we might consider in all our ship construction, from simple longboats to battleships of the line," Gaspar stated a little less enthusiastically, "the use of oak on our ships instead of teak. I have learned that teakwood is septic. After an injury that occurs in battle or on duty, an infection from the teak often forms and can kill. Whereas, if we use oak in place of teak, the wounds are usually clean and do not become infected, thereby saving our sailors' lives."

"I am sure the Spanish colonists who provide the teak to us will be supportive of your suggestion, Gaspar," Captain Colón stated coldly and with anger upon his face.

"I think we have run the course of this meeting," FloridaBlanca wisely interrupted, "I suggest that we break for lunch. Captain Gaspar, I do appreciate you sharing your unique perspectives. For myself, if I appear confused, it is because you have given me a great deal to think about. However, I must suggest to you that it is sometimes wise to consider the opinions of others before expressing your own so enthusiastically. I'll take my leave now."

When the minister arose, all the officers arose and came to attention while he exited the room. With his exit, José became aware of the fact that the only glimmer of warmth in the room toward him had been held by FloridaBlanca. Now, as a quiet murmuring engulfed the room, José was left alone as the others slowly exited in pairs or groups which he was not invited to join. Standing isolated in the room, José felt the rejection of his peers for the first time in his life.

José noted a lone figure had come forward from the shadows in the back of the room. This priest, dressed in black and wearing a silver crucifix around his neck, walked directly up to José and extended his right hand. When José knelt to kiss his hand, the priest spoke. "There is no need to do that now, my son."

José bowed before the priest and introduced himself; "I am José Gaspar, captain in the Royal Spanish Navy."

"I have had the pleasure of witnessing and hearing your discussions this morning," the priest replied gently. "It may be that I was the only one in the room who took pleasure in your presentation. I am Father Lasuen and I am on holiday from the San Diego Presidio in the Americas."

"Where in the Americas is the San Diego Presidio?" José questioned.

"Ah, it is located high on a hill, which we call Presidio Hill, overlooking the San Diego mission in California. Father Serra and José de Gálvez, leaders of the missionary expedition that was sent to the New World to convert the Native Americans to Christianity, established it in 1769. Our Presidio has been built and run by soldiers whose duty it is to protect the area from the Native Americans, the British, and even the Russians," Father Lasuen replied. "It is one of four missions built in the New World with the others being at Monterrey, San Francisco, and Santa Barbara."

"I see, but why if you are on holiday, do you spend it in a Naval officers meeting?" José asked respectfully.

"Yes, well you see, I was formerly attached to the Navy quay in Seville for a short time and there became acquainted with Admiral Castellanos," Father Lasuen answered with a smile on his face. "I wanted to inform you that he is the most influential person in our Navy in designing and supporting the building of the forty-four gun ships you lambasted in your discussion. Since I could sense his anger, I decided to stay behind and introduce myself to you and share this information with you."

"It's amazing how confidence and enthusiasm can blind one's eyes to the obvious," José countered. "I wish I had known, but you know, Father,

I am right in my opinion of the construction of these ships. They are a waste of money and will never be able to stand up to the English and French frigates."

"I know, my son, for I have recently spent weeks on Spanish ships and unfortunately must return to the New World on one," Father Lasuen laughed. "I think you need someone with whom to have lunch. If it is not me, I fear you will eat alone."

As they walked slowly to lunch at Puerto del Sol, Madrid's central plaza, José asked Father Lasuen if he believed it possible to fall in love with a woman at first sight. "I cannot answer that from experience," the priest replied, with a chuckle.

A lifelong friendship was born between them at that time and José later penned letters to Father Lasuen during times of confusion.

After lunch, the men walked across a large patio where José recognized the building housing Manuel Godoy's office. Father Lasuen bid farewell to the captain to go in search of the art museum and, as he laughingly stated, "perhaps a stop, or even fourteen of them, at the tapas."

Hoping not to repeat his performance of that morning, José pledged to try to curb his enthusiasm and not dominate the afternoon's meeting. However, he knew in his heart that our actions are normally dependent upon what we already are. He whispered a short prayer for strength and opened the thick carved wood door to Godoy's ornate conference room.

Immediately, José knew this was not going to be an easy session. The lieutenant who greeted him this afternoon was none other than Rolando Gomez, who had commanded the Asturia's patrol that had stopped him and Cousin León the previous morning. The chill that he already felt in the room belied the oppressive sultry heat outside. With the formal entrance of Manuel Godoy, dressed in new finery, and the rest of his staff, another shiver crept down José's spine. As they were seated at the hand-carved table with fine glassware and cold spring water at each place, José could sense that news of his morning performance had already filtered through to these Army veterans.

Following the formal introduction of all those present, it was obvious that Manuel Godoy was in charge of all that would transpire in this meeting. He leaned back, giving José a long appraising look, while noting his stature and poise. Behind Godoy, José saw the glowering young Lieutenant Gomez and thought that these two would present him problems as long as he stayed in Madrid.

Godoy waved his beringed hand, indicating that José should stand before him at the table where all the officers were seated. "Captain Gaspar, I am told that you seek to learn military tactics from the traditional enemies of Spain?"

"Sir, I seek to learn only that which will benefit Spain," Gaspar replied matter of factly. "I believe that we can learn a great deal from observing and studying the successes of other nations in their military campaigns. I sometimes find myself trusting that which I learn from my enemies more than what I am told by my friends."

With a mischievous cruel smile, Godoy asked young Gaspar to continue and share what he had learned with regard to military tactics so that his Army officers might benefit.

"Gentlemen, I believe that Napoleon is using military tactics which each of you in Spain's Army should consider," Gaspar began, ignoring the quiet gasps from members of the panel and their attachés.

"You believe we can learn from the French?" Godoy coldly interrupted. "Unbelievable! This morning you told your naval colleagues to learn from the rebel English colonies in America and now you are suggesting that Spain learn something from the French Army led by Napoleon? I'm beginning to doubt that you have any Spanish blood in your veins. In fact, your stature does compare to that of your French hero. Maybe you are French?"

The room was shaken with mocking laughter, the Army officers relieved that Godoy was focusing his energy towards embarrassing Gaspar instead of seriously pondering his suggestions. The Spanish Army officers knew that their traditional warfare strategies could not compare to the swift moving self-contained units that had been developed in the past twenty years by the French. They recognized a need to change but were very relieved that the young brash naval officer would not initiate it this afternoon.

"Give us some examples of what the French Army is doing that impresses you so much that you feel we should change our land forces," Godoy demanded caustically.

For the next two and one-half hours, Gaspar gave examples of how the French land forces had been changed based upon the innovative ideas of two French army officers, Pierre-Joséph de Bourcet and Comte de Guibert. Gaspar discussed Bourcet's belief that it was impossible for an enemy to be in strength everywhere. According to Bourcet, a commander who divided his forces could mislead an enemy, making him believe the main effort was coming at some point other than the primary objective. If the enemy dispersed its troops to counter, the primary target would be weakened and if it did not, the secondary targets could be captured. Gaspar approved of Bourcet's offensive strategy to disrupt and confuse the enemy with an attack on several fronts simultaneously as opposed to the Spanish army setting up singular front battlelines and spending more time in defensive as opposed to offensive movements. "The key is being able to combine your forces to overwhelm an enemy objective weakened by its division of forces," Gaspar continued.

Godoy, unable to respond to Gaspar's valid interpretation, simply waved to José to continue.

"Comte de Guibert wants to promote a more mobile type of warfare," Gaspar went on. "Guibert believes that if we divide our one large army into divisions, each of which will march in columns along different routes, we can confuse our enemies, allowing our division commanders to attack secondary or primary objectives they feel can be captured. This philosophy will combine quite well with Bourcet's teaching," Gaspar made a point of emphasis.

"The real benefit of adopting Guibert's ideas is to eliminate the wasteful and costly process we employ of using private contractors to supply our troops food and ammunition from Spain while our army is doing battle out of our country," Gaspar emphasized. "Guibert's armies are totally self-contained. With its officers knowledgeable in supply and feeding, the French army eats and lives at its enemies' expense off their land!"

Godoy, fully understanding Spain's corrupt tradition of lining the pockets of irresponsible merchants, tried to deflect this charge, "What evidence have you that private contractors have ever taken advantage of Spain?"

Gaspar couldn't control himself again. "We lost an entire armada of naval ships to the English in the past simply because we relied upon private contractors to provide our ship's casks of fresh water and fresh food. Instead they got green wood casks with tainted water and spoiled food that made our sailors sick and unable to defeat a smaller fleet."

"Enough!" Godoy bellowed. "We have heard enough. I will not attempt to hide my displeasure. Minister FloridaBlanca may be gracious and a good listener. But, we have centuries of success behind us."

"Exactly my point, Señor Godoy, those who are firmly seated in authoritarian positions or established countries for that matter soon learn to think only of security and not of progress. The world depends on progressive thinkers!"

Finally, as had happened in the forenoon, the group had enough of the presentations and dire predictions of Capt. José Gaspar, an obvious hero to the people, but who was fast becoming an enemy of the bureaucrats and the status quo in Madrid. Manuel Godoy personally saw the young officer as a challenge to the bureaucracy and military hierarchy that he had learned to deftly climb and control.

"Captain Gaspar, I find your input to be most interesting. However, I trust you will want some time to freshen up and prepare for the dinner and festivities being held in your honor tonight," Godoy stated in an agitated tone, as he struggled to gather enough composure to end the session.

Finding himself again isolated, José walked from the room and wandered through many of the series of sumptuously decorated rooms that were a part of the Royal Palace. Shortly after 4:00 P.M., Cousin León found him walking back to his room. León had made a point of coming by to help José prepare for the evening's activities.

"How did your day go, Captain Cousin Gaspar?" León asked, playfully unaware of the negative impression his young cousin had made on the military aristocracy of Spain.

"A sure way to make enemies is to suggest that those in charge change something," José replied. "The world we have created is simply a product of our thinking. Don't they understand that the world cannot be changed without changing our thinking."

"Ah, my cousin, as you age you will find that all change represents a loss of some kind—that is why we all resist change," León answered. "Many of these people with whom you spoke are quite powerful. They owe their power to the governmental bureaucracy you seek to challenge."

"But an extensive bureaucracy is the greatest threat to our individual freedom," José concluded. "Government bureaucracies can consume the individual rights of citizens."

"Maybe so, but the fact remains that the gentlemen you addressed today are both wealthy and powerful due to a bureaucratic government. They don't like their position in the bureaucracy criticized. Powerful and rich people seldom care about freedom, for they believe that what they desire can be purchased," León continued. "In fact, they purchase sex from prostitutes because they don't want to risk criticism."

José laughed heartily at León's last statement. "Come, León, you can suggest how I might salvage something from this day when I am introduced to the king."

"With Manuel Godoy introducing you, I fear there will be little to salvage," León said, as they crossed the shaded garden to José's quarters.

"With the happenings of this day, it would have been better for you to spend the day at the bullfight at the Plaza de Toros, with you being the bull, José."

CHAPTER 13

Honor and Love

*"I think the job of being a hero may well have the shortest tenure of any career.
But, I also believe that when you fall in love
there is a greater risk that everything may be lost."*
—José Gaspar, September 9, 1778

The dinner and recognition ball to honor Capt. José Gaspar was held in the great main ballroom of the king's palace and was indeed a splendid affair. As he approached the ballroom, José appreciated the beauty of the ornate carvings on the columns surrounding the hall. Inside, the tables were set with fine china and silverware, and bouquets of fresh flowers were abundant on the gold-leaf furnishings made of the finest hardwoods. The massive doorways were open to allow the fresh cool evening breeze to flow into the great hall. There were patios or balconies off each of these doorways that were decorated with royal elegance.

Lord Sergio Jiménez of the king's court was to be the official escort and attaché serving José during the evening's activities. He had arrived early at the captain's quarters to brief him in proper etiquette and the expectations of one being so honored. José liked Lord Jiménez and found him to be both frank and honest—a rare quality in Madrid. Lord Jiménez had stated early that he could not understand why someone as young as José was to be recognized by the king. "I am glad I am not as young as you, for youth believes it knows everything. Personally, I am glad to have reached an age when I am wise enough to know that I have much more to learn. But, one advantage of youth is overconfidence, which is displayed through courage. Maybe many of our heroes are young because of this."

This logic brought a smile to José Gaspar's face and he said wryly, "Yes, but aging is a great price to have to pay to gain maturity."

Ignoring José's last comment, Lord Jiménez reviewed the formality of the evening, discussing the procedures that José should follow when greeting the ladies and gentlemen of the court, as well as others who would be attending.

"Captain Sanibel told me that all the ladies of the court are beautiful," José remarked.

Lord Jiménez roared with laughter, then said, "I believe your Captain Sanibel has spread the myth that is so prevalent among those citizens living outside of Madrid. You told me you have met María Louisa of Parma? I can assure you that there are many ladies of the court who pale by comparison, so, I wouldn't get my hopes up in regards to meeting any single fair maidens."

"Well, I admit that María Louisa is not beautiful, but I didn't mean to be unfair," José replied apologetically.

"No, my Captain, you are not unfair. But, most assuredly, you will certainly meet ladies tonight who are far from beautiful. Remember, you must treat each woman in a manner that is similar to your treatment of the queen and keep your opinion to yourself," Lord Jiménez admonished.

"My hope is that Doña Rosalita Santiago will be at both the dinner and the dance which follows. I have seen her only twice, but I feel that someday she will belong to me," José said with feeling.

"I would not covet the princess too much," Lord Jiménez warned. "I know of no single man in all of Madrid who does not fantasize about your choice. In fact, many married men do, also!"

"But, when I looked into her eyes I sensed that she has strong feelings for me. I am convinced that our love is foretold in the stars above us this evening," José retorted.

"I do not know much about astrology, but I am beginning to believe you must be a Taurus with your stubbornness," Lord Jiménez chuckled. "Just be careful not to appear to compete with those powerful members of the court who share your appreciation and desire for Doña Rosalita.

The powerful, and those who would court power, started to arrive and take their official places throughout the great hall. The dinner orchestra began to play light classical fare. The prominence of the guitar in the group was a unique addition to the Spanish interpretation of the music.

With a great flourish of drums and the sound of trumpets, the official entourage of King Charles entered the great hall across from Lord Jiménez and Captain Gaspar. The group included not only the king and queen, but also the various ministers and officers whom José had addressed earlier in the day. Manuel Godoy was at the king's side and Minister FloridaBlanca was directly behind, which gave José a feeling of anxiety. *Anxiety can certainly cloud our vision of the future*, José thought to himself.

As José and Lord Jiménez went through the official receiving line, José was impressed with the overt cordiality of the group toward him— even Lieutenant Gomez and Manuel Godoy. The captain began to feel that perhaps he had misconstrued their feelings toward him earlier in the day.

Lord Jiménez, gently prodding him through the formal line, quietly whispered, "Every government I have known is run by liars and nothing you hear should be believed. I believe Plato said it best when he stated, 'Those who are too smart to engage in politics are punished by being governed by those who are dumber.' This may well be our fate as well." José smiled broadly.

When José reached the king and queen, he bowed dramatically before each. King Charles reached down and helped him to his feet and to the captain's amazement, vigorously shook his hand and held on for a long while to his arm. The king seemed to genuinely approve of the young captain, causing ill-disguised looks of disapproval from the various ministers and military leaders.

José and Lord Jiménez were seated at a table with Admiral Castellanos, Father Lasuen, and Manuel Godoy, with a number of other officers. This was the only table seating just males, which surprised him, given the reputation concerning women of the many dutifully seated with him.

Following the delicious meal and many glasses of sangria, which José compared to the juices of heaven, it was time for the formal recognition of Capt. José Gaspar by King Charles and the members of the court.

During the ceremony, José approached the head table. King Charles took an ornate sword from its scabbard—the most impressive José had ever seen. It had been handcrafted in Toledo by the most famous swordsmith in the entire world.

The king brought the sword forward and José knelt as he held it before his face. José read the inscription on the blade: CAPTAIN JOSÉ GASPAR, COURAGE AND HONOR IN SERVICE TO SPAIN.

King Charles then took the sword by the handle and tapped the point first on José's left shoulder then upon his right, officially knighting him in the Spanish tradition. Gaspar took the sword in his left hand, the king's left hand in his right, and kissed the beringed hand of the monarch.

Following a thunderous applause, José turned to face the audience for the first time. The first face drawn into his focus was that of Doña Rosalita Santiago. It seemed to leap out at him from those that surrounded her. He hoped that she knew that he was gazing at her. Then, as her eyes met his, he knew the feelings of attraction were mutual.

It is highly doubtful that even Moses could have been as skillful in parting the seas as José and Doña Rosalita were in parting the crowd, as they moved to a point where José could bow down gallantly and kiss her white-gloved right hand.

With their gaze transfixed, Doña Rosalita removed her glove so that José could hold her bare hand. Instinctively, he put the white glove in the pocket of his jacket. "My princess, there can be no flower in all of Spain as beautiful as you are this evening," he announced.

Doña Rosalita reached over and squeezed his hand, gently helping him to stand erect. "I might question that, as there are many beautiful flowers in my garden," she softly replied.

"I should like to challenge you to show me such a flower," José responded looking intently into her eyes.

"Then, I would be foolish to doubt your words, José. At this point, you may say anything to me and not worry about your words," Doña Rosalita quietly assured him, again squeezing his hand.

The band began playing, and although María Gonzalez of Cadiz had taught José to dance well, he felt a higher power must indeed be guiding his steps, for the pair flowed around the dance floor with as much smoothness as the music of the Royal orchestra.

During the later part of the evening, the perspiring pair, who had entertained most of those in attendance with their graceful dancing, decided to go out into the garden for a walk.

As they walked among the hibiscus and crotons, with hands and arms locked tightly together, José was aware of his heart pounding so loud in his chest he feared that Doña Rosalita might hear it or that it might explode. When they reached a dark, quiet spot in the garden, she tripped slightly as she stepped on an uneven brick. He caught her by the arm and when he reached over with his other arm to brace her shoulder, they held each other tightly. Her eyes were wide and her lips parted as she breathed rapidly. As they stood together, with Doña Rosalita leaning forward, José hesitated no longer. He let go of her arms and crushed her to him. They kissed and, as her tongue met his, they dropped to the grass.

José gently took the bodice of her gown in his fingers and pulled it down below her left breast. He held her breast in his hand as he brushed it with his lips. She gave a soft cry of pleasure and pulled his head more firmly against her. He continued to kiss her breast, his tongue circling the erect nipple. Time became inconsequential, but, before allowing herself to be drowned in a sea of pleasure, she pushed him away and regretfully stood up.

"I have never done this before. I know that it can't be wrong because it feels so right, yet I think we should save this activity until such time as we are truly certain of our feelings for each other. I know how we are feeling at this moment, but I am also aware that if we are to have permanent happiness together, it must be based upon a trust built over time.

With that, Rosalita ran her fingers through José's hair and ran from the garden.

CHAPTER 14

Responsibility, Obligation, and Duty

"If you want rights, you must be responsible. This means that for every opportunity you have, you accept an obligation to perform. If you avoid this duty to perform, you avoid taking action and you have failed yourself. The world only rewards those who can show results from their efforts."
—José Gaspar, September 10, 1778

Following a restless night, José finally began to doze as he listened to the birds chirping in the garden. The dark night sky was awakening with blue, gold and fuchsia tints. As sleep was finally overtaking him, his trusted cousin, León, rudely awakened him.

"José, you are to meet with Manuel Godoy and Minister FloridaBlanca this morning. I have been on duty all night and was notified to wake you and have you report in uniform shortly after sunrise," León said.

"León, lost yesterday, somewhere between sunrise and midnight, are three of the most wonderful hours of my life. Before sleep can cloud my eyes, you tell me I must now meet again with those whom I spent nearly all the remainder?" Gaspar groggily replied.

"José, remember the Spanish proverb, 'Love is a furnace, but it will not cook the stew.' You must attend to your duties, but you don't look very well. Are you ill?" León asked.

"This morning I know that I am in love and that Doña Rosalita feels the same way," José happily replied. Then a scowl covered his face. "My heart is hurting, though, because I fear that I was not a true gentleman last night with Rosalita and it pains me greatly. I now believe that lovesickness is the only cause of heartache." He jumped from his bed and left the room to go to use the facilities and prepare for another eventful day in the political forest of Spain's capital city.

Within moments, the gallant Spanish naval captain returned to the room and, now smiling, clapped León on the shoulder. José announced, "Have you noticed, my dear cousin, some of the contradictions of our times? For example, today we must deal with both *political science* and *military intelligence* issues before we can partake of the Plaza Mayor's fine bakery products."

As the pair crossed the luxurious gardens of the palace, José noticed some remarkable rose bushes inside a well-trimmed hedge area. He had never seen any roses more beautiful or with such a variety of color. He reached into his pocket and brought out Doña Rosalita's white glove. A grin covered nearly all of his face as he impulsively leaped over the hedge into the rose garden, ignoring the warnings of León who told him, aghast, that these roses were in the queen's personal flower garden. With his new Toledo, he carefully cut off a red, white, yellow, and pink rose from four different bushes. As quickly as he had entered the royal grounds, he was back on the path with Cousin León.

"My dear Cousin José, what are you going to do with these roses you have stolen from the queen's garden?" León inquired.

"I could not help myself, for last night I proclaimed to my sweet Doña Rosalita that she was prettier than any flower in Spain. To prove my point, and to hopefully make amends for my behavior, I have selected four of the most beautiful flowers that nature can produce," José proudly replied. "I chose four to celebrate each of the four days I have known her and the beauty and purity of thought that she brings to my mind."

José intertwined each of the roses with a finger of the white glove, then removed a silk scarf from under his uniform jacket and gently wrapped the glove and flowers in it. He also enclosed a note apparently written during the sleeplessness of the night.

"While I attend this meeting, my dear cousin, I want you to take this out to the lovely Doña Rosalita's house. I want her to get it directly from you," José pleaded. "Tell her that I challenge her to find any rose as beautiful in her own garden and remind her of my claim that she is fairer than these. Tell her that I will ride out this evening to offer a formal apology for my behavior in the garden last night."

"Fine, my captain. But I can't believe you risked stealing roses from the queen's own garden for such a purpose," León laughed.

"I have never before, and will never again, steal from the Spanish Crown, but in matters of love, to make a point, it is sometimes necessary to act individually and place that love above any of man's organizations," José replied.

"I will personally tell Doña Rosalita of the power she has over you," León chuckled. "The Bible tells us there is no fear in love and that perfect love casts out fear. You must feel a most perfect love."

"Aye, that I most certainly do," José responded sincerely.

Then, with a smile and a shake of León's hand, José told him, "I must go to the government building now. Another contradiction of which I am quite fond of is the term 'government organization.'"

Both men laughed and with the sun now climbing above the horizon, they went their separate ways.

The joy of the morning was soon dampened as José opened the door to Godoy's office to be met by the forbidding face of Lt. Rolando Gomez. *Gomez can have absolutely no joy in his life*, José thought to himself. Like the rest of the bureaucrats chasing around Madrid, Gomez typified the unhappiness of those who put their jobs above all else. Gaspar had determined that the fast tempo of Madrid life crowded out people's feelings for themselves and one another, making nothing seem worthwhile, and thus leaving them feeling hollow and unhappy.

Captain Gaspar followed Gomez to the main office of Manuel Godoy. The feeling of coldness evident the previous day still permeated the room. Godoy, Minister FloridaBlanca, Admiral Castellanos, and two others, whom José did not recognize, were seated at the large table.

"Captain Gaspar, you have had quite an eventful time since your arrival in Madrid earlier this week," Manuel Godoy began. "It makes me believe, as we learn from the church in the teachings of Holy Week, that much can happen in one week's time."

José found himself smiling at the irony of the happenings to him in less than one week. It was a week begun with thoughts only of triumph and adulation, but now it was a week clouded with thoughts of love on the one hand, and regret for his impulsivenes words to his leaders on the other. Godoy was right in his assessment of an eventful week.

"Captain Gaspar, we will get right to the point of this meeting," Minister FloridaBlanca said forcefully. "I have given thought to your comments of yesterday. You indicated your faith in the new American Navy, small as it is. I do not know whether you are correct in that faith, but I do know that the English have withdrawn much of their navy from the Caribbean, and American privateers and pirates are moving into the void. The American's war with England is having serious consequences upon our Spanish shipping. You will lead a fleet of vessels to the Spanish Main to escort our merchant ships and attack any pirate or privateer ship that you encounter."

"How soon do you anticipate this mission to be ready," Captain Gaspar asked, his mind and heart so full of personal thoughts that he was reluctant to accept this order.

"We are arranging for you to take command of three of my finest forty-four-gun ships," Admiral Castellanos smirked, as he thought of José having command of a ship of the type he had so firmly opposed.

"The speed with which you appear to be falling in love with the Doña Rosalita indicates that we should move quickly," Manuel Godoy stated, with envy showing through his attempted humor. "We shall see whether absence does make the heart grow fonder."

A short burst of tension-relieving laughter came forth from the table.

"Next Monday, you will go to Barcelona to assume command of this small task force. Your mission will be to escort a fleet of ships to Santiago, Cuba," Minister FloridaBlanca stated, without holding out hope for refusal.

Realizing his duty, José stiffly came to attention and briskly saluted the officers.

"Is there anything you will need?" Admiral Castellanos asked.

"Sir, I would like my cousin, León Gaspar, to be assigned as ship's carpenter, if at all possible," José requested, while still at attention.

"Go ahead, this will rid Madrid of both members of the Gaspar family," Manuel Godoy sneered. "Admiral Castellanos will prepare official orders for you and your cousin."

One of the shortest bureaucratic meetings in the history of Spain came to an abrupt close with José placed in command of three of Spain's ships, the type he most despised. Additionally, he would be forced to leave the woman of his dreams. Without doubt, Captain José Gaspar was being paid handsomely, in a negative manner, for the controversial truths he had spoken the previous day.

Later that afternoon, León returned from a much more successful mission to the princess and met with José. Although there was a brilliant sun outside, José appeared quite glum and forlorn. "I sense that you were reprimanded at the meeting this morning?" León asked.

"More than that. Although it is never pleasant when it happens, sometimes a kick in the pants can be the best thing that ever happens to you." José answered. "The fact remains that, in response to the beliefs that I outlined to the admiralty, I am being sent to the Spanish Main in command of ships that I do not believe in, to fight an enemy I do not understand, and to escort ships with cargoes of which I do not approve. Oh, León, were I only to have listened, smiled, and kept my damn mouth shut! Government people don't want to hear the truth. I'm not sure any-one in government is intelligent enough to understand that necessary changes have to be made."

When León questioned José's definition of intelligence, he replied in a serious tone, "A truly intelligent person is one who can keep two oppos-ing ideas in his mind while he can still function at his job."

"Was there any good news from your meeting?" León inquired.

"There was only one bright spot. You have always told me that you have saltwater instead of blood in your veins," José laughed, "so, you will be my flagship ship's carpenter."

León grabbed José's hand, shaking it vigorously and thanking José for getting him out of land duty. Both knew they would be glad to leave the city of Madrid and the political infighting that was a daily activity in the nation's capital. In spite of his absence from Doña Rosalita, the thought of the solitude of the sea and of being in control had a great deal of appeal given the political happenings of the last four days.

"It will be so good to use my hands to build and repair things instead of my wits to keep all these bureaucrats happy," León added.

"Please tell me that your visit with my precious Doña Rosalita went well," José inquired, concerned with losing her love during the voyage.

"My meeting with the princess went much better," León continued. "In fact, you should begin to clean up shortly. She wants you to come to her before sunset so the two of you two may seek the most beautiful flower in her garden. She will then prepare you dinner."

José's spirits rose and the gloomy room seemed brighter at the thought. "You mean she wants to see me after last night? This is wonderful. What else did she say?"

"She was pleased to receive her glove in such a unique way, though she does not wish to have the glove that she gave you at your first meet-ing returned," León responded.

José looked at León quizzically, then smiled as he felt the pouch around his neck containing the glove soiled from the muddy ditch.

León said reassuringly, "José, although it may not seem so now, this may turn out to be a great day for us both. I know a contradiction for you as well. We will both be serving together on a peace force."

Both laughed, and José hurried to get ready to go to see his love. Although he felt that his naval future had been diminished, he sang as he bathed and thought, *I may not understand the world, but do know my feelings for you, my darling Rosalita.*

CHAPTER 15

Weekend of Love

"The joy of being in love can sustain you,
in spite of the pressures of the outside world."
—José Gaspar, September 1778

José decided rather than to travel by carriage with a driver, which was customary for visiting military officers in Madrid, he would borrow a horse, and travel alone. Although the horse he was riding was easily one of the finest in the stable, José could not help but be impatient with the time it took for him to get to Doña Rosalita's estate, but he arrived with plenty of daylight left.

He was nervous as he brought his horse through the iron gate and dismounted in front of the main house. The peddler's cart looked very fetching with the paint and design that Rosalita had applied since José last saw it. *She is indeed a most talented woman*, he thought to himself. *Only Rosalita could have envisioned how charming the old peddler's cart would become.*

He looked up to the balcony and saw her watching him, as the late afternoon sun cast a glow around her. She wore a simple white off-the-shoulders-peasant blouse and maroon skirt. Her long, dark hair was loosened, cascading over her bare shoulders. José ached to rush up and hold her in his arms. Simply seeing her caused him to relax, and he felt a sense of peace as he allowed the warmth of the sunshine to wash over him.

"I am glad you came in time for us to search my garden for a beautiful flower," she called down to him, "I was so impressed with the manner in which you returned my glove to me with the roses."

"Then, as you could easily see, the queen's roses could not compare to the loveliness of your face," José called back.

Doña Rosalita laughed as she teased, "I am sure that we shall be successful in our quest, or else we must question your eyesight."

José exhaled with relief. It was as if the impulsive behavior of the previous evening had never happened. However, as is true of so many men, another part of José remembered the feel of her breasts as he saw the sun upon her bodice. His groin ached and his hands wanted to lift and caress them.

She swept from the house and was soon standing close to José. "How do you like the cart?" she asked.

José came back to reality with the question and jumped as she touched his shoulder. She was smiling and her eyes danced with amusement.

"If you had brought in the top artist in the world and given him a brush, a finer work of art could not have been duplicated. You are an artistic genius!" José proclaimed grandly.

"José, I don't know when to believe you. I do know that you make me happier than I have ever been in my entire life," Rosalita earnestly replied. He could see the honesty and sincerity in her dark eyes.

José touched the hand still on his shoulder and turned to face her. With his other arm, he enveloped her waist and pulled her to him. He kissed her nose and whispered in her ear, "I love you and want to always be with you."

"I pray that will be so, José. I slept so little last night! I think I feel the same way," she whispered in return.

"Then let's go into the garden so I can win my bet with you," he grinned.

"Although I think I love you, you may be sure that I will never allow you an easy victory," she laughed as she broke free and ran toward the garden. José, reaching for her, chased her.

After an hour in the garden, a flower to match Doña Rosalita's beauty was not to be found, according to José's judgment. On the other hand, she had at least a dozen flowers that she claimed were obviously more beautiful than she. In a deadlock not to be broken, with each complaining of the other's contrariness, a mutual decision was made to take the flowers back to the house and have dinner.

Rather than eat inside the house, the enamored pair decided to have their first dinner together sitting on the peddler's cart in the courtyard. The servants gladly complied and enjoyed the laughter and chatter coming from their normally reserved mistress.

When José looked at her, she could feel her flesh tingle. This distracted her somewhat from his words, but as he spoke, she realized not only his bravery in stating his controversial opinions, but also the creative genius that was in his mind.

After dinner, they ascended to a balcony to view the colorful sunset—a sign that fall was approaching, in spite of the continued hot weather.

"León told me that your meetings yesterday were not the successes you had intended?" she inquired.

"The meetings yesterday were, in my opinion, as close to rock bottom as they could get," he shrugged. "But since this morning's, I now think I need a shovel to begin digging even deeper. Our wise leaders have determined to bury me by assigning me convoy duty escorting soldiers and other merchant ships to the Spanish Main. I believe Spain is going to support the Americans in their revolution against England."

"Oh no! When must you leave?" she asked in shocked expression.

"We are scheduled to leave Madrid on Monday morning. The only good news is that Cousin León will be along as my ship's carpenter. Since they assigned me command of three of the forty-four-gunners, I do not think they believe I will come to approve of these slow-moving ships," José replied.

"What did you do to upset everyone in such a short time?" Rosalita asked.

"I simply told them what I know and what I believe," José answered. "If I had told them what I really foresee in the future, it would have upset them even more!"

"Like what?" she asked while running a hand softly through his hair.

"Well, for example not only are the Americans changing naval warfare on the surface of the seas, but three years ago in 1775, David Bushnell, of Connecticut, invented a submarine called the *American Turtle*. It is driven by a hand-operated screw propeller and cannot be easily seen from the surface. In fact, at the beginning of their revolution the *American Turtle* actually attached a mine to the British flagship *Eagle*. If the mine had stuck and worked, I would have definitely brought it to FloridaBlanca's attention," José earnestly replied.

"You know how stuck in their ways our naval people are," Rosalita said soothingly. She stopped stroking his head and gently grabbed his left shoulder, "I'm glad you didn't mention what the French are doing."

"Well, I did suggest to Manuel Godoy and his yes-men that perhaps the Spanish Army should consider some of the changes the French have made under Napoleon regarding unit strength and supply," José answered feeling his face going red. To justify his actions to Rosalita, he continued, "but, I didn't get into my belief that the hot air balloons the French are developing will some day have significant military value. In fact, I even believe that some day, whoever controls the airspace will have the advantage over both land and naval forces. And, I didn't tell them how my readings of Jean Jacques Rosseau have influenced my thinking. My reading of *Le Contrat Social* has inculcated the belief in my mind that the social fabric of Spain must be reformed. Of course, my reading of *Emile, ou Traite' de l'Education* has shown some good proposals for educating the masses effectively."

"But, José, his books have been burned throughout Europe," she interrupted with a laugh, "and the poor man reportedly died this summer."

"I did not know that," José responded, "I do know, however, that with all of the great civilizations known to mankind that have been lost, the cause has been either a class conflict or a war or some combination of the two. We cannot continue to segregate people in any way, or fail to educate all of our citizens. We must allow each of our citizens the right and freedom to be all that their talents and abilities allow them to become. It is simply a natural law."

"Oh, José, you have such great ideas," she reassured. "But we both know the problem with Spain, like so many other civilizations you mentioned, is that its successes have bred arrogance, incompetence, and complacency. Everyone knows the answer to the problem, but implementing a solution is much more difficult than simply discussing it. Let's go into the house and freshen up. You have had a difficult day."

After they had the opportunity to bathe and change into clean clothes, José was the first to return to the great room in the center of the house. When he heard footsteps behind him, he turned to see Rosalita wrapped with a silken robe with the collar of a matching gown underneath. He was glad she felt comfortable enough with him to appear in this manner. As he looked into her eyes, he knew that they were able to communicate their feelings directly. With their growing love and commitment, they were each attuned to the other's thoughts and emotions. This pleased them both.

Rosalita suggested that they go to the patio and enjoy the beauty of the starlit heavens and he quickly nodded in agreement. Servants brought them a pitcher of sangria as they sat together on a large, cushioned bench. José asked Rosalita to put her bare feet on his lap, and when she did, he began massaging both feet, employing the techniques taught to him by María Gonzalez. He softly kneaded each of the areas on the bottom of her foot and explained which of the parts of the body it controlled.

"I believe that rubbing the skin between your toes increases your brain's capacity," he told her as he continued to massage.

"Oh, José, I do not know when you are serious, but I do know that I am falling in love with you," she smiled, as her feet and the rest of her body relaxed.

"But, I am serious," he protested. "Drinking water also improves your brain. It is probably because sailors drink so little water that they are not as bright as they might be."

"I am so happy," Rosalita sleepily sighed, and then, with a smile on her face, she drifted off to sleep. He pulled a cover off the back of the couch and placed it over her. He then lay back, still holding her feet, until he, too, fell asleep under the stars.

The next two days seemed the shortest in José's life. He and Rosalita went horseback riding each morning. They lunched on the peddler's cart that had become a focal point in their love for one another. Each afternoon they worked together in the vegetable and flower gardens surrounding the main house. Late in the day, they would go to the damned up creek to wade in the pond.

José, an accomplished swimmer, decided to teach Rosalita how to swim. She learned quickly, but from José's standpoint, the lessons had an added benefit. She decided that her clothing was too cumbersome and weighed her down, so she simply removed it so that she could be buoyant.

Each evening the couple enjoyed each other's company on the patio, then fell asleep after discussing many topics. Although José yearned to make love, and in spite of many opportunities, the lovers were true to her desire to save herself for marriage. He teasingly agreed only on the condition that her marriage included him.

Sunday came all too soon. They attended mass at the church near her estate. José was surprised to see Father Lasuen at the mass and, after the service sought him out to introduce Rosalita.

Father Lasuen smiled and whispered into her ear, "You are very fortunate to have captured such a man's heart. You can see in his eyes the love he has for you. But, I fear you are much too beautiful and personable for him," Father Lasuen winked and smiled broadly.

"Will you marry us?" José asked earnestly.

"If you can marry before I return to San Diego next spring," Father Lasuen smiled. "Princess Rosalita, it seems that when José opens his mouth in Madrid, it is only to change whichever foot was previously there. I will marry you only if you keep him out of Madrid!"

The loving couple left the church and returned to the estate to go horseback riding, share a picnic, and have a final swim before José had to return to Madrid to assume command of his fleet and make preparations for departure.

After a long dusty ride, which included races and contests between them, they sat on the bank of the creek and shared some bread, fruit and wedges of cheese. When José noted that there were two bottles of Madeira in the basket, Rosalita replied that she wanted to drink it to numb her feelings of sorrow at José's departure.

As the sun shown golden upon her, she rose and slowly slipped off her boots and riding pants revealing the shapely, smooth legs José had come to enjoy so much. She took off her hat and undid her hair, letting it fall over her shoulders, while giving José a slow smile. She then removed her blouse revealing her taut breasts. José felt his blood hammering through his veins, as parts of his body once again became taut. She slowly slipped into the refreshing water, beckoning him to join her.

Rosalita saw the color in his face and felt a tingle between her legs as his eyes fell to the watery vision of her in the clear creek. He quickly removed his shirt, shoes, and pants and joined her, craving the warmth of her touch and longing to kiss her. Both struggled with the conflicts going on between mind and body as they grasped each other waist deep in the water.

Almost of its own accord, José's arm left her back, slid around her waist and cupped the underside of her breast. She sighed and began kissing his lips and soon they were each exploring one another with mouth and tongue. Their hands roamed over one another with a reckless abandon bringing convulsive sighs and moans from each. He reached under the water to feel her willing thighs and she reached down between his legs to grab and encourage him.

Rosalita now begged him to enter her, but in spite of his almost overwhelming desire, he determinedly pulled himself away, climbed the mossy bank, and began putting on his clothes. He then reached down to help pull her from the pond, physically regretting the action he took, but mentally knowing it was the right thing to do. He intended to spend his life married to her, and wanted her to have absolutely no regrets or guilty feelings while he was gone at sea. He wanted her trust in him to continue and endure.

He repeated to himself what his mother had told him at various times, "Good things come to those who wait," while hoping that Dulcie had not been lying to him.

As they said their good-byes, José and Doña Rosalita promised one another that as the twilight faded, they would pray for one another's safety and love for the whole time they would be apart. Together they scanned the heavens until they found a group of stars upon which to focus each night, while they thought of one another during their separation.

Peace Force Command

"In the final analysis, peace is considered more important than justice."
—Captain José Gaspar, assuming command, September 15, 1778

In his depression at leaving Rosalita, the trip from Madrid to the eastern shore of Spain and then to the port city of Barcelona seemed long and arduous. However, it gave José time to plan and discuss his goals with Cousin León. He would now not only command his own ship, but would also be the fleet commander for the two other naval escort ships and the other brigantine and transport ships—quite a privilege for someone so young and with limited experience.

José had no problem with escorting the Spanish naval ships but was concerned with the additional burden of meeting and escorting a fleet of slave ships off the west coast of Africa. José described his apprehension in accompanying the Spanish soldiers and supplies to the coast of Louisiana. The soldiers were to join the French and American troops in their war against the English.

"Our mission is to protect our fleet from England, the known enemy, and from the privateers of America, the land that our soldiers are going to protect," José complained.

"It doesn't make sense and certainly is not fair," León commiserated.

"I don't believe anything that happens in life is either fair or unfair. In the final analysis, peace is considered more important than justice and that is why we are a peace force, cousin," José concluded with a wry smile.

"Why do the Americans hire so many privateers?" León asked.

"Very simple. The entire American Navy has only thirty-four of its own ships. By enlisting more than four hundred privateers to attack British merchant shipping, they have virtually crippled British trade and matched the number of ships in Britain's Navy." José explained. "These Americans employ pirates against the very nation that encouraged piracy for centuries against Spain. Maybe there is some justice."

"But, many of these privateer ships show their true colors when they attack both Spanish and French shipping," León said.

"Yes, they attack the very ships trying to aid their cause," José rejoined, "but my original point remains. In the final analysis, peace is considered by our government to be more important than justice."

When José and León finally arrived at Navy quay, they went straight to the docks where the three Spanish warships were moored. As they ran up the gangplank of their flagship, the *Intrepido,* José asked León to summon the captains of the other two ships to join them for dinner.

José was heartened to learn that Capt. Manuel Torres, who had been a classmate of his at the Naval Academy, and for whom José had a great deal of respect and admiration, would command the *Ferdinand.*

The other ship was under the command of Gonzalvo Rodriquez, a rugged academy graduate ten years his senior. His ship, the *San Cristabol*, was the oldest of the three ships with over fifty Atlantic crossings to its credit. Rodriquez and the *San Cristabol* had sunk four enemy ships in the last six crossings with no recognition from Madrid. For that reason, Rodriquez was upset that he had not been made fleet commander instead of the youthful Capt. José Gaspar.

That afternoon, after unpacking and arranging his quarters, José decided to take a tour of his ship with his second in command, Lt. Dom Gálvez, a native of Palma, a city on the island of Mallorca.

"Tell me, lieutenant, is your island home as lovely as I have heard?" José asked as they made their way down from the quarterdeck.

"Sir, there can be no clearer water that you could find surrounding my island. The olive orchards yield more per tree than any place on mainland Spain. If there be a heaven on earth, it must be Mallorca," a proud Dom Gálvez replied.

"Perhaps I shall consider Mallorca for my honeymoon," José smiled.

After inspecting the entire ship, including the deepest recesses of the hold, Captain Gaspar and Lieutenant Gálvez returned to the captain's quarters. Shortly thereafter, León joined the group and they discussed the condition of the ship and her crew.

"Gentlemen, we have a great deal to accomplish if this ship is to become a true flagship for the fleet," José began forcefully. "If we are to become the best ship in the fleet, we must begin immediately. I'm convinced that if man were not successful in accomplishing almost everything in the last minute, nothing would ever get done. Let's get started."

"Sir, with no disrespect to our previous captain, this crew has not had any true leadership or discipline for some time," Lieutenant Gálvez volunteered.

"I plan on making this the finest ship of the fleet and this crew a disciplined and educated group," Captain Gaspar announced. "Before we are halfway across the Atlantic, I can assure you we will be ready to defend our fleet and proudly serve the flag of Spain."

Then with a broad smile to break the tension, the captain joked, "I don't want to be able to stand next to any sailor on this ship and be able to hear the ocean through his head. If anyone on board these three ships does not want to learn, then I can assure you that I don't want to deprive any village of an idiot. We'll simply put him ashore and let him find his way home!"

León laughed and added, "From what I have seen, I believe many of our crew have fallen out of the family tree."

The men left the cabin when a crewman knocked on the door and was admitted to prepare the room for the captain's dinner and meeting later that evening.

Taking advantage of fresh provisions obtained on their last night in port, they enjoyed an appetizing dinner of arroz con pollo and arrollado, a gazpacho-type soup and a flan dessert. Then José, Gomez, and the others, including the captains and their first officers gathered, around José's hand-carved desk to become better acquainted over cups of rum.

Captains Torres and Rodriquez exchanged tales of past crossings of the Atlantic and of chasing off American pirates as well as those of England. They agreed that the American privateers were every bit as dangerous as common pirates or Buccaneers. A wide-eyed cabin boy, who sat in a corner waiting to run errands, couldn't keep his silence any longer. He blurted out, "Captain, sir, what is the difference among privateers, pirates and buccaneers?"

Gaspar, delighted that the young man had asked for information, said in his opinion, they were all cut from the same sailcloth. For the first time all evening, Captain Rodriquez smiled broadly and added, "Privateers are private ships with crews who are licensed by a government through a process called a 'Letter of Marque' in order to wage wars on that country's enemies. They may or may not be citizens of the country for which they are sailing. It matters not, they are privateers because it is a way to amass a fortune almost legally."

"Then what separates them from pirates?" asked the boy.

"The line between the two is quite narrow," Rodriquez continued. "Both obviously have the same goal, that of gaining wealth, but, whereas the privateer will normally attack only ships flying the flag of an enemy nation, the pirate has no such scruples. The pirate will attack any ship of value regardless of its nationality. The holding of a Letter of Marque from the head of state is the best way to tell the difference."

"The most frustrating thing is that when a privateer acts like a pirate and commits an act of piracy, the government for which he sails seldom reprimands him."

The boy continued, "But why should a country that is profiting from a crime discipline the privateer? Isn't this why we perform escort duty? Does it mean that we will confront American privateers, the very people we are trying to help against the British."

"The difference I see between pirates and privateers is that the privateer is really often the wealthy merchant or nobleman who provides ships and crews in the interest of making a fortune," Gaspar interjected. "Whereas, the pirate may have formerly been a good citizen who has suffered an unfortunate circumstance of our society, one unfortunate enough to cause him to turn to piracy. When wars end, nations reduce the size of their navies, and persons from the working classes, who have no hope of gaining wealth or an education, often consider their only choice to 'sign on' with a captain who promises them democracy and possible riches."

"I agree, there is much truth in that," Captain Rodriquez remarked.

"I have never understood why we educate only the upper classes and persons of privilege," José offered in a contemplative mood, "even if you learn to speak and write correctly, to whom are you going to speak and write unless everyone else is educated?"

"You suggest that we educate everyone?" Lieutenant Gálvez questioned.

José laughed and replied, "We are all seaman and we realize the importance of using every bit of space on board ship. I believe it is important that if a man has a large brain, he has something in it. Otherwise it is a waste of valuable space. Right, lad?"

The cabin boy nodded.

José paused, then more seriously responded, "Yes, my friend, I believe that a society that educates all of its people can be a great society. A society that permits the ignorance of its citizens is doomed to destruction, probably through some form of revolution."

"Speaking of revolution, that is exactly what brought about the buccaneers!" Captain Rodriquez boomed. "The buccaneers were originally Europeans who settled illegally in Spanish colonies throughout the Caribbean. They were hunters who learned how to barbecue their meat over a fire called a 'boucan'—a French word and the word buccaneers came from it. Early on, the Spanish forced them from their lands and most of them moved to the island of Hispaniola. Again, our Spanish brethren attacked them and they turned from being hunters and farmers to piracy. The British took advantage of their plight and allowed many of them to locate at Port Royal in the Bahamas where they were successful until the great tidal wave destroyed the town. Many believe it was God's will to destroy their decadent city. The buccaneers whom we may face are their descendants."

"These are truly unique times in history," José sighed.

"Gentlemen, I believe that we should retire for the night, but I think we should meet again in the morning." He continued, "But before you leave, I have a navigational present for each of you. Speaking of the buccaneers in Jamaica, that was the site of the test for this instrument."

José turned from the table and reached into a large trunk. With some help from Cousin León, he handed the two ship captains each a chronometer.

"As you may know, this device was invented in 1762 by John Harrison, a carpenter from Yorkshire, England, and the British Navy has been using it," José continued. "It is a remarkable instrument for navigational accuracy. We will all learn to perfect our use of this device."

As the meeting ended, it appeared that the young captain had won them over.

CHAPTER 17

Educating the Fleet

"Having a skill is knowing how to do something well while wisdom is knowing what to do next. I want every member of our crews to be wise as well as skillful."
—Capt. José Gaspar, Fleet Commander, September 16, 1778

In the darkness of his cabin, José wondered how a man could have such diverse feelings. On one hand he yearned to be lying beside Doña Rosalita breathing in the fresh aroma of her hair and touching the silky smoothness of her skin yet, at the same time, he loved the excitement of preparing and leading a ship on a transatlantic journey. He thought of how some people seemed to have a simpler time making choices in their lives.

Unable to sleep, he climbed onto the deck where he could hear some of these more uncomplicated men who were now filled with food and too much drink. He looked down upon the cobblestone dock and saw the many sailors swaying from side to side as if on deck in a raging storm as they returned to their ships. He could see many of the youthful faces in the glow of the lantern fire. Drunken singing and laughter came from further up the dock. José could see lit pipes and cigars in the large group of men who were exchanging stories, lies, and gossip of what each had done or seen done that evening. As talk of ribald sex raised their voices, José noted sparks coming from the cigars and he was glad there was no smoking allowed on the wooden sailing ships.

As dawn lightened the sky with a vivid variety of pastel colors, he looked over the harbor. Tall ships, ships of the line, brigs, schooners, and a variety of other vessels rose and fell with the waves. He could hear the begging gulls awakening and pulled up his collar as a breeze blew through the rigging on the ship. He was nearly transfixed by the gentle rocking of the bowsprits of the merchant vessels across the bay.

"Good morning, Captain. Up early on your first day on board I see," said Lt. Rafael Alvarez, commander of the night watch, to José as he climbed up to the forecastle.

"There is much to be done if we are to sail in the morning," José said. "I want these ships to have the best crews in the entire Spanish Navy."

He went again to the shore side of the ship and looked up and down the dock in the increasing light. Warehouses and large brick buildings lined the opposite street. The roofs were square-topped rather than the familiar tile. He was surprised at the number of lights showing through the windows this early in the morning. Barcelona was waking up.

Rafael brought José a tankard of thick hot coffee, as José thought about his lovely Doña Rosalita, probably asleep at this very moment. He imagined the sunlight glowing in her hair and brown eyes as she woke up. In his mind, he knew he loved his command, while with his heart, he knew he loved her. If only he desired to run a warehouse like his father, he could have both worlds simultaneously.

José went below to his cabin where he had breakfast with Lieutenant Gálvez and prepared for the morning meeting with the two other fleet captains. Cousin León stopped by to tell José he was going to prepare the ship for the next day's sailing. Lieutenant Gálvez indicated that he would oversee the loading of food and supplies for the journey. José reminded each to be thorough and to insure that only capable seaman be put in charge of any assignment they gave.

Rafael Alvarez brought Captains Torres and Rodriquez to José's cabin and the atmosphere was much more cordial than the previous night's first meeting. Rafael left the cabin and returned with some baked goods on the shiny pewter plates common to the ships.

José began the meeting by going over his expectations of the escort. "I want each of our ships to be like a duck on the water, appearing calm and smooth on the surface, while there is great activity beneath. I expect each of you to bring your crew and ship to the highest possible level of discipline. Normally, sailors find the journey to be long and boring. This will not be the case on any ship under my command. We will train our sailors as we sail and make them truly educated individuals. We will paint and maintain the upkeep of our ships. We will practice battle drills until we can do them in our sleep. By the end of this cruise, we will have the finest ships in the King's Navy."

"You really think it wise to educate the men?" Torres asked quite seriously. "If they can think on their own, won't they begin to question some of our orders?"

"My friend Manuel, if we truly educate our sailors and give legitimate orders, we need not fear a revolt. The only requirements to begin an education are simply an empty room, the right kind of students, and dedicated teachers such as yourselves," Gaspar replied equally seriously.

Gaspar also requested that the captains order their officers to constantly look, ask, listen, and question. He believed that innovation begins with curiosity, an open mind, and analysis of the situation. He further urged the captains to begin simply and remember that any innovation or change in procedures had to be carried out by ordinary seamen and therefore needed to make sense and be enjoyable or it would not be learned or effective.

"You expect our crews to be inventors?" Rodriquez laughed out loud.

"I only expect you to respect and consider ideas from anyone on your ship. Remember, my friend, the entire progress of civilization is based upon invention," Gaspar replied.

"Well, I do like what you suggest with regard to training the crews for battle and getting our ships in shape," Rodriquez replied. "That will definitely be an innovative approach for the Spanish Navy."

As the captains returned to their ships to supervise the loading and readying of the ships for the next day's sailing, José joined Lieutenant Gálvez on deck. Gálvez was supervising the loading of live hens into the hold. "We will have good cackle-fruit on this journey for these are healthy hens," Gálvez shouted to José.

"Are the hogs on board?" José asked Gálvez.

"Aye, sir, we have a goodly number below." Gálvez reported.

José smiled, "If we are guilty of overpacking one thing on Spanish ships, I fear it is the hog."

León appeared on deck, dripping in perspiration. "We are securing the casks of beer and water below. I'd rather we brought beer in bottles than in those kegs we have had to secure. It is much easier to fasten down square crates than barrels that roll."

"Do we have adequate hardtack below?" José inquired.

"Aye, and I have attempted to seal it as well as I could. It was a good idea to use wax to seal the crates and keep out the weevils," León replied to José.

José went on to insure that enough meat and other necessary provisions were on board, and he ordered Gálvez to go and check that there were adequate medical supplies. León reported that fishing line was stowed away as well as the necessary nets so that fish could be caught on the journey. The nets were also to be used to capture sea turtles. José liked the fact that they could weigh as much as four hundred pounds thus providing a good resupply of food at sea.

The busy day had gone by quickly and evening was approaching as José met with his men on deck that evening. He announced that all able seamen could go ashore. Before dismissing them, he told them that he expected them to join him, sharp, alert, and ready for sailing at first light the next morning.

While the sailors rushed about getting ready to go ashore, José overheard a variety of descriptions as to the women that they hoped to encounter. He thought of his good fortune to have known women of quality in his life. He doubted that he would give all his money to innkeepers and whores, even if he were merely a crewman. In José's opinion, the only people who benefited financially in seaports and mining towns were prostitutes and barkeepers.

After most of the crew went ashore, José elected to have dinner alone on deck, then he walked forward past the main mast to the foremast. As twilight approached, he glanced up at the spars along which the sails were furled. In the morning, the rigging would be crowded with men as these sails were unfurled. As he looked around at his ship, *Intrepido,* he felt pride in his disciplined crew and how they had prepared her for this journey.

In his solitude at the bow of his ship, José watched the sun set over the crowded harbor and tall warehouses and thought longingly of Doña Rosalita. He leaned over the railing and drew in a large breath of salt air, as he visualized her image and realized how long it would be until he saw her again. Then, tired from the previous sleepless night, José bid Rafael good night.

Back below the stern deck in his cabin, José lay in his bed looking out the large windows at the open water and the now starry night. He thought again of Rosalita as he gazed at the same group of stars she might be looking at and said softly, "Each night when I go to sleep my love, I will count each of your many charms."

CHAPTER 18

Sailing To the Ivory Coast

"Command of an escort fleet is very simple. Only two conclusions are possible: you succeed and arrive safely or, you fail and don't live to tell about it."
—Captain José Gaspar, departing Barcelona

Early the next morning, José was up before sunrise and briskly walked down the cobblestone street along the wharf. He boarded each of the other two escort vessels, the *Ferdinand* and the *San Cristabol*, and was satisfied with the preparations for departure. Squinting through the haze, José noted sailors checking rigging, loading supplies, and packing away tools. He shivered with anticipation of the journey.

Boarding the *Ferdinand*, he breathed the early morning smells of the quay and the ship and found Capt. Manuel Torres. They leisurely chatted until Torres asked whether José had spoken yet to Miguel Rodriquez, whose ship, *La Esclavitud*, would be a part of the convoy. Captain Torres pointed across the crowded harbor to a brigantine riding low in the water. José excused himself and went directly around the harbor to visit his old friend. As he reached the merchant freighter, José noticed the handsome Captain Rodriquez. Like a child, José crouched behind some large crates and shouted up the gangway, "Permission to come aboard, sir."

"I recognize that voice. Permission granted to the fleet commander to board the finest damn merchantman in the King's Navy," Miguel shouted back with a broad smile.

José ran up the gangplank and embraced his old pal. The sailors on the *La Esclavitud* looked on in amazement as these two gentlemen sea captains jumped around enthusiastically.

"How are things in Madrid, my friend?" Miguel asked earnestly. "Is it as political as they say it is?"

José laughed and punched his shoulder. "Miguel, I found the leaders and bureaucrats of Spain willing to stand up for anything they believe will benefit them. They are willing to promise anything to the lower class except to live like them. The city is magnificent and most of the people there live the good life. I do feel sorry, however, for many of them; they rush around busily, but I can tell they are not happy inside."

"Well, José, it obviously did not make you unhappy. I notice a gleam in your eye. How do you explain that?" Miguel asked with a wide grin.

"I met and fell in love with the most beautiful woman in all of Spain. Believe me, Miguel, it was as if heaven delivered her to me. I am going to marry her and I want you to be in the wedding party. Her name is Doña Rosalita Santiago and she is a real princess."

"Marriage? Marriage?" Miguel taunted. "José don't you realize that before you marry a woman, you yearn for her; but after you are married you must earn for her?"

José laughed and remembered that Miguel had the best sense of humor of anyone he had ever known. He looked directly at Miguel as the merchant captain kept up his verbal tirade.

"Marriage is a fine example of the victory of imagination over intelligence. Are you sure you are ready to accept this intellectual defeat, my friend?" Miguel laughed.

"I tell you Miguel, that to love a woman of quality can be the greatest salvation of a man. As you know from your own experience, without a woman of substance, one can only look forward to trying to satisfy every señorita on earth. I assure you this will wear you out and make you old before your years," José responded lightly as they walked forward on the deck of the *La Esclavitud*. "Besides, both great love and great achievements require great risk and you, my friend, know better than most that I am a risk-taker!"

"Ah, José, you are so right," Miguel smiled, "to love with passion and take risks with courage is the only way to live a life. If you lose at either you may lose everything, but your life will have had both worth and character."

"Tell me, how did you get to Barcelona?" José inquired. "I thought you were being sent directly to Havana."

"That is where I will be going on this cruise," Miguel affirmed, "and I trust you will safely guard my ship to Cuba."

After José assured him of a safe journey, Miguel continued describing his trip from Cadiz to London and the return across the Mediterranean to Barcelona. "Damnedest trip I have ever taken," Miguel exclaimed. "We went all the way to England to pick up three crates of pygg for the family of the governor of Cuba. You know pygg is a dense, orange clay usually used to make dishes and cookware. But, I'll be damned if these three crates weren't filled with little fat jars shaped like orange hogs or pigs. They have a little slot in the spine in which to put coins or pieces of eight. One of the English longshoremen called them 'pygg banks' while we were loading them. Bunch of damn piggy banks, and I risk my crew's safety charting a course shaped like a pig's tail."

José leaned against the rigging and roared with laughter. "You know, as my crew was loading hogs on board the ship for provisions, I told Lieutenant Gomez that people in the Spanish Main and places like La Florida may someday not appreciate our pig shipments to the New World. In your case I'm not sure the pigs' banks will taste good, but, like ballast, they will not move around the hull of your ship like ours."

Miguel motioned José to the cargo hatch. "No doubt you noted how low in the water we are. I assure you we have ballast that weighs second only to gold or silver. Come and see."

As the two captains went below, José noted the second deck was not entirely dark. A lantern hung above their heads and he could see the twelve and twenty-four pound cannon lashed to the deck and sides of the hull. José also noticed, in the shadows, some sailors asleep in their hammocks. Miguel motioned José to follow him down a ladder to the deck below which was dark and smelled of mildew. Miguel lit a lantern that illuminated hundreds of wooden kegs of cargo. He then grabbed a pry bar from the toolbox on the deck and pried open one of the kegs. José looked inquisitively over his right shoulder in the damp, odorous, cargo hold.

"Besides pygg banks for the wives and children of Cuba we also have five hundred kegs of nails from England. Look at all these nails." Miguel stepped aside to give José a better view. "I am told the English manufacture the best nails in the world. They sell them in lots of one hundred. The nails are sold for ten pence per hundred so we call them ten penny nails. Over here, in these barrels, are smaller, twenty penny nails, which means they were bought for twenty pence per hundred. I'm glad I don't have to figure out how to pay for these things, only haul them."

José laughed. "No wonder it is difficult to describe them. You would think the British would measure them by length or width instead of cost."

"You worry so much about the proper way to speak," Miguel replied. "If everyone were as educated as you and I, we might be out of a job."

José looked wryly at Miguel and then replied, "The problem with a lack of education is clearly seen by our existence. Uneducated men will steal nails and worthless piggy banks from a merchantman. If we educated them, then we only would need to protect ships carrying precious cargoes, for they would be smart enough to know the difference."

By the time they returned to the top deck, the sun was high and the harbor was teaming with activity. Both men saw her at the same time. Moving slowly away from the wharf opposite the merchant warehouses was the *Esperanza,* a sleek, black-hulled one-hundred-twenty-foot frigate, trimmed in gold leaf and carrying forty cannons. Barely moving in the slight chop of waves, the *Esperanza* looked as if she were moving at twenty knots. Without a doubt in either captain's mind, this ship was built for speed and maneuverability.

"That ship is exactly what I was trying to describe to FloridaBlanca just days ago in Madrid," José exclaimed. "I had no idea Spain was building them. Why didn't they tell me?"

"Spain didn't build it," Miguel answered, "the ship was purchased from England. The Spanish are going to sail it and see whether it is the type we should have built. But, José, you were right. Spain is too entrenched with outdated ideas. I'll bet we give it to the Americans. I would give anything to command such a ship."

"How ironic it would be for Spain to buy ships from one combatant and sell them to their enemy," José mused, "but, with the way the world is heading, who knows? That may be what all countries do someday."

He left his friend and *La Esclavitud* and looked out in the harbor at the *Esperanza*, impressed with how soundly it was constructed and with its clean lines. Reaching his ship, José became involved with the flurry of activity prior to departure. Finally, the heavy lines holding the *Intrepido* to her dock were loosened from the dock cleats and tossed to the sailors on deck. More men were now crawling up the ratlines and taking their assigned places in the rigging. The helmsman, a burly brute of a man named Angel Castro, allowed the *Intrepido* to drift with the current of the outgoing tide until her bow was pointed out to sea. José gave the order to hoist the sails and, as they billowed from the rigging in the noonday sun, the lines went taut with strain. The sails were now set and the ship began to move out to sea.

Standing next to Lieutenant Gálvez and alongside the helmsman, José spoke in a tone of bemusement, "Setting sail on a journey is one of life's most passionate experiences. To savor this sensation, you need to sacrifice other feelings and desires. If only women were allowed on our king's ships, I could have the best of both worlds."

CHAPTER 19

Slave Fleet

*"If anyone tries to tell me this slave trade is moral, maybe we should
teach him the Golden Rule. If he still doesn't understand,
then maybe we should let him live a slave's life."*
—José Gaspar, October 1778

The morning following the departure from Barcelona, José awoke to a cool pink sunrise that would soon become a blazing, sweating orange ball in the sky. As he left his cabin, he felt the gentle roll and knew his ship was making good headway. He ascended the steps to the deck and was surprised to see Lieutenant Gálvez standing next to Angel Castro who was still at the helm after insisting on steering the *Intrepido* through the first night out of port. As the fleet of ten ships left the harbor, the smell of the fresh salt air filled José's nostrils. They were cruising south-southwest toward the Strait of Gibraltar to encounter the rest of the ships that would constitute their fleet. With the end of the stormy season approaching in the area of the tradewinds, José felt confident he could command a successful transatlantic crossing. If only all the ships in the fleet had equal capabilities it would constitute no problem. As José watched the ships, he noted *La Esclavitud*, plowing deeply into the water, creating quite a wake for the other merchantmen that followed. José thought only a supreme sailor such as Miguel could cause such a heavy-burdened ship with its decks nearly awash, to sail and maintain speed in such a manner. He admired his friend's skill and courage while feeling sorrow and pity for the way the Spanish government had treated one of its finest sea captains.

As his eyes swept the rest of the fleet, he confirmed his belief that frigates, such as the *Esperenza,* were the next generation of frontline ships. With only half of its sailcloth unfurled, the *Esperenza* easily kept pace and

José considered how significant speed was and always would be in warfare. If only Minister FloridaBlanca and the others would listen but, it was almost a certainty that they will never listen to either him or the captain of the *Esperenza*, Luis Rivas, who would undoubtedly report great news of these current sea trials.

"Captain, the most beautiful island belonging to Spain lies on the horizon," Lieutenant Gálvez interrupted José's thoughts. "The dolphins know the wonderful waters that surround Mallorca. God knows I stayed up all night to get a glimpse of the beauty He created on this earth. I wish I could show you my home," he stated with a homesick sorrow.

"When I marry my Doña Rosalita, I will bring her there and you may personally show us the wonders you proclaim for your island," José replied with a smile.

The days of sailing to the Strait of Gibraltar went smoothly and only one corsair gave any indication of probing the fleet. José smiled as he watched the *San Cristabol*, under the able command of Gonzalvo Rodriquez, come up on the corsair's stern. The men on board the intruder hustled to raise the Union Jack. José was amused as he remembered that the current rules of the sea applied equally to pirates, privateers, or ships of foreign countries *Avoid all fleets under a flag other than your own*. An experienced British sea captain would have never allowed his ship to close on a fleet of Spanish vessels escorted by warships. "One may think that obtaining an education is difficult, but that fellow proved that ignorance can be potentially costlier," José said to no one in particular as he stretched and inhaled the sea air.

Later, as the fleet approached the Ivory Coast, José felt a shiver of apprehension as he viewed the lush green coastline. *This is such a beautiful place,* he thought. *How can stories I have been told possibly be true?* As dusk came José retired to his quarters to write a letter to Rosalita.

José awoke the next morning to the nauseating smell of urine. He jumped from his bed and ran to the deck to inquire of Lt. Rafael Alvarez, the night command officer, where in God's name that smell could be coming from. The pungent odor grew stronger and he saw off the starboard side a collection of ships bobbing at anchor. José had never witnessed a gathering of such derelict craft. *The* Intrepido *must surely have sailed into a graveyard for old ships,* he thought. The beauty of the unblemished coast was secondary in his mind to the stench now permeating his nostrils.

"What is that smell?" José demanded of Alvarez. "Did the powder monkeys forget to dump the urine buckets? Did they spill?"

Lt. Rafael Alvarez pointed to the ships riding at anchor and simply inquired, "You've never seen a slave ship before, have you sir? Actually, it is not necessary to see them, you can smell them long before." He laughed at his own attempt at humor.

"Well, I am aware of the way that the Moors and the Corsairs and other Islamic nations enslave Christians. In fact, I freed some from a prison; but, I assure you the conditions were not as horrible as these appear to be," José responded.

"It is a business to which almost every rich nation has made a sizable investment," Alvarez responded, "if they are not directly involved in trading slaves themselves, they probably are at least investors in slave-trading companies. There is huge profit to be made in slavery. In fact, more money can be made by a slaver than by a legitimate merchantman or even a pirate!"

"But we are off the coast of Africa. How could native Africans allow this to happen?" José asked incredulously. "How can man be so inhumane to his fellow man?"

"Just think about it, Captain," Alvarez replied, "as long as something is lucrative to a group of people, there will be no limit to their brutality to maintain the source of the profit. The African rulers of Benin, Ashanti, and the Congo have long traded captives from other tribes for items such as cloth, iron, brass, or copper that the slavers bring them. The bars of metal are called *manillas* and they are used like pieces of eight."

"I think all men can be victims of their own greed. We might all be tyrants if we could get away with it," José answered, "If mankind would only understand that true happiness cannot be bought with riches, we would all be better for it. Actually, Señor Alvarez, the only reason we have governments is because most individuals will not *naturally* conform to reason and justice without the laws created by government."

"Aye, captain, I agree. Men like Capt. John Hawkins started the trading of African slaves two hundred years ago and it rewarded him with great profits. But, it was Queen Elizabeth herself who supported the 'Black Ivory' trade at its inception, Alvarez noted. "England's government seems to support piracy, slavery, or some other questionable practices that support their government's power."

"That's why all the governments who talk about the outlawing of slavery are guilty of speaking from both sides of their mouths," José reflected. "They work their gums before one influential group, then gum up the works afterward. Our former King Ferdinand and France's Louis XIV are as guilty as England in regard to slavery."

"I want to visit these slave ships while we stop here to load provisions," José told Alvarez and Gálvez, who had joined them on deck.

"I will arrange it, captain," Alvarez stated. Then he added, "Be sure to wear old clothes, old boots, and rags soaked in salt water and tied as a bandana. Hopefully, this will allow you to stay on board long enough to speak to the slave ship's captain."

"There must be tremendous money in this slave business, for these slavers do not seem to consider that sickening odor a problem," José noted cynically, "I guess a problem is a problem if you only think of it as a problem. I personally could not tolerate that smell."

After insuring that his breakfast had time to digest, José, along with Gálvez, Alvarez, León, and four sailors, lowered the longboat from the *Intrepido* and rowed the short distance to the nearest slave ship, *The Irish Lady*.

The Irish Lady was a merchant vessel that had been converted to a slave ship. At one time, José could see, she had been beautiful. She was one hundred and ten feet long, with three masts, but the ravages of many triangular transatlantic crossings had taken its toll. Most of the aging hull was peeled of the white paint that had once covered it. The trim on both the stern and the bowsprit had been a contrasting emerald green but they were now faded and chipped.

José thought about the diversity of his convoy. He was convinced that there are no absolutes in life, just revelations of how confusing life itself can be.

"The captain of *The Irish Lady* must be a grizzled old man," José commented to the group as they bobbed up and down through the slight chop.

"Captain, you must prepare for a shock," Alvarez smiled. "The captain is known for many things, but grizzled would not be one of them."

This aroused the curiosity of José as he leaned forward to speak into his megaphone and request permission to board the reeking slave vessel. A rope ladder snaked its way down the larboard side and the rugged first mate motioned for the group to climb aboard. As each man went up the scratchy rope ladder, he was forced to overcome a violent gagging reaction at the ghastly smell emanating from the hull. Upon reaching the deck, each placed a waterlogged scarf over his nose and mouth to avoid inhaling the revolting stench.

The slaver's first mate, a large hairy man closely resembling a jungle primate, indicated that José and the entourage should follow him to the captain's quarters in the stern.

Upon entering the cabin, José was immediately struck with the contrast between the rundown overall exterior condition of the vessel and the lavish, relatively odor-free interior of the private quarters. The panels and furniture were made of exotic teak with hand-carved designs. It was one of the most opulent cabins José had ever encountered. On the large desk and credenza were silver candelabra. The carpet on the floor was lush and not of a type normally found on a ship at sea.

"Captain Gaspar, I am so glad that you and your vessels have arrived safely," called a feminine voice from behind the group. "We have been eager for your arrival for the last three days."

José and the others turned in the direction of the melodious voice and their eyes reflected an appreciation of the beauty of the speaker.

"My name is Captain Betsy—'Brutal Betsy' as some know me," the lovely woman at the door stated. Betsy was red-haired with lively green eyes. Her fair cheeks were flushed with color and her low-cut blouse exposed bountiful breasts rising and falling in quick breaths from her rush to the cabin. Wearing trousers that fit snugly to her form, Betsy was an unexpected feast for the eyes of the entourage.

José made the introductions. "I am Capt. José Gaspar. This is Lieutenant Gálvez, Señor Alvarez, and my cousin, León, all members of the flagship *Intrepido*," he said. "I must admit that I am surprised to find a ship of this nature under the command of such a beautiful captain."

"Such was not my goal in life," Betsy replied. "At one time I lived the life of a lady in Ireland, where my father owned much land and my husband, Walter, was a successful merchant and trader. I used to sail with Walter on this very ship when he was involved in trade with the American colonies, Spain, and France. It was a great life and I never dreamed that one day I would captain a ship that was engaged in such a despicable trade."

"How did this happen? How did you get involved in the slave trade?" José asked two of the hundred questions racing through his mind. He could not help but stare at the beguiling woman in this oasis of opulence on board one of the worst ships upon which he had ever stepped foot.

"It is a long story. To make it brief, simply let it be said that religion and government caused a lady who would never harm a fly to become one of the most feared slave traders of our time," Betsy replied. "My father was killed shortly after Walter and I were married and had moved to England. You see, in Ireland, if you are of one religion, you are the enemy of those of another. My father was killed simply because he believed in Jesus Christ from a different perspective than his killers."

"And your husband?" José asked.

"Walter and I had nearly two decades of a wonderful life together." Betsy continued, "We had a country manor, two large warehouses, and a fleet of four ships doing quite well. The Crown of England decided that the royalty was not getting a sufficient percentage of our wealth and arrested my husband. They threw poor Walter into a debtor's prison without a trial. He was imprisoned for nearly a year. Walter was the type of individual who could not stand being cooped up inside for any period longer than it took to make love to me." Betsy hesitated, looking up at the ceiling, and then walked to the portrait of a handsome man behind her desk. She placed her hand on the frame and continued, "The government killed my husband. Walter never had a chance to stand trial. After all the taxes were taken, I was left with only this ship, and nothing else."

"But how did you chose slavery?" José questioned.

"That's a simple answer. My religion had betrayed me by killing my father. My government turned against me and took my beloved husband and I needed to make money quickly. Walter and I both despised the slave trade, but we knew it was the most profitable form of trading to be done. Without Walter, and with no money, I had to become a slaver," Betsy stated in a matter-of-fact tone. "Do you realize that over 100,000 slaves are shipped across the Atlantic every year? I have more than three-hundred slaves on this ship alone."

"I never gave it a thought," answered José. "I guess the enslavement of blacks must create great wealth for the whites."

"There is more money to be made off the backs of these blacks than could be made in any other manner at this time in history," Betsy replied bluntly. "The money that can be made at their expense in farming is greater than that made from mining by governments such as Spain or that stolen by pirates."

José looked intently at the female captain. The sunlight through the windows framed her intense face with tendrils of her red hair curling upon her forehead, and the unlaced bodice of her blouse revealed appealing freckles. Her appearance was striking.

Betsy returned his stare. She was attracted to this handsome young officer, with his intelligence and intensity, and her loins tingled for the first time in many years.

"Would you like to see what a slave ship is like?" Captain Betsy inquired, breaking the silence. She went to the door and waited, with a coy smile, until José opened it, then led the way into the overwhelming smell of the deck. Members of her crew quickly surrounded the group. They seemed a ferocious group who, for the most part, wore dirty canvas trousers with collarless shirts and had kerchiefs in a multitude of colors covering their heads. José admired their well-maintained pistols and shining swords. One should never judge a book by its cover, his mother had said.

As she crossed the deck to a hatchway, Betsy drew a cat-o'-nine-tails whip from the main mast. She turned to José and stated simply, "When I was happily married to Walter I used to believe you should treat people the way you want to be treated. But, now I must never allow them to mistake any kindness I might give them for a weakness. I tell you, Captain Gaspar, it is important to make people fear you, for it is your fear that makes the wolf appear more dangerous." With that, she cracked an old black man near the hatch over the back with her whip and ordered him to open the door.

José and the others followed Captain Betsy down the hatch and into the slave holds, pulling their dampened scarves up over their noses and mouths. The scene was worse than José could have imagined. Row upon row of naked, sweating, moaning slaves lay upon shelves that were stacked at least six rows high. Worse yet, each male slave had a steel collar connected by a chain to the collar of the slave lying next to him. In like manner, each man was also tethered to the person beside him with a wristband. José's covered mouth dropped open in disbelief as he moved through the narrow aisle. He saw that not only were their necks and arms chained to one another, but that they were also attached to the bulkheads with ankle fetters. There were long steel rods through the four-inch by four-inch bulkheads, and on these rods were the U-shaped steel ankle fetters that locked the slaves' feet and kept them from standing. "These devices keep the slaves immobile so they cannot riot or commit suicide," Betsy explained, noting José's puzzled look. "Dead slaves are not of any value except to the sharks we feed en route."

"Is this chaining of slaves necessary?" Lieutenant Gálvez questioned.

"Without question," Betsy snapped. "We are completely overwhelmed in numbers by our live cargo. For example, on this cruise, we have fewer than thirty sailors while we have a cargo of over three hundred slaves!"

"But, they lie in their own excrement and urine and look barely fed. Of what value can they be?" José asked.

"When we get them to land, they are cleaned and well fed. They are presentable when they are taken to the auction, Betsy replied calmly. "The ones who cannot recover are often sold in lots."

José was shocked not only by the smell but also by the absolute silence that had developed as José and Betsy walked through the area.

Whether through hunger or terror, the slaves simply stared at them with vacant eyes.

As they went to the next hold, José noted the women in this group were younger and many of them had babies or small children chained to them. He observed that they wore heavy iron collars with four rods sticking out at least three feet.

"What are those collars for?" José asked.

"It allows the pregnant women to move around and get some exercise while not allowing them to move too freely," Betsy clarified. "Also, it serves as a form of chastity belt in case a crewmen gets amorous."

"I can't take this smell or inhumane treatment anymore," José announced loudly. "Let's get out of here and away from this despicable ship. There is no way on God's earth this is right!"

Betsy grabbed José's arm as he was leaving, "It is important that you know what is and what isn't your business. Whether you like it or not, Captain Gaspar, you have a duty and a responsibility to escort us safely to Cuba."

As they left the intense smells and sights on board *The Irish Lady*, José leaned over and stated emphatically to his group, "This slavery issue is discussed by people as if it were absolutely justified, but I tell you, all absolutes must contain an opposite. I believe that in God's eyes, all mankind is equal. If anyone tries to tell me this slave trade is right, maybe we should teach him the Golden Rule. If he still doesn't learn, then maybe we should let the believer try becoming a slave himself. Slavery is a lie."

José thought of how glad he would be to have this convoy duty behind him.

Hurricane and Storm Following

"It amazes me that people who are born on a high level actually go through life thinking that they earned their station in life by themselves."
—Captain José Gaspar, October 1778

The morning that the nine ships from Barcelona were to set across the Atlantic, joined by the six slavers, José had each of the captains join him on board the *Intrepido* for a final briefing during breakfast. As they gathered around him in the galley, José was startled by the differences among the captains—the "spit and polish" captains from the four naval escort vessels, the "gentlemen captains" who commanded the merchant vessels, and the ragtag, rugged, often profane slavers. His challenge would be to motivate and inspire these different types of leaders to sail as one in a convoy. It would indeed be a great test of his leadership abilities.

He sat next to Brutal Betsy at the morning meeting. He felt that most meetings were generally a waste of time, but this meeting was vital to the success of the entire mission. One potential danger was that the convoy was transporting Spanish troops for use against England. Another was the likelihood of attack by pirates or privateers who might try to capture the slaves on the six slave ships and sell them to pocket a handsome profit. In addition, they were sailing before the end of the hurricane season. So, Mother Nature, England, or any number of pirate brotherhoods could easily challenge this convoy.

"I hope you have many four-leaf clovers," José leaned forward and whispered to Brutal Betsy. "I don't know the whole story, but I have heard that the Irish believe they bring luck. We can definitely use luck."

"Well, Captain, the four-leaf clover represents more than simply luck," Brutal Betsy replied, "the first leaf is for hope, the second, faith, the third one is for love and, of course, the fourth leaf is for luck."

"It is vital that each of us work at hope, faith, and love. This will create an atmosphere wherein luck can reside," José contemplated.

Miguel Rodriquez brought one of the slave ship captains over to José and introduced him. "Captain, this is Pedro Feliciano. Pedro was one of the most respected sea captains in all the Spanish Navy."

"How did you become a slave ship captain?" José asked with a degree of scorn.

"I hope you understand that sailing for the Spanish throne provides a great deal of uncertainty. You can be the toast of the court in Madrid one month and be relieved of command on your very next ship," Pedro Feliciano replied. "Power has always corrupted Spain and robbed it of some of the best men to serve the crown."

"I understand what you are saying." José leaned forward. "Power does corrupt, but weak kings and queens and the necessity to create deals and bribes probably corrupt even more. When you are caught in bureaucratic compromise and corruption, you may become the person who is compromised."

"That is exactly what happened in my case," Pedro sadly stated, "my command was taken away, my commission as a naval officer was limited, and I was reassigned to the merchant fleet. I decided that if I was going to risk my life to make a living at sea, then I might just as well sign on with a private shipping company. At the time, I was unaware that my company made its income in the trade of 'black gold.'"

"This is how you came to be a slaver?" José asked with a sincere interest in Pedro's reply.

"I believe that the events in one's life have a profound effect on one's future actions or reactions," Pedro stated simply. "But, I gave up worrying about the cause of my present situation and concentrate only upon dealing with whatever happens. I react rather than plan."

Brutal Betsy spoke out, "Since his own country took my husband, I now find myself looking at the dark side of things for new opportunity. Many people argue whether the glass of water on the table is half empty or half full. I don't care; I simply now go after that half instead of wishing it were all the way full."

Captain Gaspar, how do you stand on the issue of slavery?" Miguel asked his comrade.

"I believe the owning and selling of human beings to be evil. I believe that this evil will continue to grow so long as good men fail to act to stop it," José stated firmly and with a great deal of emotion. "This evil business will have a lasting impact on our children's world far, far into the future."

"Then why do you so patiently listen to those who profit from this trade?" Miguel asked incredulously. "I should think you would react more forcefully."

"I believe that in order to lead effectively, one must be disciplined enough to listen closely to the soul of the people one wants to lead. One can never inspire confidence or coordinate effective change when one is not aware of others' opinions, desires, and feelings," José quickly answered, "We must celebrate the idea that there are other ideas to be considered. What I have learned from both Betsy and Pedro is that you can understand and care for people even if they are doing something you personally abhor. On the other hand, we often tolerate those whom we could never love or understand simply because our own ideas agree with theirs. Do you agree, my friend?"

"I'm not quite sure," Miguel answered hesitantly. "Somewhat, I think."

"Simply listen my friend. True listening is a rare happening," José smiled with understanding. "It is important that you adapt conditions you find intolerable to yourself and not adapt yourself to conditions in which you do not believe. You need not change yourself to lead effectively."

Sensing a tension in the room, José broke into a large grin and posed an interesting question to those assembled around the table, "Is the problem ignorance or apathy?"

To a man, they responded, "I don't know," or "I don't care." José laughed heartily and the captains looked at each other quizzically. They finally realized that they themselves had answered in either "ignorance" or "apathy," and they began to chuckle.

"Exactly the problem!" José stated. "People either don't know or don't care."

The meeting concluded with a full understanding of how the fleet would proceed, utilizing the tradewinds, but with a strong awareness of the westerly winds that affected the onset of storms in the fall. The *Intrepido,* under command of Gaspar, would sail on the point and be responsible for the navigation of the entire fleet. The veteran *San Cristabol,* under command of Capt. Gonzalvo Rodriquez, would sail on the southern flank and the *Ferdinand,* commanded by Capt. Manuel Torres, would protect the northern side. The frigate, *Esperanza,* under the command of Joséph Figueroa, would take advantage of its speed and agility, tacking to and fro, and cover the rear of the convoy. The remaining ships would form within the perimeter and remain close to one another so as not to allow a potential intruder to penetrate the formation. The captains agreed that José had developed a good plan for the journey.

The crisp early morning turned to a blazing noon as preparations were made to the ships of the convoy.

"Make sail, Lieutenant Gálvez," José shouted. As he looked around at the convoy and then at his own ship, he watched the masts where men were climbing in the ratlines and loosening the canvas.

Like thunder rolling through a valley, the sound of sails catching the wind could be heard throughout the harbor and echoed off the tree-lined hillsides. The ships began to shudder and creak under the stress of wind catching sail. A quiet concerted ballet began as all the ships danced from the harbor, silently gliding over and through the slight chop and into the ocean. Ahead lay the open sea and one of the true joys of José's life. He appreciated the freedom he felt sailing the seas and wished everyone could experience the inner peace that true freedom brings to a man.

During the next week, the fleet moved steadily westward, taking advantage of the constant tradewinds and moving towards the turquoise-blue waters that would welcome them to the Windward Islands and into the Caribbean. On the eighth day out from Africa, José noted the Atlantic waters beginning to churn and change color. He also noticed that the cloud tops on the horizon, particularly in the eastern skies behind them, were no longer being sheared off and were becoming virtual "mountains" reaching as high as one could see into the tropical sky.

"I believe those safely on shore who said we had a fifty-fifty chance of running into a storm were one hundred percent correct," José noted to the helmsman, Angel Castro, who nodded in agreement.

"When things go too smoothly this time of year you can be sure mother nature has a surprise in store," Angel told José in no uncertain terms.

José turned the convoy over to the night watch commander, Lieutenant Alvarez, with a warning to watch for bad weather and to wake him if any change took place.

The rolling of the ship woke José the following morning. As the sun rose through the portholes he was glad to have had a good night's sleep. He went up on deck for his morning coffee and scanned the horizon then watched the ships of the fleet as well as the red glow in the east. As he looked to the southeast, José noted tall, dark clouds that reminded him of a mountain range gathering at the edge of the ocean.

"Send a message to the fleet captains that I suspect severe weather," José shouted to Lieutenant Gálvez who had just come to the quarterdeck. Gálvez immediately left to flag the message to the other ships. At that moment, the ship lurched forward, spilling coffee over José's hand and staining his trousers.

José yelled to Gálvez, "Tell the ships that heavy seas are coming from the southeast and they should leave a greater distance between to better navigate!"

By noon, the winds were picking up and the ships began scrambling hands aloft to close-reef the topsails. The crews worked feverishly to prepare the ships for the heavy weather now certain to engulf the fleet. As the bowsprits began touching the rough seas and spraying the decks, the foresails were taken in and the hatches were closed and sealed.

José heard the ships groaning and creaking as they pitched in the high seas, but over the sound and fury of the storm, he could hear the screams of terror and fear coming from the holds of the slave ships. He could think of no worse place to be in a hurricane. "Chained and lashed in a pitch black, stinking hold, watching the waters rise as the pumps struggle to pump out the bilge, and knowing that each roll of the ship could plunge the vessel under the sea." José shuddered to himself as he pictured the terrible drowning death that would take the slaves' lives, but yet give them permanent relief from the agony now taking place.

The swells became higher and more frequent, causing walls of salt water to crash over the bow of the *Intrepido* and other ships. José looked off the starboard side and was surprised to see Miguel Rodriquez up to his waist in seawater standing firm against both wind and wave, as they seemed to engulf *La Esclavitud*. The ship actually resembled the submarine that the upstart Americans allegedly invented. Miguel made eye contact with José, smiled broadly, and waved at the flagship. *The damn fool actually seems to be enjoying this storm*, José thought to himself. *Is there nothing that scares Miguel?*

José ordered all hatches battened and storm lines attached to any sailor above deck. The winds continued to increase and now the seas became mountains upon which each ship would climb before crashing abruptly into the valley created by the swell. One could even hear the wooden ships protesting the punishment the hurricane force winds and seas were inflicting upon them. As they crashed to the bottom of each swell, the bow plunged deeply into the water, causing torrents of foaming dark seawater to wash away anything not securely lashed down on the deck. It seemed as if every plank, block, halyard, spar, and bitt were crying out in anguish. The masts were swaying out of sync to the hurricane winds and the lines and stays created an eerie music as the wind passed through at varying speeds.

José clung to the ropes that tied him to the ship as he shouted corrections to the helmsman, who was on the quarterdeck. The towering waves forced Angel to struggle mightily against the wheel to keep the bow facing into the storm.

The rains, which had been spewing forth great sheets of water resembling dark curtains, began to let up enough so that José could look around the rising and falling horizon and take a mental inventory of his storm-tossed fleet. At the same time, he shouted loudly for Cousin León, the quartermaster, and ship's carpenter, to report to him any storm or structural damage to *Intrepido*. As José turned around, he was relieved to see most of his ships still afloat and smiled grimly to himself when he saw Miguel standing like a rock on the quarterdeck of his ship, drenched, but grinning broadly and shouting commands. As he continued to pan the rolling and pitching Atlantic, he was shocked to see *The Irish Lady* in shambles and listing over to larboard.

"Brutal Betsy's ship is in serious trouble," José shouted to Angel. "Bring our ship around to help." He raced to the main deck, tied a stout rope around his waist, kicked off his boots, took off his shirt and, though shuddering in the cold rain, continued to command Angel to take the *Intrepido* as close as possible to *The Irish Lady*. "We must save those poor bastards or else they will die a most horrible death."

As José and the *Intrepido* swung to aid *The Irish Lady*, Miguel Rodriquez and *La Esclavitud* circled to pick up any survivors. Not to outdone by his friend and fleet commander, Miguel followed José's example, tying a rope to his waist, and, when his ship came close to the sinking *The Irish Lady*, he jumped into the angry black foam of the sea.

José, seeing his friend jump into the sea, watched anxiously as Miguel coughed up salty sea water and yelled epitaphs audible even over the storm. José then jumped into the swells and swam toward the floundering slave ship.

The Irish Lady, broken and sinking, was beginning to roll over. The crew was leaping over the side and José was relieved to see that Betsy had jumped free and was able to swim towards him. He shouted to his own crewman on board the *Intrepido* to begin throwing lines towards the survivors. He then swam to Betsy, secured one of the lines to her waist, and ordered his crew to pull her on board. She was quite a woman, he crazily found himself thinking, and could not understand how in such a time of crisis he was taking time to admire her glistening breasts. His thought was short-lived as he heard screams coming directly from hell itself as *The Irish Lady's* beam cracked like an explosion from a cannon.

José immediately swam toward the sinking vessel and noted his comrade Miguel doing likewise from the opposite side of the ship. All José could think about was the fear and anguish of the slaves in the cracked hold of the slaver, chained within, and stinking in their own urine and excrement. He had no choice but to save these unfortunate human beings and was glad that his friend Miguel had chosen likewise.

José crawled up the side of the shattered slaver and a wave boosted him all the way to the deck. Miguel, meanwhile, grabbed a rope and joined José on the deck that was awash with wreckage.

They feverishly went to work, grabbing lashings from the deck cannon to keep from being flushed into the churning sea. Both men worked frantically to remove the batten from the hatch. As they opened it, they were horrified to see water already flowing through the broken hull. It was obvious that the slaves chained and bound in the lower shelves were drowning or already dead. Screaming loudly in their native tongues, the horror on the faces of the doomed would haunt José and Miguel the rest of their lives. Without keys to unlock the neck and arm chains, nor tools to free the leg fetters, José and Miguel knew they had no choice but to abandon those trapped in this hold and move on to the hold containing the mothers and young children.

Leaving the hatch open to help scuttle the sinking ship and not prolong the agony of the doomed slaves, José and Miguel raced to the stern of the groaning vessel and broke the hatch door to the hold containing the women, children, and pregnant mothers. Because of the women's heavy collars, José and Miguel determined that it would be necessary to lead all of them to the deck and then swim with two at a time back to one of the rescue ships. They also noticed the longboat was not damaged by the fallen mast and managed to launch it. They placed the smallest children and babies in it and prepared to swim with two adult women while towing the longboat with a rope wrapped around their waists. They then would return for more of the collared women. This impromptu plan saved twenty women and sixteen children and babies. In addition, the crew and Captain Betsy were rescued during the lull in the storm.

The eye of the storm passed shortly after *The Irish Lady* grew strangely silent and slipped quietly beneath the rough sea.

Exhausted from their valiant rescue effort, José and Miguel returned to the command of their respective ships to ride out the backside of the fierce hurricane. Evening was approaching as the sky, already darkened with storm clouds, grew even blacker and the rains began in earnest again. The winds picked up and again battered the straining ships. "Storms at night bring an even greater terror because you can't see what is going on and the sound and fury are thus magnified," José mused.

José stood on the rolling and swaying quarterdeck with the heavy rain stinging his face. Since it was his first experience with a hurricane he was amazed at the strength and stamina of both the remaining ships and their crews. José clung to the safety lines and managed to go to the main deck, then below, to visit the rescued slaves. He was pleased to see Cousin León and members of his crew cutting the oppressive neck collars off the grateful women. He was further pleased to see that the boys and girls were now free of their shackles. In a gesture of gratitude, a boy ran forward and hugged José. José returned the hug and patted the lad on the head.

As the ship rolled sharply to larboard, José held tight to the boy; then as the *Intrepido* regained its balance, José ran up to the quarterdeck. After attaining the deck, over the crashing surf, he heard Lieutenant Gálvez calling for help in the forward hold. José fought to the bow by grabbing the safety line in a hand-over-hand motion and was twice nearly swept overboard. He heard cries from below the deck and fought his way forward to the hatch.

As he peered below deck, José saw that one of the huge beer casks had broken loose and was rolling about uncontrollably. Members of the crew were attempting to stop the cask with some four-inch timbers before it rolled back again with the yawing of the ship. The lanterns that illuminated the scene were swinging wildly in the opposite direction of the ship's motion and were threatening to break loose and start a fire.

The barrel lurched forward as the ship heaved hard to starboard. One of the youngest sailors was trapped between the errant cask and the others that were properly secured. As the cask rolled toward the young man he vainly put out his arm to stop it. The cask, weighing many times more than the boy, crashed into him, and his last shrill scream was silenced. As the ship again rolled, the cask rolled off revealing the bloodied, limp body of the sailor, his open eyes staring directly at the hatch opening.

José called upon his numbed mind and exhausted body one last time and jumped to the deck below. He knew the cask must be secured or it would crash into the wooden bulkheads causing enough damage to perhaps destroy the entire ship. He yelled to two of the crewman to go aft and bring back one of the heavy cargo nets. He ordered two other sailors to go below to the chain room and bring up some iron anchor chain. The ship again rolled and the cask rolled directly at José but, just before it reached him, another wave sent the cask back in the opposite direction. As he instinctively held up his arms to fend off the cask, he realized for the first time that his hands and arms were skinned and bleeding from holding onto the scratchy hemp ropes for most of the day.

As the crew returned with the netting, José ordered them to throw it over the cask as it rolled beneath them. When the three other crew members struggled up on the deck with the heavy anchor chain, they were told to chase after the cask and wedge the chain links behind it when it hit the bulkhead, which would prohibit it from easily rolling back. With the cargo netting firmly secured, the remaining crew could then tie a number of ropes directly to the net. With luck the cask would be stabilized.

Within moments after José's plan was successfully executed, his crew cheered their captain. José was too physically and mentally exhausted to appreciate their shouts of approval, but ordered them to take care of the sailor's body.

Back on the storm-washed decks, José still had to deal with the tempest that refused to die. Yet another oncoming wave caused the ship to dive below the surface, and José again found himself thrown off his feet, clinging to the safety rope and choking on the briny water. As he broke through the second wave, José fought to get a breath of fresh air. He firmly wrapped his bleeding hands around the safety line.

The fleet, with the battered *Intrepido* still at the point, fought the storm for another eight hours. Then, about two o'clock in the morning, the rain stopped, the wind subsided, and the angry seas began to smooth. Instead of the mountains and valleys of water, the waves now became rollers that the damaged ships could traverse. The remainder of the night, José oversaw the manning of the bilge pumps to pump the seawater from the ballast. Cousin León took charge of the crew with regard to making necessary repairs. Going below, José was again shocked to see how high the water within the hold had risen. He was pleased when Alvarez reported that the pumps were working and that soon the water would not be lapping at their ankles. José told Alvarez and León that there could be no more beautiful sound than the wheezing and sucking of the pumps.

As morning dawned on the horizon, the sky was aflame with the reflection of the sun's rays on the storm clouds now moving westward ahead of the badly damaged fleet. José was relieved to find out that only two ships were sunk in the hurricane, *The Irish Lady* and *San Miguel El Archangel*, both slave ships of questionable seaworthiness.

The remaining ships had from moderate to severe damage and needed to make repairs before they could set sail on their journey again. Work began immediately on the ships as José could see the sailors repairing the rigging and climbing up to replace or repair torn sails. The sounds of the storm were now replaced with sounds of hammer and saw as the ships were made seaworthy again.

As the sun rose into the sky, José looked over at his friend Miguel, left arm in a sling and a tankard of coffee in his right hand, which he raised in salute. José raised his weary arm and waved back.

Lieutenant Gálvez came to the quarterdeck and suggested that José go to his quarters after showering with some of the rainwater caught during the storm. Never had cold water felt so good as it coursed over José's bruised body, soothing the many cuts and scrapes he had received during the storm.

Walking naked to his quarters, he felt embarrassed as he passed the bare-breasted slave women he had rescued hours earlier. Speeding up his pace, he nearly ran to his quarters, opening and closing the door quickly. As he leaned on the door breathing a sigh of relief, an equally naked Captain Brutal Betsy greeted him.

He looked at her, astounded, and asked, "What are you doing naked in my stateroom? Do you realize what you look like?"

Her green eyes flashing and looking directly at José's manhood she replied, "My ship has sunk. The only clothes I have are currently in your ship's laundry. And, what do you mean, 'Do I realize what I look like?'"

"Well, you are . . . are truly beautiful . . . I mean your skin is . . . well, let's just say you may be the most attractive woman to ever grace a Spanish warship," José quickly responded. He was confused when he found his manhood being called to action while, both his mind and remainder of his body were totally exhausted from the storm.

"Well said, my captain," Betsy quietly stated. "You need to get your rest. I will simply take a sheet and nap on your sofa until my clothes have been dried in the sunshine. You get some sleep."

With that, José dove onto the bed. Betsy sat down beside him and rubbed his aching, tired shoulders as he let go of consciousness. As he closed his eyes, he heard Betsy whisper in his ear, "Thank you for saving my life, my crew's life, and for all the heroic things you have done. You will always be my hero."

CHAPTER 21

Problems in Cuba

"I believe that it is essential that human beings should attempt
to do a variety of tasks and have numerous experiences.
This is what truly differentiates humans from animals."
—José Gaspar, Cuba, October 1778

For days following the passage of the terrible hurricane, the remaining thirteen ships of the fleet although crippled, continued on their western trek. Day after day, the industrious sailors continued making repairs while under sail.

José spent most of his time making rounds of the repairs on board the *Intrepido* while his mind was filled with many other things at one time. In addition to checking with Cousin León on the physical repairs, José met often with Lieutenant Alvarez and Lieutenant Gálvez concerning the manifests on board each ship and with the remaining supplies that each ship would need to continue to make repairs. José also needed to assure himself that the rescued slaves were being taken care of and in good health and so he checked on them often.

After a lunch of fish on a Sunday afternoon, José, Cousin León, Lieutenant Gálvez, and Brutal Betsy were enjoying coffee in the dining area. It marked the first day since the hurricane that anyone had tasted freshly baked rolls, courtesy of a group of slaves who were helping to prepare the meals under the direction of the ship's cook.

"I will be glad to get these ships to Cuba," José sighed, "It will be such a relief to deal only with Spanish ships, crewed by Spanish sailors and hauling Spanish soldiers. The trip from Cuba to Louisiana should be a vacation compared to this leg of the journey. I feel that, in spite of our efforts, this phase of our cruise is a failure."

"I disagree, Captain. This journey has been very successful," Brutal Betsy, looking fetching in a shirt of José's, commented. "Success is whatever I deem it to be and I proclaim the rescue of the slaves on this ship, along with my crew, to be a success."

"How can you call the loss of your ship and three hundred humans a success?" José asked incredulously.

"Because I have my crew alive and, when we get to Cuba and sell the slaves you rescued, I shall have enough capital to purchase another ship," she replied matter-of-factly.

"What makes you think that I will permit you to have these slaves? I rescued them and they are on my ship. I will argue to the governor that I have a right to them and if he grants my request, then I shall make them free," José retorted showing a temper that he normally kept well under control.

"We shall see, Captain, but I can assure you that these slaves are my personal property and I will sell my property at the slave auction. Besides having the law on my side, I have ways only available to a woman to convince your oversexed governor," she replied with assurance and winked at the group.

"We shall see about that," José snapped; then turning to Lieutenant Gálvez and Alvarez he ordered, "No one shall move the slave women and children off this ship until I have orders from the governor himself. Anyone who goes near the slaves is to be shot. Do you understand?"

"Does that hold true for me also, Captain?" Betsy asked in a playful tone, as she did not truly believe Gaspar's determination on this issue.

"That is especially true for you and your crew," José snarled. "I have never killed a woman, nor do I ever hope to, but I swear to you, I will blow your pretty face off with my pistol if you even go near those slaves once we get to port."

Concerned with José's antagonism, Cousin León suggested that the group adjourn and go outside to inspect the ongoing repairs of the ship. No one hesitated in leaving at this moment.

José felt it wise to transfer Betsy and her crew to Miguel's ship for the remainder of the sail to Cuba. The ships seemed to plod along over the next week as they successfully passed the Windward Islands and slipped passed Hispañola under the cover of darkness. They had set full sail before heading into the pirate-infested waters shortly before sunset and, twelve hours later, they moved west, northwest toward Cuba.

With a strong wind blowing, the ships were able to maintain a steady pace and the following morning, rising out of the western horizon, were the welcome green mountains of Cuba. As the ships approached Santiago Bay, José could see the castle and the guns of El Morro that clearly commanded the narrow channel between the Caribbean and Santiago Bay.

The ships put into port and were guided to adjacent docks in the Navy quay.

Shortly after they were secured to the dockside, José gathered his crew on deck to thank and congratulate them. As he looked over his men, he was very proud of the sweat-soaked and grizzled group. They had been forced by nature to work together as a team in order to survive and they were now veterans who appreciated each other. José ordered them to shave and clean up so they would represent the fleet and their ship well and then he gave them shore leave.

Ships of all types have always attracted women of pleasure, con-artists, and sellers of drugs and spirits to ports of call. Santiago was no different from any other port catering to these ships—in fact, it was said by some that Santiago was even more prone to these activities than the infamous city of Port Royal had ever been. Many believed that the governor, the Honorable Fidel Mota, and his bureaucracy profited from every illicit venture in the town.

Miguel came over to José's ship and, with a look of anxiety, confided to José his enjoyment in having Betsy on board his vessel and his strong feelings toward her.

"Where is the Irish Captain?" José inquired with a smile as he wondered how Betsy and Miguel would look in an embrace.

"She left immediately after we docked this morning. She went to a shop near the quay, bought a most feminine dress, cut very low in front, bathed, and had her hair washed and put up in charming ringlets," Miguel recounted. "She left in a carriage to go to the governor's and was carrying some papers. I think she wants to claim the slave women and children."

"Damn! I should have known she was an aggressive bitch," José shouted. "I need to get cleaned up myself and go directly to the governor's mansion."

"But, my friend Betsy speaks highly of you," Miguel protested. "She would do nothing to harm you. Remember, you saved her life!"

"It is not me that I am concerned about. It is the slave women and children." José exclaimed in exasperation. "She wants to get those slaves to sell at the market. I must go to the governor. If somebody is going to stab me in the back, I want to be there!"

"José, how could you not be present while being stabbed in the back?" Miguel teased, trying for some levity to lighten the mood.

José replied darkly, "I must get to the governor's mansion to verbally outwit your potential love." As he was ready to leave and awaiting the carriage, a group of women wearing provocative clothing and a surly looking man approached the gangplank. It was obvious that the women were prostitutes interested in trading their bodies for the hard-earned money of José's sailors. "It is unfortunate that women feel that they must resort to selling themselves as a product," José thought to himself. His thoughts were shattered by the bellowing shouts of the pockmarked man accompanying the ladies.

"Captain, since the sailors have obviously left your ship already and my children will go hungry this night, might I ask the least amount you would charge me for your black women?" the pimp, Manny Amadór, shouted.

"These women and their children are currently my wards and under the protection of the Spanish Navy," José sternly replied. "They are not now nor hopefully will ever be for sale, especially to you!"

"I am friends with the governor. I assure you that black slaves will never be allowed to go free in Santiago. Why not let me 'kidnap' these wenches? I will give you five hundred pieces of eight for the whole lot of them. I'll even take the damn children," Manny said as he walked, puffing, up the gangway, and pulled a pouch from his shirt. Another man, very tall and muscular, came out of the shadows and joined Amadór on the gangplank.

"I order you to get off this ship immediately!" José shouted. "These women and children are my guests, and you will not disturb them."

Amadór and the hulking, stinking giant paid no attention, but continued up the gangplank toward the women who were huddled on the deck. José stepped between the two men and the cowering women.

"Out of my way, you short piece of Spanish Navy shit," Manny shouted at José.

In a flash José drew his sword from its scabbard and, with a lightning-fast upward slash, took the right ear from the bodyguard next to Manny Amadór. The man fell, screaming, into the garbage-strewn water under the dock, his blood spattering over Manny's face and shirt. José then drew his short knife from his belt and pressed it upon Manny's genitals.

"Now, you bastard son-of-a-bitch; if you don't get the hell off my ship, I'll cut off the head of your cock, stick it in your mouth, shove that swivel gun up your ass, and blow both your God-damned heads to kingdom come," José whispered with the hiss of an angry serpent. "That way, I will be sure to kill your brain in whatever head it is located."

Manny began sobbing and begged for mercy as his women ran from the docks. The hulk in the water, who could not swim, finished thrashing, gurgled, and drowned. José then allowed Manny to crawl off the gangway and run into the darkness.

Manny shouted as he ran off, "It will do you little good. I will buy those wenches at the slave auction and turn them into whores. I will buy their damn offspring and sell them to the sugarcane plantation owners. You may have won this fight, but you cannot fight the governor and the attitudes of the Spanish Main."

CHAPTER 22

Slave Market

*"Unless we recognize our failings, our failures will shape our
thoughts and deeds. Conclusions and beliefs built upon a foundation
of human failure will lead to a bleak future for mankind."*
—Capt. José Gaspar, Cuba, 1779

José dejectedly made his way to the governor's palace located high upon a lushly vegetated mountain overlooking the turquoise waters of Santiago Bay. The whitewashed governor's mansion was located near the castle of El Morro. José gaped at the large cannon that were aimed at the narrow channel between the Caribbean Sea and the bay. Without doubt, these guns on the high ground could control who came and went from Santiago de Cuba, José thought.

As he approached the palace, he met Brutal Betsy coming out from the governor's patio. He noted that her hair was mussed and her clothes disheveled. Betsy refused to look José in the eye as they exchanged hollow pleasantries.

"José, please don't go inside and embarrass yourself," Betsy pleaded, "the governor has already been persuaded to recognize that I am the rightful owner of the slaves on the *Intrepido*. I have the signed papers and documents. All you will do is cause a scene that will diminish your fine reputation as a Spanish hero."

"I believe the true heroes are the people who do what has to be done, when it needs to be done, regardless of the consequences," José snapped back. "Betsy, damn it, sometimes when I am angry, I have a right to be angry. I must believe that someone with power in this world must believe, as I do, that the enslaving of human beings is wrong. Somewhere there must be a leader who truly cares."

"José, the governor really doesn't believe he is a bad person," Betsy interrupted, "he simply sends the Crown a list of all the good things he did in the past and puts tomorrow's dates on them. In other words, he won't listen to you. José, you really are a hero in the eyes of Spain and you are risking your excellent record. Please leave with me."

"You talk of a true Spanish hero of our time, but I tell you that none exist!" José exclaimed in disgust. "I would rather believe that God does not exist than believe that He would permit slavery!"

Betsy came forward and placed her firm hand on José's shoulder in a display of friendship and understanding. "My most dear and perfect man, I understand the frustration you feel. Were my life not turned upside down when the British government took my lifestyle and my husband, I am sure we would be in agreement on this issue. But in the course of human events, we are sometimes thrust into a position in life where our very survival depends upon our abandoning everything that we believed previously we stood for! We cannot all maintain the idealism that colors your thinking, but may need to rely on realism."

José turned and hugged Brutal Betsy, thinking how incongruous it was that he thought so highly of her as an individual and had such disgust for her actions. He looked into her pleading eyes brimming with tears, smiled at her and said with a laugh, "Just because I can't win an argument with you by using logic, doesn't mean I shouldn't be able to then satisfy my frustration by launching a barrage of profanity at your ideas. Damn it, as strongly as I believe that this is an important moral issue, I can't bring myself to swear at you or cast you out of my life."

José said his good-byes to Betsy and promised not to bring up the issue with the governor. He was let into the mansion and led to the governor, who officially welcomed him to Cuba. After discussing the latest news of Spain, the governor promised materials, supplies, and manpower to repair the Gaspar fleet so the ships could continue on toward Louisiana.

During the next week, José met daily with the other ships' captains, officers, and carpenters to insure that all required repairs were being made to the vessels to make them seaworthy. He also had an opportunity to tour Santiago and the area surrounding the port city. On two of these occasions, he chanced to meet Miguel Rodriquez and Brutal Betsy who were obviously enthralled with each other's company.

"José, my dearest friend, what is the status of things between you and your señora?" Miguel asked on one of these occasions.

"Our friendship continues to grow, even when we are long distances apart," José smiled as his thoughts focused on his lovely Rosalita. "I write to her nearly everyday. I have already sent two letters back to Spain from here in Santiago."

José and Miguel enjoyed the company of each other, able to express anything without fear of criticism, anger, or reprisal and with the knowledge that their words would go no further.

As the middle of November approached, the remaining ships of José's fleet were almost ready to continue the journey to Louisiana. Also, mid-November heralded the slave auction in Santiago. Against his better judgment, José knew he must go and witness the sale of the slave women he had risked his life to save.

As he entered the market area, José strolled down a crowded cobblestone street and observed buildings resembling horse stables on both sides of the thoroughfare. It wasn't long until he realized that these stables were actually slave pens, where those being sold at auction were held. From within the walls, José could hear both crying as well as soulful singing. The music was a stirring and unfamiliar mix of male and female voices.

The street ended at a massive building, one of the largest in Santiago. Greek columns rose to a roof about twenty feet high. The walls were made of granite with great arched windows. José walked inside with some trepidation. He saw ornate carvings of both marble and granite on the interior walls. In the center of the building, rising about four feet above the main floor, was a stage made of marble with a column on either side. In spite of the outside noonday heat, the inside of the structure was cool and José felt a chill on his back due to the temperature as well as a sense of foreboding.

He had worn civilian clothes and gone to the market alone. This allowed him to mingle with the crowd that ranged from wide-eyed children to men who were undoubtedly attending with only voyeurism in mind. Besides the variety of spectators, José recognized a sizable group of men and women who were obviously bidders in this flesh market.

José struck up a conversation with a Catholic priest who, according to his account, was attending his twentieth slave auction. Like José, the priest was opposed to slavery and attended in order to bless the slaves before they were taken away by their new owners. The priest was known for his impassioned letters to monarchies and governments around the world, imploring them to ban the practice of enslaving human beings and wrenching families apart at the market place.

"Father, I understand somewhat how governments can ignore the evil of slavery because of the immense profits generated from the production of crops such as sugar, tobacco, coffee, and chocolate that we know would be difficult to produce if not for this labor force. What I truly cannot understand is why the world's religions have long given slavery their ultimate blessing?" José asked in a tone of bewilderment.

"My son, I can only tell you what I know," the priest replied. "The people who have participated in the Atlantic slave system have included Africans, Arabs, Berbers, Italians, Portuguese, Spaniards, Dutch, Jews, Germans, Swedes, French, English, Danes, and even thousands of free blacks who have become slave-holding planters themselves. Basically, there is so much money to be made that slavery, evil as it is, has become the soul of the economic movement of the world."

"But, how can the world's religions sanction slavery?" José exploded.

"I think that because of the great expansion and change that has taken place, the churches turned their collective heads to the enslavement of human beings. After all, it has increased the money in their coffers also," the priest answered. "But, my son, from the times when the pope blessed and authorized the first Portuguese slave traders in West Africa until today, no religious organization is guilt-free when it comes to slavery. Every religion has been guilty of taking slavery for granted whether it be Catholics, Protestants, Jews, Muslims, or even Quakers!"

"I wonder if there is any hope it will end," José pondered out loud.

"My son, I do believe that when slavery is discovered for what it is, it will be a combination of religious institutions and sectarian demands that will end it," the priest stated with confidence.

"Well, it cannot be soon enough in my opinion. We must build our society upon people's strengths, regardless of who they are or what they look like," José added quickly as he turned to see the slaves, in ankle chains, being led into the building. They were wide-eyed and afraid as they shuffled slowly forward. All were dressed in ivory-colored Muslim sheets that were draped upon them like togas from the days of the Roman Empire.

José smiled when one of the young women he had rescued, carrying her infant son, smiled and yelled a greeting in her native tongue to José. One of the guards immediately cracked the woman over the head with a riding crop causing her to cry out in pain. This, in turn, caused the baby to begin wailing. José started to jump across the fence but was restrained by the Catholic priest and others in the growing crowd.

"What did she say?" José demanded as he relaxed from the grasp of the crowd.

"She called to you 'King Lion, go and produce many like yourself,'" one of the men, a black freeman, translated.

"I don't understand her meaning" José replied.

"Sir, some lions mate over fifty times a day," the old man answered. "She was recognizing you as a king of your kind and hoping you will produce many offspring like yourself."

"Maybe she has the only true answer as to how to end this sinful blemish," the priest quietly told José. "If Spain had more like you, then there would be no more slavery." The priest continued, "Her name is very fitting for you, my son, not only because you have the qualities of the King Lion, but also because you also remind me of that great English monarch we so often refer to by his French name—Richard Coeur de Lion. You are kingly in more ways than one. I shall use your heart, your 'lion's heart,' and the need for the world to have more of your kind as examples in my epistles to our religious and secular leaders in Spain."

The auction began when an extremely corpulent Anglo of questionable heritage mounted the stage and began bellowing. Although José had been taught to look for the good in all people and to overlook their physical appearance, he winced as he attempted to focus upon this behemoth. José felt that this was, by far, the most unattractive specimen of humanity that he had ever seen. He was hairy and apelike with a bulbous crimson nose and a sneering slit for a mouth.

The cowering and weeping slaves had looks of disbelief on their faces when they were separated by sex; the men were led to the left side of the stage and the women to the right side. José soon noted that the auctioneer alternated selling the men and women with children. There were numerous slaves to be sold that day.

With a sideways sweep of the crowd, José noticed Brutal Betsy and Miguel Rodriquez arm in arm near the desk where purchasers paid for their slaves and the sellers received their proceeds. Although he had a degree of understanding, José could not bring himself to go and greet them or to even recognize their presence.

On the stage, two of the women José had rescued and one of the children were brought forward. The auctioneer started the bidding, but as the bids did not seem sufficient, he stalked over to the women. He then grabbed the robe of the taller woman and stripped it from her body, revealing her sleek and well-proportioned body. The crowd roared its approval and began to clap and whistle shrilly with the voyeurs leading the applause. The slave was now shaking while trying to conceal herself. Seeing this, the auctioneer came forward and with his big hairy hands yanked hers from her breasts and crotch. She squealed in embarrassment and with a sadistic smile, the auctioneer slapped her twice across the face.

He then walked to the other woman and pulled her sheet off as well. One of his assistants came forward to carry the crying baby from the stage. The priest whispered to José that the baby and his mother would never see each other again. With tears in his eyes, José averted his face and kicked the floor in absolute revulsion.

Another cry drew José's attention back up to the stage, where two other men had jumped. He watched as they inspected the women upon whom they were bidding. José was later told that, after submitting a sufficient opening bid, a bidder could come forward to "inspect" his potential property at the Santiago auction.

The northeast breeze became quite cool in the shade of the building and the miserable women on the stage were shaking from the chill as well as fear. Their nipples were erect in the cold draft and the two bidders, encouraged and humored by the crowd, pinched and touched their breasts. José wanted nothing more than to run up on stage and rescue the pathetic slaves, but his sense of personal survival prevailed and stopped him from acting foolishly.

A familiar voice finally shouted a higher bid for the two women. José looked to his right and looking at José with a crooked smile narrowed eyes, was Manny Amadór, the pimp whom José had chased from his ship. "The bastard is making good on his promise to purchase the slaves from my ship and there isn't anything I can legally do to stop him!" José thought in dismay.

Manny then also leapt to the stage to "inspect" the sobbing women. With a look over his shoulder directly at José, Manny probed and inspected the genital areas of both women to the roaring delight of the screaming crowd.

José looked at the priest and beseechingly implored him, "Father, I can't stand to watch this; I fear I will kill those men but I know that I'll be held responsible and my imprisonment will serve no lasting purpose. What shall I do?"

"My son—with the lion's heart—please leave. Your intentions are far too noble. You would risk everything by killing those cockroaches!" The priest answered angrily.

"You are right, father," José grimly stated, "A cockroach can live nine days without its head. These men, with nothing in their heads anyway, might well live forever!"

With scalding tears burning his eyes for the first time since he had been a child of fourteen and forced to live with María Gonzalez, José fled the slave auction not stopping until he was back aboard the *Intrepido*.

He remained below deck in his cabin without appetite for two days. Finally Cousin León managed to coax him from his depression to eat. But José continued to be distraught with his participation in the slavery ordeal and shared the priest's words with his cousin.

"León, I find it so incomprehensible that two people can look at the same thing and see something so different," José mused as he thought of Brutal Betsy's attitude toward slavery. "Life can be changed in a matter of hours by people you don't even know."

"We'll soon be off to sea and your mind will clear," León stated in a fatherly tone. "Hopefully, you will become a 'King Lion' as the slave woman wished."

José at last smiled and told León that male lions mate fifty times a day. "I would enjoy being a lion with my Rosalita," he exclaimed.

"But, cousin, people and dolphins are the only species that have sex for pleasure," León replied as he clapped José on the shoulder, thrilled to see him laughing again.

"You know, León, how I always tell people that our bringing of pigs to the New World will someday be frowned upon?" José asked in mock sincerity.

"Yes," León smiled. "What do you mean?"

"Well, cousin, pigs spend a good deal of time copulating and do you know why?" José asked leaning forward.

"No, I have no idea," León replied.

"A pig's orgasm lasts for thirty minutes!" José retorted and then said, "Now if we could only take the lion and pig's abilities and put them in humans, we would be very popular with men and women alike!"

"My captain, you have been cloistered in this cabin too long. Why don't you shave and bathe and we can go into town for a good meal before we sail in the morning," León suggested.

" I feel better now," José admitted, "but to have a great world we need to be able to sacrifice what we have been for what we are capable of becoming."

CHAPTER 23

Discovery of Southwest Florida

"We often create problems in the world that we can never solve. We need to learn how to solve problems if it is our thinking or our actions that have created them."
—Captain José Gaspar, November 5, 1779

José felt relief as the fleet prepared to sail from Santiago to Louisiana. The day prior to the sail date, the crews loaded fresh supplies and the Spanish soldiers who had been on shore leave began returning to their ships. The entire slave trade experience had left José bewildered. That evening he penned a letter to Rosalita, which the governor of Cuba promised would be delivered to her in Spain.

4 November 1779

My dearest Rosalita,

This voyage has taught me that it's not what you have in your life but whom you have in your life that really counts. I am so thankful to have you in my life and I pray you feel as strongly for me. Looking forward to having you to love and to share life with makes the rest of life tolerable. The only time I feel complete and truly happy are the moments I spend in your company.

This voyage has caused me to grow older than my years. I believe that maturity has more to do with the experiences you have had and what you have learned from them and less to do with how many birthdays you have celebrated.

I have witnessed the inhumanity of man toward man and the world's religions turning a blind eye toward this cancer called slavery. These slavers are truly the dregs of society. The problem, I discovered, is that if I lower myself to com-

pete or deal with this scum, even if the argument is won, I have become scum myself. I am feeling so dirty that I look forward to leaving these people in my wake and getting away from this wretched city. Everyone is so quick to place blame and also place a burden on the black man and that is terribly wrong.

I have always believed that a person's success is relative to the sincerity in which they believe in a cause. On this night, I fear, I am not a successful human being.

Tomorrow we leave for Louisiana and I look forward to crossing the Gulf of Mexico, for everyone tells me how wonderfully clear the water is and that the fishing is outstanding, which will allow us plenty of good eating on this part of our journey.

Rosalita, the world is such a confusing place. It is larger than I imagined; but even worse is the increasing complexity. I fear that as our world continues to grow more complex, it will take all the effort we can muster simply to stay rooted. Will we become so busy with our worldly duties and activities that we will forget the importance of intimate times with those we love?

My Rosalita, I promise never to allow the world or Spain to come before my love for you. I dream only of the time when we can embrace one another and spend all of our hours together.

I shall return to you shortly after the new year begins.

Each day I love you more than the previous day . . . swelling with love whenever I think of you, which I do often, and looking upon the same stars that I know you are looking at!

With all my love,

Your Lion, José

The next cloudless morning dawned and the sun seemed to electrify the vivid blue sky with shades of pink. The tradewinds blew into the harbor as José enjoyed the flowery scents of a tropical morning while awaiting the order from the harbor master to cast off.

As he leaned on the railing of the quarterdeck, José saw a green and black carriage arrive. Going to the rail, José observed Brutal Betsy and Miguel leave the carriage and walk along the pavement stones of the wharf to the ship. Although he despised what Brutal Betsy had done and what she had become, José was glad his old friend Miguel had come to see him off once again. José knew that, no matter how firm a friendship is, that friend may hurt you occasionally and must be forgiven in order for the friendship to survive.

"Miguel, the harbor master tells me you are going to Havana and then on to Saint Augustine," José yelled down.

"Yes, Captain, since I saw you safely to Santiago, they thought it would be wise for the manifest to get to its original destination," Miguel called back. "I fear the children in Havana may not be saving any of their coins, since their 'pyggy banks' are in the hold of my ship. I leave after lunch. I also have a paying group of passengers as I am escorting Betsy and her crew to Havana where they have been promised a new ship, an older British frigate, I am told."

"Can a woman, even Irish, be capable of handling all that speed?" José shot back, attempting to solicit a fiery response from Betsy.

"José, my new ship, *The Irish Lady II,* will be able to ride the crest of waves and be as swift as anything the Spanish Navy currently has afloat," Betsy retorted. "Only an accomplished sailor can hope to stay in front of my new ship."

"Thank you, my dear, for recognizing my talent," José laughed, "I have always said that if you are not in front creating the wake, then you are doomed to always be caught up in someone else's waves."

"José, you better quit your boasting this instant, or I will challenge you and the *Intrepido* to a race," Betsy answered with her jaw jutting forward in a display of Celtic stubbornness. "But, then you would probably just cheat anyway!"

"My red-haired friend, if quitters never win, and winners never cheat, then who is the fool who said, 'quit while you're ahead'?" José laughed, "Having delusions of grandeur makes many people feel better about themselves," he continued with a smile,

"I must now prepare to shove off. I bid both of you a grand farewell until we meet again, May God be with you." With a wave, José returned to the helmsman and began shouting orders to his crew while the longshoreman began to untie the dock lines. With a groan, the *Intrepido* slipped into the channel and began to drift towards the mouth of the harbor.

Within a week the small fleet, sailing north-northwest, was now in sight of the southwestern coastline of La Florida. José was surprised at the continued clarity of the water that mirrored the cloudless blue November skies overhead. The shoreline was a series of mangrove-surrounded islands. Their charts indicated that this series of islands was referred to as "Ten Thousand Islands" and that the waters surrounding these islands were extremely shallow, which resulted in the fleet extending its course out further from shore to avoid running aground on one of the many sandbars.

Out in the deeper water, the crews delighted in watching the pods of bottlenose dolphins swimming, jumping, fishing, and playing around their ships. The dolphins had a way of comically entertaining even the crustiest of the seamen on board.

Another diversion was watching the variety of sea turtles swimming in the Gulf of Mexico. The anglers on board the ship sought loggerhead turtles, weighing up to three hundred and fifty pounds and sometimes three feet in length. They succeeded in landing a pair of these large turtles, insuring a number of hot turtle soup meals. The crew was also surprised with the number of leatherback turtles seen swimming in the water. These turtles were the largest of the sea turtles, up to ten feet long and two thousand pounds.

On the fifth day out of Santiago, the fleet discovered that not only abundant and unfamiliar sea life abounded in these opalescent waters, but also a group of pirates in small, swift, shallow draft ships. With such boats, the pirates were capable of surprising a prey, capturing a booty, and returning to the safety of the many barrier islands which, surrounded by the shallow water, could not be approached by the victim ships with their deep hulls.

The *Esperanza*, the fastest of José's fleet, had sailed west into the Gulf of Mexico in order to undergo sea trials to insure that the hurricane had not inflicted permanent damage upon it. The *San Cristabol* was escorting two of the troop ships about a mile west of the *Intrepido*, which was nearest shore, and escorting two of the small brigantine traders.

As another glorious Florida sunset began to take shape in the western sky, two of the sleek, low-sided pirate ships slipped behind and to the east side of the last brigantine where the long November afternoon shadows gave them cover from the protecting *Intrepido*. The merchant captain managed to fire off a warning shot from his swivel gun alerting José and his crew.

The echo from the gun ricocheted off the water with a violent rattle. Within seconds, José had his warship turning to larboard and heading toward the stricken ship, which now also was being attacked by the other pirate vessel. The gun decks of the *Intrepido* came alive with activity as José and the officers ordered the gunners to be ready immediately. The hours of practice that José had demanded of his sailors were now beginning to show results.

José ordered the slow matches struck and the deck batteries of twenty-four pound guns to load chain shot, that is, two cannonballs linked together with a chain. At the same time he ordered the alternate lower deck cannons to be filled with shrapnel. The sailors on the sails carried incendiary grenades to the yardarms, to be set on fire and hurled down onto the enemy ships. It was becoming clear that the *Intrepido* was determined to bring terror and total destruction to these pirate invaders.

Whether José was full of pent up frustrations caused by the hurricane and loss of the slaves he had saved, or, if destiny had merely determined that he was to become the "terror of the seas" is still open to question. What is not in question was the terror and total destruction that Captain Gaspar's *Intrepido* reigned down upon the attacking pirates.

With skillful and daring handling, the *Intrepido* lunged through the rolling waves and confronted the first vessel directly.

José pulled his sword from the scabbard and leapt high onto the gunwale shouting to his cannoneers, "On the uproll, men, fire your cannons!"

The batteries roared to life and shook the very beams of the *Intrepido*. With flash and thunder, the guns recoiled like big, black monsters belching a thick choking smoke that soon covered the decks. As soon as the breech lines relaxed and the screeching and grinding sound of the carriages stopped, the gun crews immediately began the process of reloading the cannon.

The chain shot and shrapnel scored direct hits upon the deck of the now helpless invader. The chain shot crashed into and wrapped around the masts and rigging of the smaller vessel while the shrapnel tore through the bodies of pirates who fell screaming to the decks. These decks soon glistened with the blood of the dead and dying pirates.

As the smoke cleared, José showed no mercy and commanded another salvo be fired into the crippled pirate ship. The noise again thundered across the placid gulf waters like an afternoon thunderstorm, though nature is incapable of delivering the instant wrath and destruction that spewed forth from Gaspar's gun batteries.

The few remaining pirates, still screaming in agony and slipping on their mates' blood, attempted to surrender by striking their colors. It would have been useless, as José now called for the incendiary grenades to be rained down upon the listing, sinking ship.

In addition, he ordered the ship's twenty-four pounders reloaded and had a salvo from the twenty huge guns delivered into the immobile vessel causing it to blow up in a fireball as the enemy magazine apparently suffered a direct hit.

The other pirate vessel, witnessing this brutal massacre of their fellow pirates, broke off the attack on the merchant vessel and headed east into the small islands that made up the Southwest Florida coastline. For a group who made their livelihood by instituting terror upon their prey, they were shocked at what Captain Gaspar and the *Intrepido* had unleashed.

CHAPTER 24

Gaspar's Determination

"Any man has the ability to start something,
but few have the determination to finish something successfully."
—Captain José Gaspar, somewhere near Ten Thousand Islands, November 1778

Immediately after the sinking of one pirate vessel, the *Intrepido* gave chase to the other. The pirate vessel took advantage of the distance between them and made sail for the mangrove islands where it was quickly concealed. While the heavier and slower *Intrepido* moved cautiously into the shallow waters surrounding the islands, the setting sun cast long shadows from the mangroves and twilight approached.

By keeping a constant and determined eye on the masts of the pirate ship, José was able to pinpoint the spot where the attackers had disappeared. However, his men doubted him. His lieutenants believed the pirates had gone behind a larger island surrounded with beaches. There were even fires on the large island indicating that it was inhabited. Gálvez convinced José that the *Intrepido* should anchor offshore this island and wait for sunrise before sending scouts ashore. The often shallow waters surrounding the mangrove islands were difficult to navigate, especially at night. Regardless, José was intent on following his hunch that the pirate ship had sailed beyond this island and somehow had entered a cayo or key further inland. He was determined to prove that he was right.

With a gentle splash into the dark water, the *Intrepido*'s anchor found the odorous coastal muck on the bay side of the island. Fortunately, the tradewinds continued to blow across the decks and kept biting insects from attacking the crew.

José ordered his men to prepare the longboat so that he could row alone among the darkened islands. Gálvez, aghast, pleaded with him to wait until dawn.

"This is far too dangerous an undertaking," Gálvez insisted. "You cannot risk your life. Besides, it is far too dark to see. It simply cannot be done!"

"I guess people will always say that I tried the impossible," José responded. "But, my friend, if you attempt the impossible, there is no competition, which means you get to try simply because no one else dares to."

"But, sir, the fleet needs you in command. You need not take foolish chances," Gálvez protested in frustration.

"Lieutenant Gálvez, what is your first name?" José asked.

"Why it's Marco, sir," Lieutenant Gálvez responded taken aback.

"Then, Marco, if I do not return by morning, you take the marines and charge ashore on the large island with the lights." José continued, "You can claim it in your name for the crown of Spain. Call it Marco Island if you wish."

With a laugh, José crawled over the side of the *Intrepido* and disappeared into the moonlit semidarkness, rowing silently towards the darkened keys. The nearly full moon began to illuminate the waters as it rose. As he placed the oars in the rippling waters, he could hear the mullet splashing and noticed the sour smell of the shore beneath the mangroves.

As he reached the island he could find no inlets or bays into which a two-masted schooner could vanish. This fact puzzled him, as he was sure the ship had disappeared into very center of the island. He rowed slowly back the way he had come, again seeking an obvious entrance. The outgoing tide created a strong current in the pass between two islands, which pulled him away from the land. He rowed furiously against the current until he reached the mangroves hanging over the water's edge. He tied his boat to a branch, and was about to step on shore when he noted with surprise that the branches were actually growing and floating on a raft of logs and covered with a foot of soil. *How ingenious*, he thought. *These pirates have constructed gates that, when closed, conceal the entry to the island. From the sea, no one would ever expect this island to be inhabited or to conceal a ship.*

José decided for the sake of protecting Spanish fleets, he would scout the island to learn what he could about the pirates and their compound. Mosquitoes attacked him mercilessly and he felt sticky blood each time he swiped at his face. Sodden, sweating, and dirty, he could not remember another time in his life when he itched or smelled as bad as he did that night.

He fought his way through the jungle of multi-trunked mangroves and onto the sandy mounds beyond. In the moonlight, José could see there were trees tall enough to camouflage a ship's masts, and that branches had been hoisted up the halyards to add to the disguise. As he moved carefully up the low dunes, José heard the sound of voices, both male and female, from the other side of the mound. He dropped to his knees and crawled slowly to the top, hesitating briefly when a snake crossed his path.

Ahead in a clearing were eight small huts and one larger house, arranged in a circle. The roofs were made of thatched palm fronds. Near each hut was a small fire burning inside a gourd-like fireplace. The flames illuminated men, women and children, who were sitting around the tabby furnace. José counted forty-five men or large boys, twenty-three women, and fifteen small children.

As his eyes became accustomed to the scene, he noticed that a sand dune ran about two-thirds of the way around the encampment before blending into a thick woods on the northern side. On the western side lay the false mangrove gate. It concealed the schooner, which was tied securely to a dock. Nearby were piles of cargo and crates, the apparent booty of the pirates.

Grateful that he had not been discovered, José quietly returned to his boat and began rowing back to the ship, this time with, rather than against, the tide.

The sky was beginning to turn to early morning pink as José, exhausted, bloodied, and agitated, returned to the *Intrepido*. He stripped off his clothes, jumped into the water, and let the refreshing salt water engulf his multiple bites and scratches. Then he climbed naked up the rope ladder to the center deck where a broadly smiling Alvarez welcomed him. José went directly to his cabin for a clean clothes.

As the sun rose higher in the east, José assembled the crews from the *Intrepido*, the two merchant vessels and the *San Cristabol*. He shared with them what he had discovered and his plan.

Since they had all seen campfires on Cayo "Marco," José determined that Marco Gálvez would take the marines from the two merchantmen and the *San Cristabol* and effect a landing and assault with the intent of capturing any pirates on that island.

José would take the marines from the *Intrepido*. They would row in longboats to land on the smaller key that looked blacker from its dense foliage, and surround the encampment on the south, east, and northern sides. The *Intrepido*, under temporary command of Lieutenant Alvarez, would maneuver into position in order to lay cannon fire into the mangrove gates on the west side of the island.

When the signal was given, both the *Intrepido* and the *San Cristabol* would begin a massive artillery barrage on the respective islands which, combined with the musket fire of the marines, should create terror to those on the islands and cause a quick surrender.

By mid-morning all units were in position and José lit a cigar from which he then lit a flare grenade. He threw the grenade high into the air and the bright pink flame illuminated the crystal-clear blue sky.

The quiet morning sounds of birds and surf were replaced with thundering blasts and recurrent echoes as the twenty-four pounders from both ships let go simultaneously with forty cannon shots. The screaming shells found their marks in the towering trees and the resulting explosions sent splinters and burning branches flying in all directions. One shell hit the onshore magazine of the pirate island, as flames and secondary explosions reverberated. To the pirates, roused from their beds and breakfast, it seemed as if hell had come up from the ground in a fiery volcano.

After the last of the explosions, José stood on the hill overlooking the pirate compound, with his sword drawn, and fired a shot from his handgun into the air. This served to immediately capture the attention of those below as everyone looked up in José's direction. "Surrender or die!" he shouted.

Nearly all those below stopped in their tracks and raised their arms. However, one small group of men attempted to sneak off toward their moored ship that was concealed with a blanket of swirling smoke. José grabbed a musket from one of his prone soldiers and took aim, firing a shot that tore into and shattered the skull of the apparent leader. Immediately, the three survivors thrust their hands and arms into the air signifying their surrender.

As the marines from the *Intrepido* rose and swept down the hill to take control of the prisoners, José motioned for Cousin León and some of the sailors to climb the hill and join him.

"Your plan was brilliant," León exclaimed. "I was not sure that it would work."

As the men gathered the prisoners and searched the pirate village, José received word that the attack on the nearby "Marco Island" was equally successful.

Sitting with his men, he spoke to them with passion, "There is nothing more exhilarating than to be in battle, to face down your enemy and survive. It gives a rush of pure triumph that can never be rivaled."

C HAPTE R 25

Paradise Discovered

"A person who enjoys nature and fishes almost always becomes a philosopher. You see, enjoying nature and fishing gives a man time to think. I often fish without hook or bait."
—José Gaspar, November 10, 1778

After the three leaders of the pirate colony were shackled and brought on board the *Intrepido*, José ordered that their families and the others who made up this island community should be allowed to stay and resume their lives. He made them promise not to return to piracy, at least against Spanish-flagged ships.

José decided to tour the pirate island and what was becoming known as Key Marco to inspect the communities that had developed there.

Both islands had a diverse terrain that included small sand hills and swampy areas, tall trees, sandy soil and a wide variety of vegetation. In addition, the islands had citrus, coconut, avocado and mango groves. The citrus trees were apparently brought from Spain. From the days of Ponce de León, sailors were required to carry at least one hundred citrus seeds to plant to help combat scurvy. The pirate farmers were also cultivating bananas, pineapples, onions, tomatoes, cabbages, peppers and other garden crops to supplement their diet of fish. They seemed to be a well-fed and healthy group. José was intrigued by the concept of healthy individuals attacking dehydrated, underfed, and ill sailors manning ships that had been at sea for weeks with no fresh fruits or vegetables. "Indeed," José thought, "scurvy has scuttled many more ships than actual sea battles!"

And the fishing! One sunny afternoon, as a young pirate of about nineteen years of age, León, Gálvez, and José walked barefoot on the shell-strewn beach, they noticed seven or eight snook close to shore. One fish, weighing at least twenty-five pounds, hovered near where the gentle waves lapped the sand. It seemed to be showing off its body with the yellow dorsal fin and tail.

The pirate lad explained that off these secluded beaches, snook, pompano, and even tarpon were caught regularly simply for the fight they give. "Tarpon come close to here," the boy added. "Near the passes there are often schools of both large and small, especially at dawn and dusk and when the tide is going out. Do you want to fish with us?"

"You also mentioned redfish?" José questioned.

"Yes, redfish are also here and of course, there are always sharks," the pirate lad replied with wide eyes. "And they are not afraid of anything. They swim up and down the beach as the masters of the water."

The boy continued describing other types of water animals surrounding these islands. The unusual sawfish, blowfish, and eagle rays sounded like creatures of the imagination. As the group listened, the boy pointed to a school of lethal-looking, gray stingrays sliding effortlessly through the gentle surf.

"These islands are a true paradise," José declared to the group, "except for the buzz and bite of the mosquitoes. If one could only escape the insects and the nocturnal habits of much of the wildlife!"

The Spanish fleet spent two more days enjoying the warmth and beauty of these subtropical isles as the pirates' heavy cannon were removed from their schooner and placed upon the Spanish vessels. The fleet also took on board a quantity of citrus fruit and garden vegetables from the hapless pirates.

As the crews regretfully departed and moved back into the placid Gulf, José watched roseate spoonbills feed, sweeping their long, flat bills rapidly from side to side as they scooped in their dinner. José smiled as he remembered the pink wading birds described as "flamingos" by Angel Castro to Lieutenant Gálvez.

While the convoy picked up the southeasterly wind and moved northwesterly, the peculiar brown pelicans sailed by overhead in flowing single lines, gracefully gliding on wind currents, appearing to stop in mid-flight before diving directly into the water to gobble up unsuspecting fish. Although a thing of beauty in flight, the pelican looked awkward when it took off and when it suddenly splash-landed.

As the ships approached Estero Island, a majestic bald eagle stopped in mid-flight to dive and snatch a fish with its talons. This female eagle was at least three feet in height with a wingspan of eight feet—an unusually large specimen.

Later, José felt privileged to witness eagles, paired for life, in a court-ship display. As the pair flew high over the *Intrepido,* they grasped the claws of the other and plummeted towards the gulf waters, cartwheeling with their wings and legs outstretched before releasing each other just above the surface of the water.

As the ship moved just off of what would later become known as Black Key, José could see the huge nest, ten feet across, high in the trees overlooking both the Gulf of Mexico and Estero Bay.

The sun began to rapidly disappear in the western horizon when José directed his fleet of nine ships to proceed to the bay formed at the mouth of the Indian-named Caloosahatchee—a river near the inviting island marked as "Santa Isabella" on their map.

Cousin León and Angel Castro began arguing over the proper name of this barrier island. "I tell you it is SanyBal Island," Angel said to Cousin León.

"No, it is Santa Bella," León earnestly told Angel.

"It almost sounds like our dear Captain Sanibel's name to me," José interjected with a broad smile. "Perhaps we should simply call it 'Sanibel' in honor of our friend."

The next morning, the fleet lifted anchor and headed back into the Gulf of Mexico, skirting the island called Santa Isabella, Sanybal, Santa Bella, or Sanibel. As on previous days, the ships plowed easily through the gently rolling turquoise water while running parallel to the pale beaches of numerous islands.

As evening again approached, the fleet neared the island of La Costa and decided to enter the deep harbor called Charlotte. A group of Cuban fisherman, who operated a fishery on La Costa, warned them to proceed west and north around the hidden sandbars. José was thankful for the assistance since the maps on board the *Intrepido* did not indicate obstacles. These maps had been drawn when the Spanish had a chain of missions along the west coast of Florida in the period from 1565 to 1568. Charts from the eighteenth century indicated only major landfalls and bodies of water.

The ships safely passed through Boca Grande Pass between the tropical outer islands and made for anchorage in the bay marked "South Bayou" on the eastern side of the island. This hidden harbor and bay offered camouflage to any ships passing by in the Gulf of Mexico.

José grew excited as he spotted a special island he had been studying on his map. He had noticed that there was an inlet between two keys at the mouth of Charlotte Harbor, each bearing the name of Friar Gaspar—Gasparilla Island, Gasparilla Inlet and Little Gasparilla. "I tell you, this area is a paradise," he shouted to his men.

A number of fishing ranchos were operating in northern Charlotte Harbor. Since this was November, Spaniards from Cuba had returned to fish during the winter season. José learned that there were also many year-round residents—outlaws from Cuba. They had cohabited with the Spanish-Indians who also worked the ranchos so many children were a Cuban-Indian mix. Since both Spanish and Indians ran the ranchos, a trading system had developed between the ranchos, and the Seminole Indians of the interior. José learned of its effectiveness as he was given blankets from the Indians of the interior and fishing tools fashioned of shells from the Indians of the ranchos.

José enjoyed the time he spent with these rancho residents and always remembered what he learned of the Cuban trade with the Seminole Indians. "I tell you, this is truly a paradise," José repeated to those living in the ranchos on these islands.

After a fitful night of sleep on the placid lagoon, José rose to have coffee on the quarterdeck. Leaning over the rail, José called to Lieutenant Alvarez to come quickly and see what was quietly rubbing against the side of their ship. Below swam a large animal resembling a seal, but with a beaver-like tail, two forelimbs with four nails on each, gray-brown skin, and stiff whiskers on its upper lip.

"It has whiskers like yours, Alvarez," José laughed.

Just then the animal seemed to voice its disapproval with that comparison by blowing hot air through the nostrils on the upper surface of its snout.

"Look over there. It has a calf!" Alvarez pointed out.

"This is one of nature's most perfect creatures. It has no natural enemies," José told Alvarez, "It is the West Indian manatee, and this one must weigh 2,000 pounds!"

"Look over there!" Cousin León shouted as he joined the other two officers on deck. "There is a wood stork wading in the lagoon. Up in the trees . . . look, there is a whole colony nesting up there."

"How are you so sure they are wood storks?" Alvarez asked León.

"Simple, the wood stork has a dark featherless head, a stout bill, and that white plumage trimmed with black," León answered confidently. "They are unusual birds that require many fish that these waters evidently provide. I learned that a pair of wood storks need nearly five hundred pounds of fish during a breeding season. I learned about the birds in this strange land from my earlier travels."

"We have been here only one and one-half days and I have already seen snook, redfish, sea trout, grouper, snapper, cobia, mackerel, barracuda, blacktip shark, sheepshead, and sea bass," José marvelled.

That afternoon, José and his party went ashore on Gasparilla Island. He was quite pleasantly surprised to find that some of the Spanish fisherman and Indian women had developed a number of small farms and grew mangoes, pineapple, citrus fruit, and a wide variety of exotic tropical fruits.

"If we were smart enough to purchase these fruits to eat on our ships, we could eliminate sickness and the weakness of our sailors," José exclaimed to members of the party. "But, since we are on Gasparilla Island, how could we not expect smart people to populate it?"

The next day, with island birds filling the sky, the fleet ventured again into the Gulf of Mexico and up the coast, past another pass between the barrier islands. There they were met by the frigate *Esperanza,* which had anchored the previous night on a large point of land jutting into a bay about fifteen miles north of the mouth of Charlotte Harbor. The anchorage site in present-day Lemon Bay was near what is now called Cedar Point.

The captain told José that during their exploration, they had seen many island birds including osprey, heron, egrets, woodpeckers, ibis, and an array of hawks, owls, and songbirds.

The fleet continued north, moving effortlessly over the frothy blue waters of the Gulf, sending either the small boats into and out of many of the shallow bays and waterways to more closely explore this fascinating subtropical haven. The crews continued to report on myriad sea life in the gentle water and around the spectacular beaches.

The ships stopped to anchor in Terra Ceia Bay. Three of them later left to go miles into the harbor, even larger than Charlotte Harbor, and returned to claim that it was one of the finest natural ones in the world.

"Someday, if all you tell me is true, I predict one of the world's great seaports might well be located there," José told Captain Manual Torres of the *Ferdinand,* who had led the explorations. In later years, following José's prediction, that great seaport would be known as Tampa.

The fleet spent the next three days further exploring this huge harbor by sailing from what is now Sarasota Bay on the south, then back north past Anna María Island, and into the large harbor. The fleet then lifted anchor and journeyed on, north and then west, past many miles of wooded shore and long stretches of white beaches, to Spanish Louisiana. Spanish Louisiana's young governor, Bernardo de Gálvez Madrid Cabrera Ramirez Y Marguez, was providing covert, but crucial, support to the Americans operating in the western theater of operations. With the addition of the troops delivered by Gaspar, plans were made to consolidate resources to reconquer British West Florida for Spain.

The pirate prisoners were turned over by José to the young governor, and José was welcomed to the Spanish enclave.

C^{HAPTE}R 26

Return To Doña Rosalita

"Cuando amor no es locura, no es amor."
(When love is not madness, it is not love.)
—Pedro Calderon de la Barca, Spanish dramatist (1600–1681)

After the ships discharged the troops at Louisiana, supplies and a cargo of tobacco, cotton, and other items needed in Spain were loaded into the holds of the ships. Meanwhile, the crew enjoyed their time ashore.

When it was time to set sail, José decided that the fleet should return the way they had come, in the shallow waters near the coast, in order to avoid contact with British ships and American privateers.

As the *Intrepido* and the other three ships navigated the placid Gulf waters along the verdant Florida peninsula, José again marveled at the coast's isolated beauty and potential.

"This land is a paradise with bountiful resources. One of the great nations of the world will establish itself here someday," José mused, then added, "Spain is wise to keep Florida; my fear is that the Americans will covet this land. They seem to have an insatiable appetite and ambition for power."

Later that afternoon, José ordered the fleet into Terra Ceia Bay, which opened into the mouth of the bay the Indians called "Tanpa." The ships were taken up to the soft, white beaches where the *Intrepido*, the *San Cristabol*, and *Ferdinand* could be careened and take on fresh water for the voyage around the southern tip of Florida, then up the east coast to St. Augustine. He dispatched the *Esperanza* to conduct more explorations while maintenance was done on the rest of the fleet.

The men worked vigorously using the adze for chipping off barnacles and seaweed from the hull of the ships. "These three days will save us many on our trip home," José proclaimed to the captains. "A clean, smooth hull means more speed!"

After three warm days spent caulking and cleaning the three forty-four-gun vessels, the ships were eased back into deep water and made ready to sail. At mid-morning of the following day, the *Esperanza* with sails fully set and billowing, moved into the gentle chop of the bay.

As the fleet made its way down the west coast, José tried to capture and secure in his memory a lasting image of the dazzling beaches inching into the clear blue waters and the lush, green subtropical vegetation.

While the ships rounded the southern tip of scattered islands that formed a chain of keys separating the smooth Florida Bay from the gently rolling Atlantic Ocean, José and the crew alike were in awe of the beautiful coral reefs and colorful fish that inhabited these warm transparent waters.

"Having traversed the Gulf of Mexico, along the colorful coast of Florida one can easily understand why Ponce de León named this land 'Florida' when he explored it in the spring of 1513," José remarked to Lt. Gálvez and Cousin León. "As *pascua florida* means the feast of flowers, and as we have seen, something is always flowering in this sun-drenched land, it is a good name, Florida."

Almost always at dusk, as the current colorful sunset topped the previous evening's beauty, José would feel a pang of longing for Rosalita.

Standing at the ship's stern, José would look up into the sky at the emerging stars and hope that his Rosalita was viewing them also. During their absence, his love for her had grown to such an extent that all other thoughts became meaningless. It was becoming his obsession; he wanted to spend every waking hour talking to, loving, and sharing this beauty with the beautiful princess. Night after night, José imagined her slim body moving at the railing with the *Intrepido's* gentle rhythm. He could visualize her hair blowing gently in the breeze, lifted high enough for his eyes to caress her bare shoulders reflected in the starlight. As they crossed the Atlantic, he spent most of his evenings following this ritual and fighting sleep so this nightly vision would not dissipate.

"Sir, you must go below to rest," Lt. Rafael Alvarez would encourage him each night as he made his rounds of the ship. "You need sleep for an alert mind."

"Lieutenant Alvarez, the amount of sleep each of us believes to be necessary for a good night's rest is about thirty minutes more than we actually get," José laughed, as he finally agreed to retire to his cabin. "There is an old Irish proverb that Brutal Betsy loves to quote: A good laugh and a long sleep are the two best cures."

After rounding the tip of Florida, they noticed that the waters of the Atlantic were a darker color blue and the waves were stronger than those of the Gulf. After stopping at St. Augustine to load more provisions and to make repairs, the fleet was ready to return to Spain.

Fortunately, they had a smooth crossing. Before the fleet reached the coast of Spain, they passed an aging three-masted French warship, the *Duo de Duras*, which was also sailing north towards the coast of France. When the ships came alongside each other a conversation ensued between José and the captain of the other vessel. During the discussion the French captain indicated that he thought he might be on his last cruise aboard the *Duo de Duras* as he had heard that the ship was going to be given to the American revolutionaries. The rumor was that John Paul Jones, an American captain would assume command and that the ship would be renamed the *Bonhomme Richard*.

"That is astounding," José exclaimed across the railings. "This Jones fellow apprenticed on a merchant ship, became a mate on a dreaded slaver, allegedly committed murder, fled to the Caribbean, joined the American Continental Navy and will probably end up a hero."

"Captain Gaspar, I agree with the French philosopher Molière that it is the ultimate stupidity to busy oneself with trying to correct all the world's problems," the French captain called back as the ships parted. *"C'est la vie! Au revoir."*

Within days, José had safely guided his fleet back to Barcelona and was back in Madrid meeting with his superior officers before being allowed to return to Rosalita's estate.

"Captain Gaspar, your exploits and courage continue to become legend here in Madrid," Minister FloridaBlanca stated, as José was welcomed at the Navy headquarters. "Obviously, not everyone is pleased, because of your youth, but I will be recommending that you receive the rank of admiral within the next few days. In the interim, you will be the Navy Department's official liaison to a secret meeting.

On April 12, we need for you to go to Aranjuez. We need insurance that our government is guaranteed a number of advantages as Spain joins with France in supporting the American rebels battling with England."

"That is fine, so long as there are no crisis situations in May, for that is when I intend to marry Rosalita," José beamed proudly at the frowning Minister FloridaBlanca, "I will be on my honeymoon in Mallorca."

"But, my dear Captain, you are a hero of the people," FloridaBlanca growled as his scowl deepened. "They look to you to make history. Your duty to them must be the primary goal in your life."

"But no single man is capable of making history," José quickly replied. "The history of the world is really a product of perceptive leaders who struggle to sustain and better that world."

"Public opinion is sometimes stronger than the monarchy or the legislature," FloridaBlanca shouted angrily. "And the public has chosen to follow you and your career. It makes no sense to ignore that devotion and only makes those who detest you despise you more."

"Politicians often spend so much of their time keeping their ears to the ground that they allow their own behinds to become targets," José responded, with irony creeping into his voice. "I can't be responsible for that. I am not a politician. I act on what I believe to be right and not necessarily what might ingratiate me into the favor of others."

"Regardless, you will represent the Spanish Navy at the secret meeting with the French and Americans in April," FloridaBlanca replied emphatically and abruptly ended the meeting.

José couldn't wait to get back to his quarters. He stripped to the waist as he entered the building and, as usual with any military organization, a lower-ranking officer stopped him and proceeded to verbally "dress him down." With his mind consumed on his upcoming reunion with Rosalita, José humbly stood at attention, while the young officer harangued him. After the tirade ebbed, and the flushed officer calmed enough to write a discipline report, the color drained from his face as he realized he had been harassing his new commanding officer.

"What is your name, Lieutenant?" José inquired with a stern look.

"Captain Gaspar, I beg your pardon, sir, I had no idea. . . ." The youthful officer stammered, "My name is Lt. Emmanuel Ortíz, sir."

"Very good, Lieutenant Ortíz," José replied, now smiling. "Never apologize to anyone for doing your job. Discipline is at the heart of any successful organization. I made an error and you did the right thing by bringing it to my attention."

"Thank you, Sir," Ortíz replied, still frozen at attention.

"Perhaps you could see that I have a horse within the hour, Lieutenant?" José asked cheerily. "For I am off to be with the lady I love."

José rushed into the barracks, bathed, and dressed in civilian clothes for the ride out to Rosalita's estate.

The journey seemed to last an eternity, but judging by the lather and the panting of his mount, it could not have been accomplished any quicker.

José felt a twinge of concern as he approached the large gate and could see no sign of servants or activity within. He tethered his horse and tentatively walked into the courtyard.

To his surprise, Rosalita was sitting seductively upon the peddler's cart. She beckoned to him and opened her arms wide as he ran to her. José leapt agilely onto the cart and they passionately embraced and kissed repeatedly. No words were necessary.

Finally, José managed to whisper in a husky voice, "My love, I have spent months dreaming of this moment. How I have hungered for your kiss and yearned for your touch. I love you with all my heart and soul."

"I missed you so," she whispered back. "I hope that we will never need to be apart this long again. The moment I met you was the beginning of my life. Our absence had made me positive of my feelings toward you and I want our wedding to take place soon."

"The story of my life begins and ends with you as well, my love," José said as he gently pressed her down on the cart and began to disrobe her. He no longer was concerned with feelings of guilt or worried about a loss of respect. In fact, all thoughts except that of his hunger for Rosalita were driven from his mind. The sunset seemed the most spectacular of their lives as it formed a backdrop for their love upon the cart.

Later that evening, José learned that Rosalita had given all her servants the night off so they could be alone together. Together they prepared a simple meal and conversed excitedly as they tried to make up for their separation.

"Sailing from port to port, running around the world in antiquated ships; I wonder why, when all I really want is to be with you," José exclaimed to Rosalita. "No career, no challenge, can be as important as loving and holding you."

"José, you give so much of yourself to others," she protested pressing her fingers to his face. "I worry that sometimes you care about others so much you forget to take care of yourself. This concerns me, since I know you would give your life to protect them."

As they moved into the living area and sat close together, José responded seriously, "My darling Rosalita, you will always be the most important thing in my life. With you, I can be anything. Without you, I fear, I would be nothing. I would never jeopardize losing you through my duty to others."

"That is not altogether true, my love, for you were already a naval hero when we first met and you saved my peddler's cart," she reminded him.

"Oh, it may be true that I could become what the world might expect of me, but I would be only a hollow shell of a person without the completion that you give me," José answered. "You make me a whole person."

"José, one of the things I admire about you is that you always open your mind to change, but you never let go of your values," she whispered in his ear as she cuddled up comfortably next to him and closed her drowsy brown eyes. José heard her mumble softly, as she drifted into sleep, "I will always love you, my José."

Over the next week, they spent their days riding horses, eating leisurely picnic lunches, swimming naked in the small stream, and lying on the decorated peddler's cart gazing up at the stars. Each evening José delighted in bathing Rosalita, then drying her, and rubbing her body until she fell asleep. He would then cover her with a satin cover and hold her until he also fell asleep. He felt sole responsibility for her happiness and safety.

A messenger from the Navy barracks interrupted this idyllic time—José was ordered to Madrid to prepare for the upcoming meetings in April 1779 with the French and the Americans in northwestern Spain. The meetings went well and José's empowerment extended far beyond what he had expected.

When he returned, Manuel Godoy and Minister FloridaBlanca insisted that José and Rosalita attend a dinner and ball at the palace that weekend. José would be officially promoted to admiral, the youngest naval officer in Spanish history to have that honor.

On his way back to Rosalita's estate that Friday afternoon, José was forced to ride in a Navy carriage with an armed escort through orders from the minister himself—a restriction that bothered him greatly. He was also uncomfortable and in a foul mood. As he glumly peered into the neighborhoods they passed through, he noticed two obviously drunk, shabby men laughing as they beat a cowering small hound.

José ordered that the driver stop the carriage and drawing his cutlass, immediately ran to the aid of the whimpering dog. He yelled at the men as he ran to halt further abuse. The two men turned with shocked looks upon their faces. In their drunken state, they aggressively stood ready to fight this slight figure intruding on their recreation.

The taller one swung his right arm in José's direction but was soon screaming in pain as José's right foot landed solidly in his groin. He fell to the ground in agony, clutching his genitals. The other man attempted to swing a club at José's head only to be blocked by José's free left arm. An instant later, José's razor sharp cutlass sliced the left side of the bully's face. The drunk tried to stop the flow of blood as he staggered down the alley. The first man, still doubled up in pain, was helped up by José's guards and ordered to leave or face arrest.

José went to the whining, quivering dog and picked it up. His face was bathed with the tongue of the grateful puppy, as he held it to his chest. He gingerly carried the animal to his carriage and continued on his way to Rosalita's estate with an unexpected present.

On his arrival, Rosalita tenderly carried the young animal into the house to clean it and tend to its wounds; the dog's tail wagged furiously during this lavish attention.

"You know, many people believe that true contentment and happiness cannot be achieved by a human," José remarked, "but I believe that having a dog can be very beneficial to human relationships and often incite happiness."

"Yes, José, my little boy, we can *keep* the dog," she smiled indulgently.

"You know, my lovely Rosalita, I think men are like dogs and it is up to the woman to train them. If a woman sets the standards, the dog, or man, will be loyal and lay around ready to cuddle her when she grows old," José smiled as he hugged her.

"Then come on, you old dog, now that we have bathed the pup, it is time for you to bathe me," she smiled, "and you can dress me for the dinner where you will become Admiral Dog."

"During my whole life I have fantasized about undressing women," José complained. "I have no idea of what it is like to dress one!"

As they prepared for the state dinner, José lovingly dried her smooth, olive skin. As he lifted the satin dress over her head he admired her form and the luxuriant hair flowing loosely around her face and shoulders. He began to stroke her bare back and his heart raced as his fingers touched her body. The white satin hugged her bosom as she pressed against him. Her hands and arms were displayed under the elbow length sleeves. He imagined the curve of her hips and legs under the skirt with its lace petticoats and velvet ribbons. José dropped to his knees to slip on her shoes and could not stop the erection that was painfully encased in his tight trousers. While on his knees, and looking up at her with pleading eyes, he softly said, "I cannot live without you. Will you make me the happiest man in Spain and marry me as soon as I come back from Aranjuez?"

"Well, my soon-to-be admiral, only if you marry me at the earliest possible date," Rosalita answered with a warm smile.

CHAPTER 27

Making Mortal Enemies

"If only a person were given the choice of enemies. It bothers me when
I cannot respect the public ideas of a person whom I like, but like the ideas
of one I do not respect. I wonder if there is anyone in the world whom
I love and publicly admire besides you, my lovely Rosalita."
—Letter from José to Rosalita, April 13, 1779, from the secret meeting in Aranjuez

The day before José was to depart for the secret meeting, he spent the day at Rosalita's estate. They had an exhilarating morning together on horseback and returned to the main house for lunch.

As they entered the patio, the rescued hound limped up to greet them, its tail wagging so strongly that Rosalita worried that the dog might fall down. José laughed and bent down to get his face licked enthusiastically, while Rosalita stroked the small animal and rubbed its belly.

Out of the corner of his eye, José was aware of a figure lurking in the shadows. "Come out of there, I command you!" José shouted, scaring the little dog with his outburst.

A small, dirty, wide-eyed boy, the son of one of the servants, fearfully came forward and softly asked, "Is that your dog?"

Rosalita smiled and nodded and José, feeling guilty for being abrupt, smiled, and in a milder tone replied, "Yes, it is. I just got him yesterday."

"What is his name?" the boy asked.

"His name?" José looked quizzically at Rosalita.

"The dog's name is Lucky," she said. "You see he was lucky my José came along to save him from some cruel men. Also, the dog's name is Lucky because, like the dog, I am lucky to have José and we are all lucky to be a family together."

"Lucky," José murmured aloud, "a good name indeed. He is a very special dog, but I fear he will not be able to run and jump like other dogs."

To José and Rosalita's surprise, the boy reached down and rolled up his own pant leg to reveal a badly twisted right leg, supported by a crude, carved, wooden brace. His luminous brown eyes looked up at them and in a soft voice he replied, "Well, I don't run so well myself, and I think your puppy needs someone who understands him to take care of him."

She and José knelt by the boy, gave him a big hug and José, with Rosalita's approval, declared Carlos to be Lucky's official caretaker.

The boy beamed with pride as he and the small dog limped out of the patio. José and Doña could hear him announce proudly to his friends that he was the personal dog trainer.

"That is the difference between sympathy and empathy," José whispered as he tightly held Rosaita. "If you haven't suffered in the same way, you can only give *sympathy*. Whereas, like Carlos, you can give *empathy* if you have suffered a similar fate. Our dog is well-named."

She replied flirtatiously, "I am the lucky one. To have such a famous man love me."

"I will never understand how some people become famous," José said thoughtfully. "The only great thing I have done is to fall in love with you. There are many people like my friend, Miguel, who work hard and do great things every day and yet get no recognition. This fame thing is truly difficult to understand."

* * *

The next day, José and the Spanish entourage made the trip to Aranjuez, on the Tajuna River northeast of Toledo. The meeting was to be held in this remote village to avoid the suspicion that such a meeting would have had in the cosmopolitan cities of Madrid or Barcelona.

That afternoon, the representatives gathered in the meeting room of the small government building located in the Plaza Mayor of Aranjuez. The room was cramped, dark, and dank compared to the palatial government buildings in Madrid.

Representing the American Revolutionary government was the recently assigned Mr. John Jay, minister plenipotentiary, and Adm. John Paul Jones of the American Navy, who claimed to speak for Benjamin Franklin, the American ambassador to France.

The French were represented by Marshal Jean Baptiste Rochambeau and Adm. François Grasse and were clearly intent upon bringing the government of Spain into a joint alliance with America and France against their archenemy, England.

The first day's meeting went fairly well with the parties each stating their country's positions and expectations to the others.

That evening, José hosted a dinner in the government hall. His purpose was to aid understanding by having them enjoy and understand each other on a more intimate basis. He believed that if people understood their similarities, regardless of nationality, the world would better be able to hope for a lasting peace.

Minister John Jay introduced his pregnant wife to José and the others. Sarah Jay was a lovely and gracious woman whom José soon realized was as devoted to her husband as he was to her. It was refreshing to see another couple as much in love as he and Rosalita.

José was seated between John Jay and John Paul Jones. He took an immediate liking to John Jay whom he found to be moral, self-reliant and deeply religious, yet spirited and optimistic, with a good sense of humor. He admired Jay not only for his devotion to his wife, but also for his mind, which, like José's, looked not only at details but also at the whole picture. He believed that people who possess a comprehensive vision of the future and who are tireless in the application of their beliefs are rare throughout history.

José had heard much about Jones. As in the case of Brutal Betsy, he admired many of his ideas but he found it difficult to condone the behavior they both showed to their fellow human beings, especially regarding participation in the slave trade.

José discovered that Jones had been an officer in the American Continental Navy since 1775. In 1776, Jones had taken command of a square-topsail, gaff-rigged sloop, one of the first ships commissioned into the Continental Navy. Originally the merchant vessel *Katy*, she had been refitted with twelve cannon and was reborn as the battle-ready warship *Providence*. Under Jones's command, she had become the most victorious American ship of the entire Revolutionary War.

"I tell you Admiral Gaspar, she was the first ship and the very best and the best crew I've ever commanded," Jones stated emphatically. "We captured or sank seven British fighting ships."

"A sloop? How could you be successful?" José inquired earnestly, while wondering if having a quick, swiftly attacking navy fleet would not be of benefit to Spain.

"Speed and quickness afloat!" Jones exclaimed. "We have found that rapid ships that dart in, do damage to an enemy, and withdraw to attack again, like a swarm of bees in a blossoming vineyard, is a strategy quite foreign to European naval captains, whose ships lumber along like turtles."

"I understand the concept. You have a goal of creating terror by making daring raids, versus standing and fighting to the death," José nodded.

"That is correct, Admiral Gaspar," Jay interjected with a confident grin that José thought seemed symbolic of the upstart Americans. In fact, Admiral Jones came to France aboard our ship, the *Ranger*, last year and with only an eighteen-gun ship, managed to terrorize the coastal population of Scotland and England."

"How do you view your new ship, Admiral Jones?" José asked.

"As you know, she is a rebuilt French merchant ship," Jones answered in a patronizing manner, "but she has more cannon on board than any other ship I have commanded." He continued boastfully, "Later this year, the *Bonhomme Richard* will be well known to the British shipping lanes."

The next day was not to be nearly as pleasant for either José or Minister John Jay as they disagreed on nearly almost every point that Jay attempted to resolutely present to the delegations.

"The issue of using Spanish currency as your currency is one that should be given serious consideration," José agreed. But on another point he heatedly argued, "Mr. Jay, you want to claim for America all the lands to the Mississippi River instead of only to the Appalachian Mountains. Sir, this would double the current size of your country! Then you want both Spain and France to not trade or navigate that great river without your approval?"

"That is basically our position!" Jay shouted back.

"It doesn't matter how loudly you yell," José countered firmly. "I just delivered Spanish troops to fight for your country in the Mississippi Valley. I'll be damned if Spanish blood will be shed on your country's behalf along that river with no gain for us!"

"Sir, you are part of a self-serving monarchy. Your king will benefit ultimately with increased trade, but I am a Federalist!" Jay angrily replied. "I believe we need that land to form a strong central government and a strong central government is necessary to survive! That does not make me popular with some people with a different idea of a people's democracy. For that reason, I was forbidden from attending the constitutional convention in Philadelphia."

"Mr. Jay, in your American ideal you believe everybody has a right to express what he thinks, even the village idiot. I am concerned that people won't be able to tell the difference between a politician like you and the village idiot."

"My dear friends, are we not allies?" Jean Baptiste Rochambeau, marshal of France interrupted, irritated at the constant debating between José Gaspar and John Jay, "I know that I will be commanding a large French army of six thousand men and I would like to feel confident that the Spanish and French ships upon which we travel are commanded by friends, not foes."

"You are quite right, sir," José apologized. "I do hope you understand my conviction that a person who doesn't sometimes lose his temper over certain beliefs doesn't believe in them strongly enough."

"Aye, Admiral Gaspar, I can now see how your reputation as an attacking commander has been well deserved," French Adm. François Joséph Paul Grasse stated with a quiet voice and a broad smile. "I am sure we can sail together to America but, I believe you would not be content with the blockade tactic I have planned for the British at Yorktown."

José smiled and apologized for his outburst directed against Jay, but indirectly towards his French allies. He left the meeting for the noon meal and a short meeting with his staff.

"This American, John Jay, concerns me," José stated to the Spanish delegation. "The last person I believe you can trust with power is the person who is overly eager to have it."

"Then who would you trust?" Lieutenant Gálvez asked with a curious look on his face.

"The person you can trust most to wield power wisely is the one who is reluctant to seek it," José replied, "someone who only leads out of a sense of patriotic duty to his country while wishing to be home enjoying his private life."

Before the meetings resumed, José did strike a bargain, on behalf of his future bride, with Marshal Rochambeau for a portrait of Marie Antoinette of France. Rochambeau was a friend of the artist Elisabeth Louis Vigie Le Brun, who often painted portraits of the queen.

"I never understand why we military men spend so much time arguing about things that can simply be proven by introducing the facts," José told Rochambeau.

"I agree, Gaspar, that we sound like politicians," Rochambeau laughed. "Only politicians can say the things they say without having to rely upon facts."

The afternoon of the second day, a general agreement was reached on how the Spanish, French, and American forces would transport troops and naval vessels to the colonies. José thanked both the American and French delegations for their input and accomplishments.

"Small deeds that are finished are more important than great deeds proposed," José stated. "Since we have completed our plans for the steps to success, we will postpone our larger philosophical discussions until we have been successful on the battlefield."

That evening as the group sat drinking wine, José offered to help John Jay and his wife, Sarah, find suitable lodgings, as well the name of a good physician for their forthcoming baby. He invited the Jays to his wedding, which was scheduled for the fourth of May in Madrid.

Although they accepted José's invitation, Jay later confided to his wife that José Gaspar would always be a thorn in the side of Americans and, so long as he remained a Spanish hero, relations between the two countries could never be totally cordial.

Marriage

"My love is your love and your love is my love; but, the secret to our love
is that we share rather then control each other's lives."
—Commitment made by José Gaspar and his wife, Rosalita, May 4, 1779

The broad cobblestone streets of Madrid were alive with excitement as the wedding day of Spanish hero, Admiral José Gaspar and Doña Rosalita Santiago finally dawned. The shops were uncharacteristically shuttered on the morning of the wedding, and the streets were thronged with excited citizens awaiting a glimpse of the handsome couple.

The wedding had many notables attending, not only Spanish royalty, but representatives of other European countries as well. King Charles III, thought of as one of Spain's best kings, was the first to enter the beautiful cathedral. Following the king were Manuel Godoy, Minister FloridaBlanca, and others who represented the monarchy. The American ambassador, John Jay, arrived with his wife and entered the church to sit behind the king and his entourage, as Father Lasuen, along with the archbishop of Madrid, prepared to officiate the service.

José entered the cathedral by a side entrance amid the cheers of the many onlookers surrounding the large church. José presented a striking appearance in his perfectly pressed white admiral's uniform complete with his Toledo sheathed inside its ceremonial scabbard. Capt. Miguel Rodriquez, on leave from his duties in the Spanish Main, arrived with him. Both men disappeared inside the church smiling broadly at the prospect of the wedding ceremony.

Shortly thereafter, Doña Rosalita Santiago arrived in a lavishly decorated white wedding carriage. The crowd smiled in amusement as a single horse pulling the charming two-wheeled peddler's cart pulled up directly behind the wedding carriage. Leading the small horse was Carlos, dressed in his finest church clothes, and with him the little hound, Lucky, his tail wagging enthusiastically.

The crowd gasped at the beauty of the bride as she exited the coach and entered the church. Four attendants were needed to keep the wedding train from touching the stone stairs of the church entrance. Rosalita's wedding gown was a dazzling white, lacy creation with the sleeves slashed to reveal ruffles. The skirt was held up in scallops by velvet ties, and layers of petticoats peeped from underneath. The lacy, scooped bodice revealed a hint of cleavage, while effectively hiding her bosom. She was as stunning as any bride to ever grace the capital city.

It is easy to understand how the men and women who gathered either admired or loved Rosalita or were jealous of her classic Spanish beauty. Since Rosalita did not have a scandalous history or reputation, which was unusual in Madrid, it was understandable that many were envious of this radiant bride and her dashing bridegroom.

Within the large, ornate cathedral, the aroma of burning candles and incense filled the air. Volumes of colorful flowers lent their scent to the solemn procession proceeding down the aisle. The archbishop led the high mass. José's friend, Father Lasuen, who had traveled from San Diego to officiate the ceremony, began the wedding vows. When asked if they wished to add anything, the bride and groom looked directly into each other's eyes and, in unison, vowed, *"My love is your love and your love is my love, but the secret of our love is that we share rather than control each other's lives."*

As the recessional wedding march blared forth from the huge pipe organ, the audience inside began to clap. The applause and cheers followed the couple outside as they left the church.

The pageantry of the wedding continued as the military honor guards moved out in front of the carriage and began leading the cortege down the boulevard to the Renaissance Palace built by Philip II in the sixteenth century.

Arriving at the palace, the newlyweds were escorted into the great hall through the magnificent library in the escorial. The highly polished marble floors were complemented by decorative brilliant frescoes. Entering one of the massive rooms, the joyous couple went to the front table and was joined by the wedding party, as well as King Charles III and his royal delegation.

A sumptuous meal of ensalada verde, sopa de ajo, pimient de piquillo, pescado a la sal, faisan a la alcantara, ending with filloa al licor was served, and toasts to the newlyweds rang out from throughout the ornate hall. As the orchestra provided music for dancing, many in the festive crowd felt fortunate to be in attendance.

As the afternoon wore on, a messenger slipped a note to José. The Princess María Louisa wanted to see him in her quarters at four o'clock. Curiosity instantly filled him as to what the princess wanted with him on the afternoon of his wedding.

He excused himself at the appointed time and insisted that everyone stay at the party to enjoy themselves while he left briefly. He then asked a servant the way and hurried to María Louisa's private quarters.

Upon arriving, he was surprised that no one was in the sitting room. He then heard María Louisa's voice calling him. Cautiously, José walked through the sitting room into the bedroom, which was awash with the golden rays of the afternoon sun. On the bed near the far wall, José was astonished to see the princess completely naked, lying with her back arched, and gently rubbing her pendulous breasts with both hands as she struck a seductive pose.

"Come over here, my young newlywed." María Louisa coaxed in a throaty voice while beckoning the open-mouthed young admiral to her bed. "I have wanted you since the first time I met you here in Madrid, but you have been unavailable until now."

"But this is my wedding day. I don't understand," protested José.

"I want to bear children from a handsome, intelligent, genuine man like you, José. Before your marriage is consummated with your skinny new wife, I want you to make love to me. I have always desired you," María continued seductively.

As José was trying to regain his poise and deciding how best to diplomatically refuse and quickly extricate himself, María Louisa sprang from her prone position to grab José's pants. She frantically pulled them down and started to caress his penis. Astonishment rooted José to the floor, then to his horror, as María Louisa's hands continued to manipulate him, his penis, of its own accord, began to stiffen. Waves of embarrassment flooded over José as he found himself unable to move. María Louisa took advantage of this and proceeded to arouse him, much to José's dismay. Before he could react, she encircled his penis with her large mouth and started to massage it vigorously with her tongue.

José finally began to gain a semblance of control and, grabbing her hair, managed to pull her head back as she yelled out in pain. She let go of him, and he quickly backed away from the bed. José gazed in incredulity as María Louisa rose to her knees on the bed.

"José Gaspar, if you don't make love to me now, I swear I will make your career an absolute hell on earth!" María Louisa screamed with tears running from her face and dripping on her naked breasts.

As José pulled up his pants, he looked at her in disgust and spat out, "Princess, this is my wedding day. I have no interest in making love to any woman except my lovely Rosalita. Unlike many men, I am content to have only my wife in my bed. I believe in the holy sacrament I swore to this morning."

"You will be sorry, Gaspar! As long as you serve in my Navy I can assure you that you will receive the worst possible assignments," María Louisa shouted angrily.

"I must go back to my bride," José said formally. "It would be wise of you to forget this happened. If you do, I promise I will never tell anyone." He then stalked from the room.

On what had once been the happiest day of his life, José Gaspar returned to the wedding hall with tears of frustration in his eyes. He felt he had been sexually compromised and was sure he would be punished for his actions in the future. When he reached the great hall, Rosalita was incensed that José had left her alone on their wedding day. Rather than telling her what had happened, José simply apologized, telling her that it was a matter of state.

Within the hour the wedding party prepared to depart the Renaissance Palace. Almost alone with his bride at last, José suggested that she ride on the peddler's cart with Lucky, while he and Carlos led the pony back to her estate, so that well-wishers could continue to greet her. José enjoyed the attention and adoration his lovely bride received from the peasants on the route home.

When they arrived at the estate, Carlos and Lucky ran off, pleased to be able to run and play after a day of being restricted by the formalities. José unhitched the horse and turned to his bride, who was still on the cart. He removed his uniform and then began to undress Rosalita. The hardened muscles on his chest flexed and quivered as he unbuttoned her garments. She touched his taut muscles gently and then slid her hands down his torso. As she found his hardened penis, they both shivered. The sky was still ablaze, and purple and pink rays were dancing off the clouds in the western heavens when he eased her down onto the floorboards of the cart.

He looked into her large dark eyes and touched her breasts, letting his hands softly travel down over her bare hips to her thighs. As they kissed, with their tongues probing one other, José caressed her body. They pressed against one another on the floor of the peddler's cart, and the rhythm of their lovemaking caused the cart to creak with a steady cadence.

After an intimate hour, José and Rosalita lay spent together in the cart, softly stroking one another. José ran his hand through her long, soft hair and looked up at the starlit night. As he gently ran three fingers along the side of her head, he professed his love and devotion and told her how much he was looking forward to their honeymoon in Mallorca.

Rosalita smiled up at him and quietly whispered, "I was concerned about you after you returned to the hall this afternoon. You seemed so distant, but now I feel relieved."

José silenced her lips with a kiss.

A Perfect Love

"The true story of my life began the day we met and will end the day we part."
—*José Gaspar, May 9, 1779*

The honeymoon was truly a celebration of one of history's greatest love affairs. During the voyage south across the beautiful Mediterranean Sea to the historic port city of Palma, on the northwest coast of Mallorca, José found it impossible to leave Rosalita's side.

Mallorca was not only the largest, but also one of the loveliest of the Balearics. As the ship approached Palma, the couple walked to the bow to drink in the beauty of the island as the late afternoon sun cast a golden aura on land and sea alike.

"Lieutenant Gálvez was correct," José spoke, "except for possibly some areas along the west coast of Florida, this has to be the most beautiful place on earth."

"The water is so pristine," she exclaimed, "and the beaches so bright."

"And since so many of this island's enemies came from the sea, the only city that breaks the panorama is Palma," he added. And then, with a wink and a smile, "Most of the population and cities are located further inland, leaving you and I able to enjoy this natural beauty in a most natural of state of undress."

Rosalita's blushing face matched the change in the setting sun's color as she smiled and gently slapped his grinning face.

Changing the subject, he explained how Palma was built on the coast with elaborate and expensive atalayas, or watchtowers, to protect the port city from the likes of the famous pirate, Antoni Barcelo.

Rosalita relaxed and settled into the warm arms of her husband. He smiled and casually remarked, "Were it not for my love and desire to spend my life with you, being a pirate has some appeal. At least, I wouldn't need to worry about pleasing the bureaucrats. I find myself perpetually on the wrong side of their issues."

"You are the most intelligent man I have ever known," she interrupted. "I can't see how people can disagree with you."

"Well, when I told Miguel I had half a mind to get married to you, he told me that's all the brain I have," José laughed and broke away, backing toward their cabin.

"Well, I have half a mind to brain you, José," she shrieked and ran after him. The princess and the admiral chased gleefully after one another as the ship slipped into the darkening port.

After a passionate evening and a restful night's sleep, they woke to the first of many days of bright sunshine on the island. Following more lovemaking and breakfast on the terrace, the newlyweds strode down the street, hand in hand, to the stables for a ride. Since Spanish horsemanship is second to none, both were premier riders.

The midday sun felt warm upon their backs as they galloped into the country. They admired the windmills they saw in the century-old olive groves and laughed as they raced competitively during their afternoon romp.

Later, as the evening twilight settled around them, José leaned across the dinner table and held Rosalita's hands in his. He said quietly, "My mother told me when I was a child, 'If you become a sailor you will become an admiral, and if you become a politician you'll end up a king. But, my son, if you truly want happiness, no matter what you are, you will find it only in a perfect love.' I now know what she was telling me. I may have a successful career, but my real fortune was in finding you to share my life. I pledge you my love forever."

* * *

In the week that followed, José and Rosalita enjoyed the isolated beaches with the warm, turquoise, water and soft sand, often romping naked through the surf. They spent their afternoons lying on the beach, sharing a picnic lunch and bottles of the fine French wine that the couple had received as a wedding present from Marshal Jean Baptiste Rochambeau.

On the last day of their honeymoon, they went to the amateur bull-fighting arena where José had the opportunity to fight a one-year-old bull. Rosalita sat in the stands and cheered wildly as he entered the ring. However, as the "cute" young bull entered on the opposite side, she began to cheer for the bull.

During the playful romp, the bull would charge, and José would deftly step aside allowing the bull to run through the red cape and safely past him. Each time this happened, José would furl the cape to his waist, bow, and throw a kiss in the direction of his bride. He was caught by surprise, however, in the middle of a gallant bow, when the young bull turned quickly and rammed his head squarely into the newlywed's rump. The shocked look upon her husband's face brought both laughter and concern to Rosalita.

Within moments, he picked himself up and dusted off his trousers, wincing in pain and embarrassment. When she ran down to him and they embraced in the bull ring, José quietly asked if she would promise to massage his injury. The sound of a slap echoed through the small arena as Rosalita responded playfully to his request.

C_{HAPTE}R

Serious Problems in Madrid

"All bureaucrats have one thing in common and that is the notion that the bureaucracy is never wrong; it has to be someone else's fault. One of the characteristics of bureaucrats is they avoid personal responsibility."
—José Gaspar, on being banished to sail on a worldwide cruise, June 21, 1779

The newlyweds were met on their return from Mallorca by Cousin León, little Carlos, and Lucky. It was a joyous reunion on the dock and, after the trunks were loaded on the carriage, the friends decided go to an open-air café.

"I have never seen you so happy!" Cousin León explained. "You must have had a delightful honeymoon."

José reached over and gently touched Rosalita's shoulder, then looking her straight in the eyes, he nodded. "I am married to the most wonderful woman on this earth, so our honeymoon was perfect."

"José," she smiled, "only two kinds of people appreciate flattery such as yours." Then with a large grin and a gentle poke at his chin that made everyone laugh, she continued, "women and men."

As their polenta and spicy sausage was served," Carlos asked José why they called this vacation after marriage a honeymoon.

"Well, it was the accepted practice in Babylon long, long ago that, for a month after the wedding, the bride's father would supply his new son-in-law with all the mead he could drink. Mead was an ancient honey beer, so this period was called the 'honey month' which has become commonly known as a honeymoon."

"So, how are things going in Madrid?" José asked León, "Are they getting my ships ready to escort the French vessels to the American colonists?"

León's smile disappeared. His face turned ashen and his lowered head spoke volumes to the others at the table. Finally, after a lengthy silence, he slowly raised it and with moist eyes answered José. "There is bad news regarding your relationship to the Americans in general and to Señor John Jay and his wife, in particular," León spoke, almost whispering.

"How can that be? I have not seen nor spoken to John or Sarah since the day after my wedding in Madrid. I disagree with his policy ideas, but I admire his devotion to his wife and family." José spoke with disbelief that anything could have injured their relationship.

"While you and Roslita were on your honeymoon, the baby daughter that was born two days after your wedding suddenly died," León continued. "Since you recommended the doctor to them and he was at fault, they are blaming you, also, for the infant's death."

"That's ridiculous," José retorted hotly. "All I did was tell them of a physician I had heard good things about. I didn't even know they went to him. There must be more to it! As far as I knew, he was a good doctor."

"That may be, José. I think perhaps it is because of your strong opposition to his plan for the American rebels to lay claim to all the land to the Mississippi River, including land we already claim, if they defeat the British. In addition, Señor Jay has had a difficult time dealing with the bureaucrats in Madrid and feels his time in Spain has been fruitless," León replied sadly. "He has been frustrated since you left and can't get anything done. So, in a way, he also blames you for deserting him."

"I don't understand," José moaned, "I got married and went on a short honeymoon and all hell has broken loose, none of which is my doing. You mentioned that the Americans 'in general' were also upset?"

"Well, remember that John Jay's wife is Sarah Van Brugh Livingston, whose father is the governor of New Jersey and a leading American patriot," León went on. "And, without you here to cut the red tape, the Spanish bureaucrats have not been cooperative to Mr. Jay or any of the other Americans. So, along with death of the governor's first granddaughter, your absence, and frustration, well. . . ."

"I can't believe this," José exploded. "Don't these Americans understand what a bureaucracy really is? It's an organization in which people get paid a salary for following prescribed routines and not violating the artificial rules that are of no consequence! Someday if they succeed in becoming a nation, they'll become a bureaucracy just as Spain is today."

"Regardless, José, John Jay and his wife are blaming you for contributing to the death of their newborn daughter and the inability to get Spain to move more quickly on their requests," León reported.

"I wonder how Minister FloridaBlanca is reacting to this?" José inquired.

"Well, cousin, he has given me orders to have you come to Madrid and meet with him as soon as you return," León answered hopefully. "Perhaps he will have your fleet ready to escort the French to America."

"I pray that you are correct, but I want to discuss with him my resignation from the Spanish Navy," José revealed gravely, to the shock of everyone at the table, "I have given this issue great thought and I don't want to ever again leave the side of my wife. I love her so much that I even find myself missing her when I leave the room for only a few minutes."

"José, my love, I fear that you would soon be bored with only me to occupy your time," Rosalita interrupted."

"Never, my dear," José smiled.

"But, if you resign from the Navy you will have nothing," León protested. "It is not manly to live off the estate of your wife."

José chuckled and retorted, "My cousin, I started out with nothing and I still have most of it! Besides, getting out of the Navy will mean I won't have to worry about putting my foot in my mouth. A closed mouth gathers no feet."

By now the tension had lessened. In fact, León also seemed relieved that José had decided to resign his admiralty at a young age and spend his days enjoying life with Rosalita in Madrid. They boarded the carriage and left Barcelona for Madrid.

The day following their arrival at Rosalita's estate, León accompanied José to Minister FloridaBlanca's office. The day was unusually hot and humid and, for the summer, uncharacteristically cloudy so early in the day. "This could be a stormy day, I fear," José mentioned to León as they entered the building. He was referring to the weather, unaware that his life was about to turn into a tempest.

When he entered the minister's ornate office, José was surprised to find Manuel Godoy seated next to Minister FloridaBlanca. Both men forced a smile as José came forward and tendered a salute.

"Admiral Gaspar, how was your honeymoon on Mallorca?" Godoy asked with formality.

"Excellent, Manuel. Mallorca is very close to what I believe heaven must be like," José replied slowly as he recognized the tone in Godoy's voice.

"Admiral Gaspar, being so young, perhaps you are not aware of the responsibility of your rank?" FloridaBlanca interjected.

"If someone would have told me one day I would be an admiral, I would have definitely studied harder," José replied as he tried to interject some humor.

"Admiral Gaspar, since you have left Madrid, many unfortunate things have happened which require us to take action in your regard," FloridaBlanca continued in a serious tone. "With the American, John Jay, questioning openly your leadership capability, we need to resolve the issue of your command of the Atlantic fleet."

"You mean the escort fleet to America?" José interrupted.

"Yes, Admiral. I see no way you can remain in command of the Atlantic fleet. Godoy suggested that we might, instead, send you, publicly, on a goodwill cruise to China and other countries to deal with the problem of piracy," FloridaBlanca said in a manner that brooked no appeal.

"I was considering resignation from the Navy," José began. "In fact, I have discussed it with my wife, and I think it would be best for everyone if you could accept my resignation. . . ."

"Impossible!" Godoy boomed, "you have managed to become the hero to all of Spain. The citizens wait for you to accomplish yet another deed so they can stand on the curb to applaud you as you pass by. There is no way we can let you resign at this time! Since they consider you a hero, by damned, you will continue that role as long as they continue to worship you!"

"But, I want to resign. I can explain my position to the people." José protested, "I love my wife and no longer wish to leave her to spend months at sea."

"When we achieve a public status, we no longer have the freedom to do as we please!" Godoy shouted. "Now, get the hell out of here. Be prepared to begin a worldwide voyage by the weekend."

"But, I only want to be with my wife," José cried out.

"Your country loves you and you have an obligation to love your country," FloridaBlanca snarled. "We need to recognize what is best for Spain. You have to understand that you are larger than life itself in the eyes of the common Spaniard."

José left the office emotionally drained, nearly stumbling down the flight of stone steps outside the naval headquarters building and joined León. His eyes were moist and he was distraught, feeling emptiness at the thought of such an extended absence from his Rosalita. Only two days remained before he was ordered to go to sea for a yearlong voyage, merely because, he knew, they were afraid of the power of his growing popularity with the Spanish people. How insecure they must be!

That evening, an extremely subdued José broke the news to his bride of five weeks. "A cruise of a whole year, around the world? What happened to your escort fleet duty?" Rosalita asked, with tears streaming down her cheeks. "I thought you were going to resign from the Navy?"

"I tried to resign," José cried out with emotion choking his reply. "Godoy and FloridaBlanca would not let me. They set this world cruise up as a way to get rid of me and save face with the French and Americans. They want me out of the picture."

"But, my love, I don't understand," Rosalita cried out, as she began shaking.

"Politicians and bureaucrats justify their lies by saying it is for everyone's mutual good," José moaned. "I have never accepted this altruism. To me a lie is always a lie. God damn that John Jay and his American phonies!"

After dinner, José and Rosalita went to the patio and lay upon the peddler's cart, as they looked up at the starlit sky. "Each night, my love, again look up into the sky at this time and view those stars. Know that, at the same moment, I will be watching them also and so, indirectly, be watching over you," he whispered in her ear.

The next morning, José rose early to pack his sea chest and load it on the carriage. León then took it to the city to be loaded on a military convoy. After he left, José and Rosalita went for a horseback ride and a picnic along their favorite creekbed.

As they frolicked naked one last time before his departure, they made love numerous times. Both returned with sunburns on previously pale parts of their body.

He felt that to leave his new wife in the morning would be the most difficult thing he would ever have to do. He decided that he and Rosalita would have a sumptuous dinner and a spectacular evening; then he would sneak away before sunrise, thus avoiding the hardest good-bye of his life.

After dinner and a walk through the garden, she ran to him and flung herself into his arms. "I never want you to leave me, José," she said passionately, "but I know that you must."

As he smelled her hair, inhaling the fragrance of her natural odor, he mumbled the words, "Duty and honor . . . I wish I'd never heard of them. I love you so."

CHAPTER 31

Ship's Tour before Setting Sail

"The world is in a constant state of chaos, so it is only fitting that armed ships patrol it. I will never see the day that there will truly be peace on earth."
—José Gaspar, just prior to embarking on world cruise, 1779

José's attempt to sneak away from Rosalita proved impossible since the lovers tightly embraced each other after their night of lovemaking. When the cool morning breeze gently blew over the couple, awakening them, José knew that, at some point, a sad good-bye to his bride would be inevitable.

He decided to allow Rosalita, her servants, and Carlos to accompany him to the port of Seville from which his ship, the *Intrepido*, would depart on the dreaded worldwide cruise.

Arriving at the dock, José boarded the ship and after a brief inspection of the decks, sent for his lovely bride and her traveling party to tour the ship. He thought it was important for her to have an understanding of the environment in which he and his men would be living for the next year.

Rosalita and her party arrived shortly before noon. She was dressed in a lacy white cotton dress that revealed her shoulders, and the noonday sun showed the red highlights in her dark hair. As she gracefully came on board, she gave a salute to her love and asked permission to board the gleaming warship. After a return salute, José bowed gallantly and took her hand to show her the ship on which he would spend the next year. It was a bittersweet moment for both but important to Rosalita that she could visualize José's environment during their year of separation.

Giving a sniff, she then asked José what the unusual odor was on the ship. Grinning, José replied, "There are so many smells in these wooden

178

ships that I could give a variety of replies to your question. Someday, man will learn to use something besides wood in building ships if for no other reason than to eliminate the strong odors."

"I can't describe it, but 'musty' is in my mind," she began.

"Mildew and mold are as much a part of this ship as the sails and rigging," José interrupted. "These ships leak constantly. When we are in rough seas the waves rush over the upper decks and down the hatches to the lower decks. As you can see, once the inside of the hull of the ship gets wet, there is no way to dry it out and the mold is everywhere."

"But, there is something else," she mused inquisitively.

"If we go down to the bilge, it's possible to find almost anything there," José answered. "Also, you are smelling the perspiration of the sailors as well as accidents of a natural sense that often occur—vomit, urine and worse."

"Ugh, stop José! I think you have made your point," Rosalita hoarsely cried out. "Is there nothing to prevent this from happening?"

"Not as long as we send ships out on cruises over long distances that require men to be at sea for months at a time," José stated. "If ships spend only a limited time at sea, like the ferry we took to Mallorca, then the hygiene and cleanliness of the ship can be guaranteed. My ideal Navy ship would be used primarily for defense and would never be out at sea more than two weeks at a time."

As the party went below the main deck to the first gun deck, Rosalita was amazed at the immense size of the iron cannon and the huge wooden carriages upon which they sat.

The massive rope that José called the "breeching" was anchored to the walls and attached to the knob of the cannon. He also explained the use of the shot garland, a huge rack that held the cannon balls and other "shot" fired from the cannons, the "crow," a long iron bar with two claws on the end that was used to move the ship's guns, and a brush end, called the swabbing sponge, that was used to clean the cannon barrel after firing to put out any fire or remaining sparks.

Rosalita looked at José and sniffed again.

"Yes, my love, another source of the perfume of a fighting ship at sea," José smiled. "You see, saltwater cannot be used to clean a iron cannon, and fresh water is at a premium on long voyages. So, the men relieve themselves of urine into the oaken buckets between each of the gun batteries and. . . ."

"Stop it, José. Again, I can guess the rest," Rosalita said with disgust. "What other smelly things can your mind conjure up?"

"Well, I haven't shown you the galley area below deck where the live turtles, chickens, and pigs are kept until slaughtered for food at sea," José laughed, amused with her discomfiture. "I can assure you that pigs and chickens do excrete quite a smelly product."

"Quit it this minute, José," she scolded. "Let's get out of here."

Back up on deck in the warm sunshine, the group walked around the ship as José indicated out various other points of interest. They then adjourned to José's quarters where Rosalita was impressed with the ornate furniture and the view from the pair of large windows overlooking the stern. After walking around the large conference table in the center of the room, she ran her hand along the bed, glanced over her shoulder, and gave José a broad smile and a wink.

Carlos, who had been extremely quiet throughout the early afternoon, ran outside, with the rest following, to the brass swivel guns mounted just inside the windows. "What are these for?" the wide-eyed youngster asked.

"The stern of any ship is the weakest point and all sailors realize this truth," José began. "These are called culverins and are of small caliber. As you can see, they are easy to swivel and aim at different angles. When we are at sea they are loaded with old nails, glass and shot so they can spray a large area. They are very effective in discouraging any unwelcome men who would board us," José laughed. "We also have these culverins fore and aft and on the railing of the starboard and port sides of the ship."

Toward evening, José had dinner brought to his cabin for the group. After they had finished eating, he sent Carlos back to their lodging with León, explaining that he would bring Rosalita later. The inquisitive youngster had more questions. He wanted to know why the ship would not be leaving on Friday. José told him sailors felt it was unlucky for any ship to begin a voyage on a Friday. Carlos smiled at the thought of grown men harboring such superstitions.

When José and Rosalita were finally alone on the bed in his cabin, they vowed to cherish the memories of their brief time on board the ship together—especially these parting moments in the captain's bed.

CHAPTER 32

World Tour—a Year of Excitement

"To really live life, one needs to sacrifice the need to chase a career."
—José Gaspar, sadly departing Spain on World Tour, 1779

Early on Saturday morning, while his crew made sure that everything was in readiness, José boarded the *Intrepido* to begin preparations for sailing at mid-morning.

Before they left one another, José and Rosalita made a commitment to continue to grow individually so that when they were together again, each would have much to contribute to the relationship. "If we cannot have constant companionship, by developing our own interests and talents we will be able to appreciate one another even more when we are together," José whispered in her ear during their last embrace.

The ship was alive with men on the rigging unfurling the sails, and those who loaded the last-minute supplies. José awaited the arrival of a delegation of Catholic cardinals and priests who would be passengers on the first leg of the journey from Seville. Although it was an honor to escort the Vatican clergy, José yearned instead to be escorting troopships and warships to North America as part of a fighting armada.

The religious group, led by Father Serra, arrived in three carriages and José ordered the marines to assist the clergymen with their trunks. The marine commander, Captain Paules, remarked after his men had loaded the gear, "I thought priests took a vow of poverty. I tell you Admiral Gaspar, indigence can weigh a great deal."

The journey took them around the southern tip of Spain, through the Mediterranean Sea, and past the southern side of the island of Mallorca, with all its pleasant memories. Only summer thunderstorms and some brief rolling seas broke the boredom of bright sun and heat as the *In-*

trepido sailed past the island of Sardinia, into the Tyrrhenian Sea, and on to the seaport of Ostia near Rome.

José had an audience with Pope Pius VI on the afternoon following the party's arrival in the Vatican City. Only a blind atheist or one not attuned to the arts might not appreciate the beauty and splendor of the Vatican. *Centuries of power, often absolute, have emanated from these walls*, José thought to himself as he awaited the arrival of the Most Holy Pontiff.

José had studied the background of Pope Pius VI and knew that he had been born Giangelo Braschi on Christmas Day, December 25, 1717, at Cesena of noble parents. Under the Jesuits, Braschi had studied law and took his degree when he was only seventeen years old. He became a renowned lawyer and Pope Benedict XIV offered him a canonry in St. Peter's. Braschi was engaged at the time to a beautiful woman he planned to marry. He later decided to become a priest and his fiancée entered a convent. Braschi quickly became papal treasurer and, in 1773, a cardinal. Shortly thereafter, at the death of Pope Clement XIV, he was selected as the pope.

The doors to the great room opened, awakening José from his reverie and the pope appeared in the room. José's thoughts as he knelt down were that the Italians were correct when they described Pope Pius VI as "handsome as he is holy." José was in such awe of the stately, noble pope that he shook visibly as he kissed the papal ring on the hand of the ornately clad prelate.

Following the formal presentation of credentials and papers from Madrid, José was issued an invitation to join His Holiness for dinner, which he eagerly accepted.

They went into a dining room that overlooked the historic courtyard of St. Peter's Basilica, and José remarked that he was impressed with all of Vatican City. "Without a doubt, God is in residence here," José stated.

"If only the French would believe it to be so," Pius replied somewhat sadly. He continued, "the problems of the Catholic Church are many, but the biggest issue we face is pleasing one group without displeasing another, because our church serves so many different nationalities. Our church should be like an octopus and have eight hands in order to meet the individual demands of its various segments. Since it does not, I concentrate on acting as the head of the church, telling our parishioners what God and the Bible tells us. The French, however, do not like our Italian hierarchy."

"Aye, Father, the French are a unique people," José answered, nodding his head in affirmation. "They are creative, artistic, intelligent people. They build the finest ships and have some of the best wines; their art is sought after worldwide, and they have many geniuses in all areas of scholarly and military backgrounds."

"Yes, the young fellow Napoleon comes to mind," the pope mused. "He is one who believes the Catholic Church should be headquartered on French soil."

"Your Holiness, the French believe they have created or invented everything, or are at least willing to take credit for it," José laughed as he looked at the decanter of French wine on the table. "On the other hand, we Spanish know better and so we enjoy trading with them and of late have chosen to be their ally in most instances. My friend, the French moralist Joséph Joubert, often questions whether anyone is capable of respect or even worthy of it."

"Admiral Gaspar, I find your ideas to be multifaceted," Pope Pius VI smiled. "This is quite unlike so many of our leaders today."

"I believe that some of our leaders have found two ways to go through life without having to think," José said with a wry smile, "and that is to believe everything *carte blanche* or to doubt absolutely everything. Either way they are always right in their own mind and their decisions are simple ones."

"My dear Admiral, the Lord is waiting for men like you," Pius smiled.

"I pray you are right. I know the Lord is waiting but, so is my bride, Rosalita," José quietly replied as he knelt on both knees before the Holy Prelate. "With all due respect, I hope this journey goes well and that I see her often before I meet our Lord and Savior."

"I will pray for you, my son," the pontiff replied. "Be of good character and remember that a clear concience creates a soft pillow. Bless you and your crew."

"Holy Father, rest assured that God is the captain of my ship of life and I am but a seaman," José replied reverently.

The following weeks saw the *Intrepido* sail west through the calm, blue waters of the Mediterranean, back past Spain and the Rock of Gibraltar, with José remarking to Lieutenant Gálvez, "If we simply sailed back to Spain now, would anybody know or even question whether we sailed around the world? Were it not for John Jay and the Americans, we would be now in sight of North America instead of being kept out of sight sailing around the African continent."

As they sailed through the shipping lanes off Africa, José noticed an increased number of slave ships sailing westward into the Atlantic Ocean. Sickened by the thought of the slaves in the stinking holds, José promised himself that whenever he was in a position to free slaves, he would do so.

Two months later, the Spanish man-of-war sailed into the China Sea and met a ship of China's Qing dynasty. It was obvious to José, by the condition of the vessel and age and ability of the crew, who were mostly very young boys or old men, why Qing's dynasty was crumbling. The one-hundred-foot, three-masted junk had fourteen cannon on either side and was manned by at least four hundred sailors. It was barnacled and rode extremely low in the water. The men operating the pumps were barely able to keep her afloat.

Meeting with the ship's captain, Ching Chih-Lung, a great-grandson of the famous pirate of one hundred years earlier as he proudly told José, was a learning experience. Ching Chih-Lung was a Christian pirate, also known as Gaspar Nicholas, which caused José to chuckle at the number of times he had heard his last name used by famous people. "Perhaps, my ancestors took the name of Gaspar from your famous great-grandfather," José told the old captain.

Ching Chih-Lung warned Gaspar to be careful sailing in the China Sea and Pacific Ocean. He mentioned not only the famous Chinese pirate, Ching Yih but told of British pirates operating in the area as well. Since the *Intrepido* would be sailing through the Straight of Mallaca between Malaysia and Sumatra, Gaspar was warned to be careful of the Bugi-men, a fierce group of unusual pirates, who hid in trees that grew to the very water's edge, and generally attacked with small boats launched from the cover of the tree line. These were slaver pirates who captured people from the Philippine Islands and sold them as slaves.

As the *Intrepido* sailed through the Straits of Mallaca, being a man-of-war, it had no problem until it came upon a British ship being wildly attacked by at least thirty small boats. The pirates were using blowpipes made from bamboo tubes to launch salvo after salvo of poison-tipped darts that kept the English from manning the cannon on the decks. The assault allowed the other pirates to begin boarding the British vessel.

Admiral Gaspar ordered the cannon on board the *Intrepido* to be loaded with grapeshot. He also ordered the marines and others on the deck to load their muskets and "rain holy terror down upon the pirates!" The sailors carried fire pots up in the rigging. When lit, the pots would be thrown at the small pirate crafts.

As he skillfully ordered the Spanish ship into position, José snarled, "Ancient weapons are no match for modern technology. We will blast them out of the damn water!"

When the surprised Bugis finally noticed the oncoming man-of-war, it was too late for them to retreat. As they tried, Gaspar pulled his Toledo from its scabbard and gave the order to fire the starboard cannon on the helpless pirates. "I would rather avoid a fight; but, if we must fight, then we will fight with everything we have!" he shouted.

The *Intrepido* shook violently as a firestorm of metallic death was rained down upon the Bugis. The grapeshot, made up of rusting metal, glass shards, and splinters of wood, tore into their flesh and shredded their small crafts, sinking them almost instantly. As the *Intrepido* rocked back, the snipers and marines on deck fired a volley of shot at the helpless, bleeding Bugis, now drowning. "Kill every god-damned one of the devils!" José screamed, "I want them to know the terror they have brought to innocent victims!"

The sea turned red from the blood of the pirates dying in the water while José and the crew guided the *Intrepido* to the British ship. Launching grappling hooks, the Spanish marines were successful in "marrying" the two ships. The remaining Bugis were crouched behind bulkheads and English bags of tea to avoid the hail of bullets riddling the top decks.

As the Bugis recognized their hopeless situation, they raised flags of surrender on their Dao swords. These were the razor sharp swords decorated with the human hair of previous victims that the Bugis cherished and used in their campaigns.

The marines ceased fire and quiet settled over the battle scene. The only sound was the creaking of oak plank upon oak plank as the two ships rubbed against one another in the gently rolling water.

As the Spanish sailors and marines boarded the British ship, rounding up the pirates, the tension of battle began to ebb. Just then, the doors from the quarterdeck burst open. A wild-eyed Bugi lurched out with his right arm collaring a bleeding Englishman, while in his left hand he held a Dao to the man's throat. The Bugi was screaming and enraged, threatening to kill his captive.

José leapt from the *Intrepido* and before the crazed Bugi could react, the Spanish admiral severed the pirate's head with one swing of his blade. Blood spurted over the Englishman as both fell to the deck. In shock, the Englishman lapsed into unconsciousness.

Later that afternoon, the Englishman, washed and clean, woke up in the captain's quarters of the British ship with José at his side. He smiled at the Spanish admiral and reached out to grasp his hand. Although in considerable physical pain, the patient smiled and made an effort to sit up on the bed, mumbling, "I am glad at times like these that I don't sleep in a sailor's hammock."

José laughed and agreed.

"My name is Benjamin Raffles and as you can see, I am a captain in the East-West Indies merchant trade," the man stated.

"I am José Gaspar, admiral in service to my king and the country of Spain." José replied, "I am glad we were able to be of aid to you and your crew."

"Sir, although our countries' leaders officially choose to be at war with one another, I have never been happier to see a handsome Spaniard," said Raffles gratefully. "My thanks to you and your crew, and allow me to share some of our fine provisions with you as a measure of our indebtedness."

Remaining lashed together for the rest of the night, the ship's crews enjoyed an evening of merriment and dancing as the musicians from both ships formed one band, playing everything from Irish jigs to the flamenco.

Years later, José would learn that the captain was the father of Thomas Stamford Raffles. Sir Thomas Raffles was the famous British governor who suppressed the slave trade and liberalized the rules of the British colonial system. Sir Thomas also established a settlement on the island of Singapore and is looked upon as its founding father.

The thankful Captain Raffles gave José some potted banyan trees, asking him to plant these ageless trees throughout the remainder of his cruise around the world. José agreed, as he knew that the trees grew to such height and breadth they were valuable to coastal, low-lying areas.

"Over time, these trees could give refuge and safety to coastal people in case of gravity or tidal waves," José told Cousin León and Lieutenant Gálvez back on board the *Intrepido*, "of course only our grandchildren will benefit."

One month later the *Intrepido* was sailing off the coast of Malaya when it first came into contact with one of the ships of the pirate confederation headed up by Ching Yih. This was the first time that José learned that one of the most powerful navies the world had ever seen owed no allegiance to any nation or ethnic group.

In the first wave of Yih's attack, the pirate vessels were small and quickly positioned themselves around the *Intrepido*. These quick light vessels were no match for the cannon on the Spanish ship. Later that afternoon, a larger Ching Yih ship came from the southwest to join the smaller craft.

"Admiral Gaspar, we have enemy craft off the bow, off both the starboard and port side, as well as following our stern. We are completely surrounded!" Lieutenant Gálvez reported to José, an element of fear in his quavering voice.

Calmly José gestured to gather the officers and men around him and stated in a stern, matter-of-fact voice, "Very good, Lieutenant. Now that we know the position of the enemy we can deal with them."

"Sir, many of the pirate vessels are under the command of women!" Gálvez shouted in surprise.

"Order all men to battle stations and load the cannon and swivel guns, Lt. Gálvez," José barked out. I want grape and chain shot loaded alternately into each cannon. I want the rigging and upper decks lined with snipers and marines," he continued confidently. "Bring our ship hard to port. We want to position it to the stern of their main flagship. Chinese pirate captains sail with their families. We want this fleet captain to realize that our first volley will be directly into the cabins housing his wife and children, should they be on board!

Within the hour, the Chinese captain raised a flag of truce and José agreed to meet with him, providing he agreed to escort the *Intrepido* to a meeting with the Pirate Patriarch, Ching Yih.

Two weeks later, Admiral Gaspar with only one ship and two hundred and forty-four men at his command, met with Ching Yih, who commanded more than one thousand ships, divided into six fleets, with nearly 60,000 men and women. Yih's pirate confederation was assigned to plunder and control an assigned part of the Chinese coastline.

"Admiral Gaspar, the stories of your daring and courage are obviously true," Ching Yih stated at the first meeting. "We admire and respect courage, although I must tell you that, were you a merchant vessel, your failure to surrender your ship without a fight would have resulted in your terrible death," Yih smiled. "In fact, many of our captains would have delighted in nailing your feet to the deck of your ship and beating you to death slowly. The women would have enjoyed other brutalities before they castrated you and choked you to death with your own penis."

"I hesitate to think of what you do to those who meekly surrender their ships and cargo," José smiled, leaning forward to look Ching directly in the eyes.

"Quite the contrary, my dear Admiral," Ching replied, "all the fleets of our confederation are under orders to allow those ships to proceed in peace as soon as we have taken their cargo. You see, Gaspar, a ship that surrenders without a fight is good for us, as we lose no men or women in battle and gain the cargo as prize. It is a good business practice, in the long term, to let them go, as these captains become confident that they will be allowed to safely pass. It is such a good practice that many of our regular prizes are permitted to keep one half or more of their cargoes."

"That is a unique concept," Gaspar stated thoughtfully. "I can see that it might benefit you to sell passes or licenses to ships using your waters."

"My wife, Ching Shih, has suggested the same thing," Ching Yih laughed loudly. "Perhaps, we could arrange such a system for Spanish merchant vessels, say for ten percent of the total value of their cargo?"

"Let us draw up a treaty to that effect," José suggested, in what would be one of the most positive results of his worldwide journey and would result in increased trade for Spain.

After an agreement had been drafted and signed, José gave Ching Yih an expensive vase of gold, crafted in Mexico. Ching Yih took a Chinese sword from his waist and gave it to José. As José looked at the short sword and its unusual handle, Ching Yih leered and proclaimed, "the Chinese Sword, a blade to kill any man, with a handle to please any woman." José cast a knowing smile at the Chinese pirate king.

Before sailing to the Pacific, José had the opportunity to meet Madam Ching Shih, a former prostitute and the current wife of Ching Yih. Years later she would command the largest independent confederation of pirates numbering more 80,000 men and women and nearly 2,000 ships.

The *Intrepido* survived a typhoon while crossing the Pacific Ocean and the veteran crew, who had survived Atlantic hurricanes, laughed and joked afterwards as to how they couldn't tell the difference between a typhoon and a hurricane. "Both storms tear at the ship, ruin sails and rigging, and cause you to pray to your God," José exclaimed.

Weeks after successfully rounding Cape Horn and the southern tip of South America, the ship landed in Havana, and the weary crew was given leave, while the *Intrepido* was repaired and new rigging and provisions were brought aboard.

José was pleased to find his dearest friend, Miguel Rodriquez, on board the *La Esclavitud* and surprised the unsuspecting merchant captain by sneaking up behind him and tossing him overboard off his own ship. This delighted the crew who remembered the men's friendship.

After the two famous sea captains spent the better part of the day zestfully engaged in a good-natured wrestling match, a fencing contest, and a tug of war, they went below to clean up and prepare for dinner.

"This is a dinner of great celebration, my dearest friend," Miguel stated as he proposed a toast to José, "May the child of your marriage be half the man of his father."

"What are you saying, Miguel?" José stammered in surprise.

"You don't know, do you?" Miguel laughed, "My friend, your Rosalita is with child. In fact, you might already be a father!"

José was suddenly filled with the satisfaction and peace that only a father can feel upon knowing that he has fulfilled his biological destiny.

However, before he could begin the voyage home, the *Intrepido* was ordered by the Navy commandant to go to New Orleans to escort three merchant vessels back to Cuba. A British man-of-war still thought to be in the Gulf of Mexico had sunk their escort vessel, a French frigate.

En route to New Orleans, José ordered his ship to hug the shallow coastline of Florida, stopping often in the sandy, safe harborages he remembered fondly. At each landing, José would take one of the small banyan trees given him by the British captain, Benjamin Raffles, and plant it in the Florida soil.

On beautiful Gasparilla island, Gaspar planted many of the banyan trees for fear that planting them further north would endanger them from frost and other weather problems. "How ironic the world is," José thought to himself. "Here I am planting living trees given me by a grateful British ship captain, while another English captain out in the Gulf of Mexico would like to kill my crew and me. I know not if these trees will grow, but I know we must all plant seeds or seedlings of all kinds, with the hope of these trees helping those who survive us."

The *Intrepido* never did meet the English man-of-war as it escorted the three ships to Cuba. Within days, the *Intrepido* began the last leg of the fifteen-month journey around the world, returning to Spain in October 1780.

CHAPTER 33

Boredom and Bliss

"I have a position that allows me to be a witness to history and bores me. I have a marriage that excites me and keeps me in ecstasy."
—Admiral José Gaspar, at Treaty of Versailles, January 20, 1783

As soon as José could get away from his duties on the *Intrepido* when they arrived back at Seville, he climbed impatiently into the carriage that León had come in to transport him to Madrid. After a dusty ride, they continued on to the estate. José swept Rosalita off her feet in a lengthy embrace and was then presented to his son. He felt a thrill of excitement as he held the chubby-cheeked, brown-eyed alert baby who grinned widely at his long-absent father and grasped José's finger tightly with his hand. José had a conflict in deciding whether to carry his son around the house or make love to Rosalita. It was a dilemma that the young husband and father delighted in solving after his arrival home.

Rosalita had waited until his arrival to name the child. She wanted to name the boy after his father, but after some discussion, José suggested that the boy also should have his great-grandfather's name: José Pedro Gonzalvo. He whispered in her ear, "You have made me the proudest man in Spain. No man has ever been prouder to have his first-born son carry his name. He will carry the Gaspar name into the 1800s. And perhaps, like my grandfather, and me, my little José Pedro, my Josélito, will one day also become an admiral."

Rosalita decided that it was necessary for her to accompany the two men in her life everywhere they went. When she didn't, she worried because when the baby pointed to objects and grunted, José would explain them in too much detail. José was unaware that hours often slipped by while he described things the baby could not understand. Although she pretended interest, José sometimes bored her with hs pontifications on many subjects. While at sea, he was used to having a capitve audience for his lectures.

José lived a life of ecstasy at home, never seeming to get enough time with his family. At work, as José described it, "I have a desk and office, where I read and sign paperwork. My main job however, is riding around in carriages and being seen with the leaders of Spain. The most important thing I did in the whole year of 1781 was to insure that the name Sanibel be given to an island off the west coast of La Florida to honor the queen of Spain. I shortened the name from Santa Isabella to Sanibel because it is such a small island; I wanted the mapmakers to be able to get the name fully on the chart without totally covering the island. Also, using the name Sanibel brings honor to the first captain under whom I was privileged to serve."

The homecoming year of 1781 was also when Rosalita and José conceived their second child and playfully argued over whether this child, too, was conceived upon the peddler's cart or some other traditional location.

Their personal joy was tempered somewhat by José's knowledge that his former ship, *Intrepido*, now commanded by Capt. Alferez de Navio Margues del Moral, was having a successful campaign against the British in the Gulf of Mexico. José felt it a personal insult that his choice for a successor, Captain Andromaca, was ignored and the command given to another captain whom he did not respect. In fact British Capt. Robert Deans burned his ship, *Mentor*, at Pensacola on May 8, 1781, to avoid capture by the *Intrepido*.

José was also discouraged when he learned that Captain Andromaca had run his own ship, the frigate *Francesca*, aground on a shoal in Pensacola Bay on April 19, 1781. The *Francesca* lost her large cargo of war materials. The *Intrepido* rescued Andromaca, adding one insult upon another in José's mind. He was still irate about not commanding the *Intrepido* in battle but instead having to make his worldwide voyage to mollify the personal jealousies of FloridaBlanca and Godoy. This anger was tempered, however, with the joy of being home with his wife and child.

Early in 1782, José met with representatives of Thomas Jefferson to encourage them to adopt the Spanish dollar as the unit of currency for the new United States government. Jefferson later used Gaspar's reasoning in urging the adoption stating, "the Spanish dollar or peso was picked because it was a known coin and most familiar in the minds of the people."

During these discussions, José earnestly proclaimed that having a currency and coin accepted by all nations of the world would promote trade and improve economic conditions worldwide. Privately, José believed that Spain, which had been the leader in world exploration, should have its coin used.

Years later, Gaspar would chuckle to himself that the symbol of the American dollar, the $ sign, was really derived from the Spanish peso of the day. The Spanish coin on one side had two pillars, representing the pillars of Hercules at Gibraltar. In writing, it was symbolized by two vertical lines with an S over top of them to indicate plural.

He considered it amusing that suggesting another country's copying of your nation's coin could become the most significant event in one year of a man's career.

June 6, 1782 brought about another of the happiest days in José Gaspar's life—the birth of a seven-pound baby girl. For the second time, José had become the father of a child whose beauty, in his opinion, was unmatched by any other baby. José insisted the girl be called Rosalita Dulcie in tribute to his wife, and his mother.

Carlos, who was growing into quite a good-looking young man, continued to be a part of the family and to be the de facto keeper of Lucky, although young José Pedro was now enjoying romps with the dog. Lucky had the cheerful and friendly disposition of most hounds and adapted with noisy enthusiasm to all the beloved humans in his environment.

Two days after the Christmas feast, though it was an unusually cool day with heavy gray clouds pressing down, José was enjoying the playful antics of José Pedro and Lucky, as he held five-month-old Rosalita Dulcie in his arms outside the patio near the road. Shortly before the group was to return to the house, a group of twelve Asturias cavalry rode recklessly up the road, causing swirling great clouds of dirt and causing José, in civilian clothes, to shake his hand in protest and disgust as they galloped by.

The column came to an abrupt stop at a signal from the leader and wheeled to quickly ride back toward the angry father. As the cavalry detachment came closer, the leader raised his left hand to call the riders to a halt. As he rode forward slowly and deliberately, José recognized Capt. Gomez, who was also the personal escort of Manuel Godoy. The fierce mutual dislike both felt from their first meeting had escalated through the years to intense hatred. Gomez was overbearing and arrogant and never hesitated to exceed his authority. He seemed to take perverse pleasure in baiting the admiral, knowing that Godoy, who loathed José, would protect him. Lucky, as well as José, sensed danger, and barked incessantly at the swarthy cavalry captain.

"Admiral Gaspar, I did not know it was you walking unescorted along the road," a surprised Gomez said gruffly. "It can be dangerous walking along these roads."

"I think the danger is dependent upon who else is on the road. People riding carefully are not normally a threat to us," José replied in a biting voice.

"We were riding to find you, Admiral. The king wants you to come to the palace tomorrow so that you can be part of the delegation going to Paris, to solve the world's problems," Gomez announced sarcastically.

"I believe it is fruitless to solve the world's problems until we can resolve our own problems here," José retorted, "Why would we go to Paris?"

"The treaty to end the American Revolutionary War will be discussed. One of the American ambassadors, John Jay, will be there to try and confiscate as much land as possible." Gomez continued, "Our king specifically wants you there to represent the Spanish interests, stymie Jay's demands, and insure that Spain retains a strong presence in North America. Sounds simple, for a people's hero like you, Gaspar."

José nodded silently, noting the envy and resentfulness in Gomez's voice.

Acknowledging his duty to his country and sadly leaving his family, in January 1783 Gaspar went with the delegation to participate in the Treaty of Paris.

Upon his arrival, José soon discovered that his role in the talks would indeed be important. The British recognized publicly their trust of the Spanish naval hero who, in spite of the hostilities between their two countries, had risked his life and crew to save their ship and its famous captain, Benjamin Raffles, in the Straits of Mallaca. José felt somewhat uncomfortable with his lofty standing in the minds of both the British and the French, as both confirmed that Admiral Gaspar was a person whom they could trust in these negotiations.

Benjamin Franklin, the American ambassador to France, warmly greeted José and told him that his role in the Treaty of Paris would have lasting effects on all the countries represented. Franklin cautioned Gaspar, "Trust is built over time. It can take years to build and can be lost in a heartbeat."

"I believe trust is built upon two values, justice and integrity, and I will not sacrifice either. You can count on that," José assured him.

José responded to his new role by announcing at the first meeting, "I believe that greediness has diluted not only our Spanish culture but also the world as we know it. If the nations gathered here cannot halt this 'all or nothing' attitude and stop their craving of material possessions, then our mission will become diluted and meaningless. The wealthy individuals in our world today want to live apart from the poor, partly through fear and partly because they feel they deserve such a lifestyle and are superior to those who have less. As nations, so as to not live in similar fear, we must adhere to justice and fairness and we must share or we will end by having nothing!"

As discussions continued and meeting followed meeting, the relationship between John Jay, Benjamin Franklin's chief aide, and José grew more strained. José discovered that Jay was ignoring instructions from the American Congress to claim land only to the Appalachian Mountains and, instead, had taken it upon himself to negotiate for territory all the way to the Mississippi River. José remembered Jay telling him of his intentions in Spain four years earlier and, even after José's heated objections. Damned if Jay wasn't now doing it!

Gaspar pleaded with the parties not to allow the American to get away with this abuse of power not even granted to Jay. "This grabbing of land will double the size of their new country," José protested at every opportunity, "and even their Congress does not approve! Soon the rest of us will be forced out of the territory."

Although Jay and the Americans were successful in securing the land they sought, Gaspar's relentless protestations at the Treaty of Paris were responsible for the Florida territory being retained as a Spanish colony.

José was heralded as a hero and a great negotiator though he did not feel he deserved such adulation from the Spanish people. He confided to Cousin León one evening, that, "Many people believe that information is power but what good is that power if it is based on wrong information." José mused, "I am not sure that our decisions were correct and in the best interests of anyone but the Americans."

Although Jay and José Gaspar spoke openly in public and argued privately, the chill between them was obvious to everyone. One evening a carriage came to the Spanish embassy carrying Mrs. Sarah Jay and her two daughters, Maria, born in 1782, and Ann, a newborn. José was pleased to see Sarah and talked animatedly with her about his own son and daughter whom he missed terribly. Unlike her husband, Sarah Jay, knowing that José had simply passed the name of a doctor to them, never blamed José or Rosalita for the tragic death of their first daughter.

Before she left, she grabbed José by the arm and in a rueful voice warned, " José, my husband John admires your courage, appreciates your conviction, respects your positions on issues, and gives great thought to your suggestions. He does this because he deeply loves America and desires to make sound decisions and because Benjamin Franklin insists he work with you. However, since the death of our first daughter, he cannot overcome his hatred of you and will not be happy until your career is destroyed. Please be careful, for John will do all he can to aid in that destruction."

José thanked her and they quietly embraced, knowing it would become increasingly dangerous for them to communicate.

Returning to Spain after the Treaty of Paris was signed, José was heralded throughout Spain for his leadership. He spent the late spring and most of the summer traveling the country and insisted on taking Rosalita and the two children with him to represent the crown at festivals and parades.

The people of Spain grew to know and appreciate the famous admiral and his family. The love and adoration heaped upon the Gaspar family caused the royal family in general, and Manuel Godoy in particular, to stoke the flames of hatred. But Godoy and the throne could not cope nor overcome the overwhelming affection that the people of Spain accorded the handsome admiral.

As fall waned into early winter and the queen's resentment's grew, José came home from Madrid one evening and announced that he had yet another task assigned to him.

Rosalita asked excitedly, "Oh, José, are they finally giving you command of a ship?"

José answered sarcastically, "No, I have been given the dangerous task of taking the queen's jewels to Seville. Perhaps they will let me visit the docks after I deliver the baubles of our overweight monarch."

CHAPTER 34

Theft of Crown Jewels

*"In order for one to be effectively blamed for something,
the accuser must have many accomplices. I never realized that jealousy
would be a sufficient cause to destroy another's career."*
—José Gaspar, proclaiming his innocence to Cousin León, January 21, 1784

The summer of 1783 had sped by quickly. In August, José and Rosalita had gone to Seville to bring Dulcie Gaspar, now a striking widow with streaks of silver in her ebony hair, back to Madrid. They were looking forward to the Christmas season. José and Rosalita felt that they would feel more comfortable in leaving their two children under the watchful eye of José's mother.

But, as it happened, José was named the presiding officer in the task of taking the crown jewels back to Seville to be reset for the queen. The violent fury of a thunderstorm caused the postponement of the trip, allowing José and Rosalita another night together before the rescheduled convoy left the next morning.

Carlos wanted to know if a presiding officer was also a commanding officer. José laughed and shook his head stating, "No, a commanding officer is in charge of the troops. I am a presiding officer, which means that I simply act like a courtroom judge, by keeping my mouth shut, nodding off, and simply going along for the ride to insure the jewels arrive safely. Upon arrival, I hand the jewels over to the jeweler and get a receipt. On the return trip I am only a glorified passenger!"

Carlos laughed, roughed up Lucky's head, and they ran off through the courtyard with José Pedro giggling and awkwardly running behind.

Rosalita came out into the courtyard and sighed, "I love the air after a thunderstorm; it is so fresh." She shivered a little and José put his muscular arm around her shoulders.

"Darling, I didn't realize you were chilled," José said, with concern.

"I really am not cold. I don't understand why, but I have a premonition," Rosalita replied, with wide, pleading eyes. "I don't want you to go tomorrow. Please stay with me."

"I would like nothing better," José smiled. "But, this journey tomorrow should not be a problem. The Asturias Cavalry will be escorting me and no one would dare to attack a royal carriage guarded by the king's finest troops. Since last year we have not been at war with anyone. The crime within Spain is less than in previous years. I think everything will be fine. Besides, until they let me retire gracefully, I still have an obligation to our country."

"I pray you are right, José," she whispered, "I don't want to live without you by my side. We are blessed with two wonderful children and a fine home. These are the best of times but things can change so quickly."

"Don't worry, my dear," José answered trying to reassure her, "I'll be back by the end of this month. Nothing evil can happen to me. Am I not still your hero? That knowledge will keep me safe."

That night, after little José was worn out from playing with his father and taken to bed, Rosalita went to bathe. José waited until he thought she would be undressed then sprinted to the bedroom.

"José!" she shrieked in shocked pleasure as he charged into their room, surprised at his sudden entry, yet glad that he still desired to see her naked.

"José, I am going to beat you," she yelled playfully.

"You can try, but I might invoke the rule of thumb law that I learned about in Paris," José shot back.

"What do you mean by rule of thumb?" she asked.

"My dear Rosalita, the rule of thumb is the English Law that says you can't beat your wife with anything wider than your thumb," José laughed as he ducked a wet, crumpled towel hurled at him by his wife.

"José, you enjoy teasing me, but you have always treated me like royalty," she quietly whispered as she moved into his waiting arms. José began gently stroking her soft, bare back and kissed the top of her head.

His hands moved tenderly over her skin and his right hand delicately cupped her left breast as they searched frantically for each other's lips with open mouths. Another thunderstorm approached the estate and the lightning flashes illuminated the pair as José swept her off the floor and carried her to the bed. She was grateful that the claps of thunder were able to muffle her loud cries of joy, and on this night there was no doubt in her mind that they had created their third child!

The next morning they repeated their lovemaking activity, more subdued, but still passionate, as rays of the early sunlight crept across into the window beside the open draperies moving in the gentle breeze.

At breakfast on the patio with the children, the couple became somber with the inevitability of José's departure.

"If I had known the future when I was growing up, I would have become a farmer," José spoke trying to lift their spirits.

"José, the children and I need you," she quietly whispered. "Please be careful. I can only hope that Manuel Godoy cares enough for the crown's jewels to worry about you as much as I do."

"Godoy is only concerned with advancing himself, no matter what he promises," José replied with anger in his voice. "Although he swears to oaths, his lack of a conscience always releases him from any inconvenient promises he makes. He is an egomaniac, a liar, and not to be trusted."

"Then why do you serve him so gallantly?" Rosalita asked sadly.

"My love, please understand. We who are in the military serve our country in spite of who is leading it. It has always been that way and it always will be," José replied as he got up to pick little Rosalita Dulcie off the floor. "History has taught us that, regardless of the country, often the best leaders are not those who are charged with actually governing that nation."

"José, the military is asinine to follow a weak leader," his wife smiled.

As he tickled his children, José stated flatly, "Remember the Spanish proverb: Every person is a fool in somebody's opinion. Sometimes the military suffers fools in the name of duty."

Two hours later, the carriage came from Madrid to pick José up. After hugging the children, scratching Lucky's belly, and shaking hands with young Carlos, José again held Rosalita. He whispered, "I want you to know that when we first met, I shared a prayer with the sand and the sea, praying that you would come to me. I thank God for you. I love you so much."

José strode quickly to the coach, then turned and smiled, waving to his family.

When José arrived at the palace in Madrid, he went into the room where the crown jewels were placed in ornate strong boxes, grumbling that the rich should learn to not advertise their wealth so publicly.

After inspecting the jewels and signing the inventory list, José learned that the Asturias Cavalry unit, under Captain Gomez, was not assigned to escort him to Seville. Despite his dislike of Gomez and his men, he respected them for their ability to fight. "Where are they?" José asked incredulously. "I can't believe the crown would risk their gold and jewels with an ordinary army unit."

"Admiral Gaspar, there has been a terrible calamity in Italy with 100,000 Italians killed," the agent of the crown stated, "and Manuel Godoy sent Captain Gomez and his troops to guard the supplies being sent to Barcelona for shipment to Italy."

"That makes no sense to me, as a regular army unit could be entrusted with guarding supplies," José replied. "I am sure the king must have a plan, I just don't know what it is." José continued as he walked toward the carriage. "I only hope the right decision has been made, so we will have no regrets."

The convoy consisted of two royal carriages and twenty cavalry troops. Moving away from the palace, the coaches rumbled over the cobblestone streets of Madrid.

On the second day, the convoy stopped to water the horses at a swift-flowing stream. As he walked to the knob of a grassy knoll to stretch his cramped muscles, José noticed a group of about fifteen riders looking down upon them from a ridge above the valley. He felt a chill go through him that raised the hair on the back of his head. With a sense of foreboding, he realized these riders might well be a danger to the jeweled cargo they were carrying. José scrambled down the hill to join the young, recently conscripted, soldiers who were loudly arguing about which of them would spend the following night in the arms of a señorita in Seville. This novice cavalry was totally inexperienced when compared to the veteran, rugged and flamboyant Asturias Cavalrymen who normally accompanied José.

José knew that he needed to rouse the soldiers' awareness and alert them to a possible confrontation with the horsemen, so he hastily gathered the troops around him at the edge of the creek. Standing on the step board of the nearest carriage, he cried, "Men, before the sun sets, I fear we may be attacked by that group of riders following us along the ridge line." He pointed to the ridge where the riders sat motionless. "You need to remain alert as we travel. I have taken men into battle aboard ship and on land and I urge you to fight with enthusiasm if the need arises. Don't think you can win the battle; know that you can win. Don't simply look to your own survival; be determined to prevail. If you don't fight with enthusiasm, you will surely die. Remember always that you are the brave soldiers of Spain!" With a flourish, Admiral Gaspar removed his sword and raised it high into the air, the sun reflecting off the gleaming surface of the Toledo.

The caravan again began the trek south towards Seville, this time with the men alert and cautious as the road twisted between a series of rolling hills. At mid-afternoon, the first wagon and eight troops rounded a bend in the low-lying road. A crack of gunfire echoed throughout the valley as shots were fired at the first group of soldiers. Piercing screams muffled the sounds of the musket fire raining down on the convoy.

José's face jerked around toward the window of the carriage in which he was riding. As he stuck his head outside the carriage to look up, blood from the driver's head splattered over his face and white uniform. A veteran of many battles, José instantly overcame his shock, and anger seethed through his body.

He climbed out the window as the masked riders on their frothing mounts galloped down the hill with swords drawn. Although they wore civilian clothing, José was sure he recognized some of the horses as well as the bearing of the attackers themselves.

As he crawled to the driver's seat, José reached over the corpse and grabbed the reins of the horse team. He then snatched up the whip and applied it fiercely to the horses, urging them on. As he looked over his right shoulder and saw one of the riders come along side the coach, José tugged the Chinese dagger from its scabbard at his waist, and, with his right hand, plunged it into the eye of his attacker, who screamed and grabbed his face thus losing his balance and falling beneath the wheels of the carriage. José gave a curious look at his dagger and shook the victim's eyeball from its tip.

Glancing up, José saw that one of the riders had jumped from his horse onto one of José's team in an attempt to stop the carriage. He calmly pulled his pistol from his belt and whistled shrilly. As the attacker turned and faced José, terror showed in his eyes. José smiled coldly at the man, and pulled the trigger, watching with fascination as his bullet shattered the man's teeth, scattering them like pieces of broken glass before it tore off the left side of his head.

José now turned his attention to the leader of the group who was galloping along the left side of the carriage. Throwing his pistol down, he stood up to draw his Toledo.

The lead rider of the banditos tried to level his pistol but, as he was attempting to find Gaspar as his target, the hardened steel of the Toledo sliced through his biceps, causing him to shout in pain and drop the pistol. José recognized the shout as the voice of Captain Gomez!

The sounds of battle surrounded José and the acrid odor of gunpowder assailed his nostrils. As he glanced around he could see that the inexperienced troops under his command were quickly falling victim to the more-experienced fake bandits.

José pulled the horses to a stop. He fought on, killing two more of the attackers, then stood on top of the carriage to fight off three more with both sword and dagger, when a heavy blow landed on the back of his head. As he lost consciousness, José continued to swing his sword wildly.

When he awoke, José found himself covered in blood. From the way he ached he felt sure that the blood must be his, but as he slowly began to move, he realized that in spite of his head, he was very much alive.

Looking around, he saw the visages of death all around him. As he stood up and slowly walked among the bodies, he became numb at the violence of the slaughter. All members of his escort party had been killed. The crown jewels were gone, as was the other carriage.

Remembering Gomez's cry as his arm was sliced, José realized that the immoral Manuel Godoy, María Louisa, and the others who were jealous of him, had set him up.

"They will accuse me of stealing the crown's jewels and either imprison or kill me," José thought. He realized that no matter what he said, it would be their charge against the word of the crown's representatives. As the blood pounded in his temples, he raised his fist and shouted, "Only God can judge me!"

José said a prayer for his fallen comrades, and then, his mind still whirling, mounted one of the horses and headed back north towards Rosalita and his family.

"I will take my family to La Florida and begin a new life. Perhaps I will form a new government that gives rights to the people, rather than enslaving them in a bureaucracy like Spain's," he vowed.

CHAPTER 35

Death of Living

"It is a fact of life that people we love touch our lives even after they are gone."
—José Gaspar to his son, José Pedro

Realizing that he was now a fugitive and a thief in the eyes of the crown, José waited until after midnight to sneak into Madrid. So as not to raise suspicion, he shed his military attire by trading his dress uniform to a peasant for the peasant's pants and cape. After further dickering, the man also gave José his straw hat.

Remaining in the shadows on a bright, moonlit night was somewhat difficult even on the narrow city streets. Twice he was forced to duck into doorways when he hard the nearby clatter of mounted patrols of the Spanish Army.

Each time that José was forced to evade capture by crouching, his head throbbed in pain. He was certain that the blow to his head had fractured his skull. But even if his injuries needed medical attention, he could not risk seeking a doctor, so he simply endured the agony and moved forward towards the naval barracks at the palace where Cousin León would be sleeping.

Some time before dawn, José crept into León's room, clapped his hand over León's mouth, and roused him. León awoke with a start and sat upright in bed before his sleep-filled eyes opened.

"José, what are you doing here? Why are you dressed so?" León hoarsely whispered after José removed his hand. Then sniffing, he asked, "What is that odor? It smells like a barnyard!"

"León, some people believe that you count life in years; but, let me tell you, I have suffered a lifetime just this past fifteen hours," José answered in a low, tired voice. "I have become older and wiser in the time between sunrise and sunset. I am dog-tired, but you must help me get to Rosalita."

León sat in the bed, shaking his head and mumbling to himself, confused and unsure of what to say or do next. He stalled by asking, "I wonder where the phrase dog-tired came from?"

"León, after the fall of the Roman Empire, the dogs that had been used as military messengers became hunting dogs and were forced to work hard in order to survive," José said impatiently. "That is where the phrases 'dog tired' and 'die like a dog' came from. Now that you have had your history lesson, get your ass out of bed and help me sneak home!"

León and José made a series of stealthy moves to the palace laundry, near León's room. There, José chose some gowns and dresses belonging to María Louisa. He stole back to León's room with them and, after showering and shaving, he dressed himself in a lovely white gown with a lacey bodice and veil. Fortunately, José was of small stature and although muscular, was thin, so the gown fit him nicely.

León couldn't stop laughing at how his famous cousin looked, in spite of the tragic circumstances that forced this disguise. León located his civilian clothing in his locker and dressed as a natty-looking gentleman.

Still in León's quarters, José explained his plan and invited León to go with him and his family to La Florida. José planned to sneak into his estate, dressed as a woman, and have Rosalita and the children leave later that afternoon as if going into Madrid to the marketplace. José would leave shortly after with his mother, Dulcie, behaving as if they were two old friends going for a walk. Then they would all meet at the clump of trees on the road to Seville, just east of the manor.

They would then proceed in two carriages, one-half day apart, to María Gonzalez's estate outside of Seville. There they could stay safely until José would be able to arrange passage for all to the Florida territory he had been so instrumental in assuring for Spain in the Treaty of 1783.

The cousins moved quietly to the stable, chose a carriage and two horses, and as the sun rose, casting a golden glow over the stately Spanish capital, the two left Madrid for the last time.

Soon the cobblestone street turned into a dusty road and, as the pair neared the city gate, they became even more vigilant to their surroundings. Both smiled broadly when a guard near the gate saluted and wished the "lady" a good morning.

José suspected that Godoy would have his henchmen watching the estate so, as they approached the woods on the western side, he ordered León to stop the carriage.

With a feline quickness, in spite of his dress, José disappeared into the woods. León continued on with the carriage to the other side of the estate where he had agreed to wait in a clump of trees until José arrived with Rosalita and his children.

José moved furtively through the woods, oblivious to the chirping birds and the earthy smells of nature coming into full bloom. As he moved from point to point, José became aware of the fact that not only were the guilty cavalrymen watching the estate, they were already inside. He felt nauseated as he contemplated what these traitors might do to those whom he loved most in the world.

Pausing at the creek, José saw his reflection in the clear water. As he flung off the dress, he thought wryly that he could never look like a real lady. He then hid the outfit behind the log where he and Rosalita had so often piled their clothing when they joyfully swam naked in the chilly stream. Wearing only tight-fitting riding trousers and boots, José now hung the Chinese sword and Toledo from his waist, stuck another knife in his right boot and shoved the pistol in his trousers.

Moving cautiously from the woods, he crawled along the creek bed toward the main house. The creek ran into the courtyard, the source of water for Rosalita's enchanting flower garden.

José finally reached the outside wall and began to carefully remove the grate so he could pass through it into the courtyard. As he was removing the grating, José saw that Captain Gomez was slumped in a chair on the patio next to the peddler's cart, which was resplendent with flowers. Gomez's right arm was heavily bandaged and encased in a crudely made sling. José found grim humor in the knowledge that his blade had successfully found its intended mark.

Still surveying the courtyard, José now saw the other cavalrymen, still dressed in their civilian robbers' clothing, helping themselves to the expensive wines from his wine cellar. They appeared to be at various stages of drunkenness. He could not see any of his family members and deduced they were safely inside the house.

How often José had remarked to friends that "a dream is something that only comes around once, while nightmares seem to be a daily occurrence." He knew this was a nightmare he could not have dreamed!

José decided to wait until the cavalrymen had an opportunity to drink even more wine before making his move. Since only eleven remained, José felt that the odds were fairly even, particularly since they would be drunk and not able to react quickly, if at all. As a young, brash midshipman, José had often bragged he was better than ten men in a swordfight.

This plan might have worked if José's mother had not demanded to take the crying baby Rosalita for a walk in the courtyard. Although Dulcie was José's mentor and hero, because of her independent and rebellious nature, this was not the time for her to show it to the world, he apprehensively thought to himself as he heard her imperious demand.

The sun was nearly at its noontime zenith and shining brightly, when Dulcie and the baby woke Gomez from his pain and drunken stupor, startled and angry at this commanding old woman.

"Who in the hell do you think is in charge here?" Gomez demanded of Dulcie.

"I really don't care, Captain," Dulcie coldly snapped back, "I am taking my granddaughter for a walk. It is much too beautiful outside to be imprisoned in one's own home."

"Like hell you are!" Gomez shouted loudly. "Get back inside the goddamn house!"

"You'll not use that language in the presence of my granddaughter, young man," Dulcie angrily yelled back at Gomez, who was teetering to stand up. "We'll be going for our daily walk now."

Instantly, Gomez reached out and grabbed the front of her peasant shirt pulling it down to reveal her breasts. Dulcie turned sideways to slap Gomez sharply across the face with her free right arm. He growled as he grabbed an empty wine bottle from the table with his good left hand and, in a backhanded motion, smashed it on the right side of Dulcie's skull.

Dulcie gaped at Gomez in disbelief as she crumpled to the ground, landing on top of the baby. The shock of the weight of her unconscious grandmother caused the child to scream out in pain and then wail loudly.

This harsh crying further aroused Gomez's anger and he began to kick the helpless baby. A crack sounded at his first sharp kick, and blood gushed from the baby's mouth and nose. The wails suddenly stopped; the silence was eerie.

Seeing his own half-naked mother bleeding from the wound to her head and his daughter being kicked by this despicable animal, José uncontrollably jumped, screaming, from his hiding place.

With his Toledo held high in his right hand and the Chinese sword in his left, the snarling José ran toward Gomez.

The cavalrymen, who had been in a state of shock as they watched their leader beat an elderly woman unconscious and brutalize a baby, reacted slowly to José's assault. As Eliazad Colón, one of the largest of the soldiers, tried to get to his feet, he was struck across the chest by the battle-tested sword of José. The blade found its mark as the bleeding Colón looked curiously down upon his newly opened chest and watched his heart beat the last few beats of his life.

José moved quickly to another rising cavalry trooper and, with his left hand, plunged the Chinese dagger into the man's throat, severing the carotid artery and causing him to die almost instantly with his blood spurting higher than his head as he fell forward into the dirt.

The other men came running, swords in hand, and surrounded Gaspar who was fighting valiantly to reach his fallen mother and daughter. José's sword flashed repeatedly as he slashed wildly at those circling him.

As he attempted to jump up on a stairwell to a defensive position, José slipped and fell. Fists pounded his face and body as the shaken and angry men crowded in. Gomez ordered the beating stopped as José lapsed into unconsciousness. He then had his men strip Gaspar and hang him from the gate by his wrists, his feet dangling above the ground.

After a period of time, the bruised Gaspar began to regain consciousness, the taste of his own blood fresh in his mouth and pain wracking his body. His outstretched arms were being drawn tight by his own body's weight and the ropes were clearly cutting off the circulation of blood to his hands. José's eyes were swollen nearly shut and his head throbbed so fiercely that he could not raise it fully. Blood also poured from his battered nose, so José was barely able to breathe. Through his intense pain, in a surreal moment, he envisioned Jesus suffering on the cross.

The sound of a woman's outcry was the reality that brought him back to his agonized senses. José lifted his head enough to see Rosalita kneeling over his prostrate mother and mortally injured daughter. As she cradled the baby to her chest, her blouse covered with the child's blood, Rosalita looked in the direction of José and shrieked with alarm. He could keep his head up only long enough to make eye contact with the love of his life, communicating his empathy for the pain she was enduring.

At that moment, Gomez grabbed the young mother's long hair with his bloody left hand and pulled her to her feet. Another of the guardsman came forward, took the dying baby from her arms, and laid it upon the peddler's cart, with its tiny hollow staring eyes showing through the blood-stained child's face. José felt tears stream from his eyes, blurring the scene as his head again fell forward.

Rosalita's cries and screams shook him back to reality and he again struggled to raise his weary head, now tasting both his own blood and salty tears of grief.

The drunken cavalrymen now grouped around the peddler's cart staring at the horrible scene. They were looking to Gomez for direction, realizing that the plan to steal the jewels and capture Admiral Gaspar before taking him to Madrid to stand trial had gone terribly wrong.

Three of the men were holding the emotional and crying Rosalita while the others were shouting excitedly and asking Gomez, "What shall we do now?"

Gomez, who was dazed, drunk, and shocked by what had transpired, was no longer a disciplined soldier but was acting now with animal instincts. Rather than thinking logically, as a military officer, Gomez instead focused his stare directly on Rosalita's bosom, lusting after her as a prize.

"For now, we will all enjoy the most prized fruit of passion in all of Madrid," Gomez growled as his left hand roughly grabbed her right breast. "After we have drunk all Gaspar's wine and each given his wife the taste of a real man, we shall kill them both. We will then take all the bodies into the main house and set it on fire. We will claim to Godoy and the queen that we trapped the jewel thief in his house and that they killed themselves after setting the house on fire."

Gomez ordered the peddler's cart cleared of Rosalita's prized flowers and plants. Gomez, himself, grabbed the baby' body by the left leg and threw it carelessly on the ground under the cart as if she were nothing but a rag doll. Rosalita screamed loudly as the terracotta pots crashed to the ground and the potting soil and shards of planters covered her dead child.

When the cart was cleared, Gomez ordered it rolled to the gate where the semi-conscious admiral was tied. José was slipping in and out of consciousness from the beating. The cart bumped twice as the left wheel ran first over the dying Dulcie's midsection, then the dead baby's legs. Gomez made sure the cart was placed so that, even as Gaspar's head sagged to his chest, the top of the cart would remain in full view.

Gomez then ordered the men holding Rosalita to bring her to the edge of the cart and to strip naked the delirious, sobbing princess. José awakened enough from his semiconscious state to make eye contact with his beloved Rosalita and they visually shared the horror of the nightmare. José, shouting obscenities at Gomez, struggled furiously with his bindings as Rosalita also began to struggle in a vain attempt to escape the many hands holding her hostage.

As José's efforts proved fruitless, he continued his shouting through sobs, as he was forced to watch the blouse being torn from his wife's upper torso by the swarthy calvarymen. It seemed that the more she struggled, the more excited the soldiers became, now intoxicated not only with alcohol but also with lust. One leaned forward to bite her left breast savagely, leaving angry red marks on her pale skin.

Two soldiers held her legs up while others tore her riding trousers from her body. As her shredded trousers were being torn off, another yanked off her boots revealing the shapely feet José had loved to hold in his lap. Seeing this, the one holding her left calf grabbed her ankle and put her foot in his mouth. As he bit down, Rosalita screamed out in pain.

As she continued to writhe in a vain attempt to escape, the soldiers rolled the peddler's cart over and strapped her arms and legs to each corner of the cart's top. After tying her securely, Gomez unsnapped his trousers and, aroused from watching the happenings, crawled upon the prone, sobbing princess and raped her as the helpless José could only watch while screaming in utter pain and revulsion.

As Gomez was assaulting Rosalita, the other men were groping, grabbing, and rubbing other parts of her body. The swarthy biter now unsnapped his trousers and, while Gomez was still atop her, took out his penis and shoved it into her mouth. This hellish scene, coupled with his own injuries, which were worsened by his struggle to free himself, caused Gaspar to again lapse into unconsciousness.

When he awoke, another man had climbed upon his moaning bride and three others, only wearing boots, had either just finished raping Rosalita or were waiting their turn. As Gaspar averted his eyes from this scene, he noticed two of the cavalrymen on their knees in the corner with rosaries out and praying, obviously repulsed and not a part of the sexual mayhem that was taking place.

Gomez came forward to the weeping admiral and threw wine in his face to assure that he was fully awake. The grape stung his eyes as Gomez commanded, "Watch this, hero. See how I treat your perfect wife, you bastard!" And, Gomez, sporting another erection walked to the head of the cart and stuck it into Rosalita's mouth. As she gasped for air, with her head hung over the edge of the cart, he continued to thrust into her mouth as another soldier pumped her limp torso in the opposite direction. Her battered body writhed in a last act of survival. This movement only heightened the intensity of both men as they increased their efforts. Unable to breathe, she choked; life faded from Doña Rosalita. Her husband screamed in agony.

The appalling scene became too much for José to handle, and he lapsed again into unconsciousness, the numbness of his bound hands now cascading over his whole being. Then, the sudden release of his right arm and the feeling of losing his balance jarred him back into a cognizant state. His eyes were crusted with a combination of blood and mucous, but he forced them open to see the blurred, friendly face of Cousin León solemnly cutting away the ropes holding him to the cold, iron, gate. He held a finger to his lips to indicate silence to José.

A shiver swept over his naked body as he realized that it was now late at night and a cold breeze was blowing over him. Squinting into the darkness, José could see a large campfire in the middle of the courtyard with the soldiers sleeping in various positions around the perimeter.

As his eyes adjusted to the combination of firelight and moonlight, he could see the bodies of his mother and daughter still lying face up under the pile of broken pots and flowers. As his eyes searched the area closer to where he was leaning on León, he was even more shocked to see the bruised and violated body of his love, her eyes staring blankly into the heavens and her face frozen in a mask of terror.

Cousin León grabbed the groggy José as he fell from the gate and carried him quietly inside the main house. Once inside, León quickly swabbed the cuts, bruises, and open wounds that covered José's body. After giving him water, León carefully helped him into a pair of pants, boots, and a shirt. Meanwhile, José's mind was furiously plotting a course of violence.

The two men whispered to one another as José insisted upon gaining immediate revenge. "I have been forced to kill enemies in the name of Spain. Most of us claim to abhor murder, however, when our loved ones are involved, we look forward with delight for an opportunity to take the enemy's life," José quietly stated with a cruel coldness that brought a chill to León. It marked the first time that León had ever seen the "kill" in his cousin's eyes. José continued emphatically, "I will, this night, have my revenge!"

José laid out a plan for León to follow. León's responsibility was to check out the entire house to look for his little son and any others hiding in the building. Another objective for León was to knock unconscious and tie up the two cavalrymen who did not participate in the brutal violence. "I want them left as witnesses to tell what Gomez and his soldiers did here this day!" José snarled.

As the moon moved into the western sky, and the campfire was now glowing embers, José Gaspar silently moved among the drunken, sleeping cavalry with his garrote and sword. With the skill of a surgeon, he slipped the steel garrote around the neck of each sleeping man and, with a strength born of seething hatred, quickly jerked the deadly Spanish weapon, severing the head of the victim and allowing no cry of pain or plea for help. The feel of the razor sharp steel slicing cleanly to the vertebrae of each casualty gave José some measure of gratification.

This feeling of intense revenge continued to fuel José with a sense of euphoric satisfaction and gave him the energy to continue the noiseless slaughter through the rest of the night. Never before had he felt exhilaration in hot blood flowing over his hands. For the first time, taking the life of another felt and caused an adrenaline rush similar to a sexual orgasm. José now understood the "thrill of the kill."

As the eastern sky turned a pale pink, José had killed the men who had participated in the debacle, with the exception of their leader, snoring loudly barely ten feet from the body of José's dead daughter. Gomez was "dead to the world," a term that would soon be fact.

José was now filled with a frenzied energy as he kneeled over the sleeping Gomez. He removed his sword once again from his waist and with an experienced swing brought the blade down upon the backs of both of Gomez's calves severing tendons and striking the raw bones.

Gomez's outcry echoed throughout the valley. He attempted to jump to his feet, but instead crumpled to the ground. Gaspar wasted no time in plunging his sword into the fallen man's only good arm. When Gomez raised his left arm, the backhand slash of Gaspar's sword disjoined the hand from the arm. The severed hand flew into the fire with a sizzling sound.

Gomez looked up at Gaspar in terror as the now-brutal admiral took the garrote from his waist. Gomez began pleading for his life as blood flowed from his cut and amputated limbs. Gaspar smiled an icy smile, and replied, "Gomez, you showed me how lethal your cock could be, so I can think of no better weapon to kill you with."

The garrote encircled the cavalry captain's penis and José took great joy in pulling the two handles together, severing the captain's prized member. As it fell at his side, Gomez looked at it with complete bewilderment as he bent to grasp his penis with his handless arm.

José picked up the penis and held it, dripping blood, above Gomez' face. He shouted at the dying captain, "Now I am going to do to you what you did to my love. You will choke to death on your own penis."

With that, José pried open the mouth of Gomez and thrust the penis inside. He then leaned over him, squeezing the nostrils with his other hand. As the choking man fought to breathe, José whispered in his ear, "May your soul rot in hell! I shall, from this day, be the mortal enemy of any who pledges allegiance to the criminal crown of Spain."

To display his contempt of these men and the Spanish crown, José severed the heads of each of the dead cavalrymen. He then plunged their swords into the ground and impaled the severed heads on the handles. To add greater insult, Gaspar amputated their penises and without regard as to whose was whose, stuck one in each mouth. The two living cavalry-men captured and tied up by León, cried and begged for forgiveness as they witnessed this gory scene.

"I will spare your miserable lives, but you must tell the truth of what happened here," José said as he elicited a promise from each.

He then turned to the task of preparing his wife, mother, and daughter for burial. He went into the house to select their finest clothes, then loaded their bodies on the peddler's cart, which had represented such joy and such despair in his life, and hauled them to the creek where they had so often bathed and picnicked.

With tears streaming down his face, José gently washed each of the bodies and carefully dressed them in the clothes he had selected. He closed their eyes and closed Rosalita's mouth and kissed her lips. He was thank-ful that each looked at peace and that the terror on their faces had disap-peared. It was almost as if each were taking a siesta.

He then took the bodies back, loaded them on a carriage, harnessed the horses, and drove them to the rectory of the church in which they had been married so few years before. The kindly priest accepted the bodies and promised a Christian burial.

José returned to the carnage of the estate and heard, on his arrival, a barking dog. A flicker of a smile came to his face as he saw Lucky run-ning towards him and behind the dog, Carlos and León. León was hold-ing little José Pedro and anxious to tell José how the children had sur-vived by running from the estate to Carlo's mother's house when the rob-ber calvarymen had first appeared at the iron gate.

Quickly he packed some clothes, including the fine dress unform he had worn on his wedding day. José had decided they would proceed to Seville and the María Gonzalez estate as planned. The knowledge that his son was alive brought some measure of relief to José as he struggled to find any blessing in his ordeal.

In the afternoon, the wind picked up and sent heavy black clouds across the sky. José hugged his son to his chest to shield the child from the cold wind. He thought about how easy it was to protect loved ones from the elements and how difficult to shield them from death. As he wondered how to tell a two-year-old about death, a sharp pain knifed through him, cutting at his heart like a rapier.

As León handed him a torch to burn the main house, José crawled to the top of the carriage. He raised his face to the sky and in a loud, resolute voice, repeated his pledge as an oath, "Oh my God, please hear me. I,

José Gaspar, swear on the graves of my mother, wife, and daughter that from this day forward, I will be the enemy of Spain and to anyone who pledges allegiance to Spain!"

As they drove out of the gate, José looked out over the fields and the woods. He could almost see two lovers frolicking together. As the wind continued to blow, José felt that he could hear the sounds of Rosalita's laughter. He seemed to also feel her soft touch. Tears again stung his eyes, but he knew that it was time to turn his back on the comfort of these memories and begin a new life of revenge.

CHAPTER 36

Escape From Spain

"In order to form the perfect democracy, I must choose a select group of men of like mind and help them escape the miserable monarchy of Spain."
—José Gaspar, March 6, 1784

"Today is all we can be sure of. Tomorrow may never be," José sadly said to Cousin León as they journeyed slowly towards Seville and the estate of María Gonzalez. The expedition was forced to make many stops for food and water. Transporting a toddler, a boy and a hound over hundreds of miles was quite a task for two grown men. José quietly confided to his wise cousin, "Being alone scares me, León. I have never sought solitude in my life."

"Cousin, you will survive this crisis," León replied with an arm around his shoulder. "After awhile you will again be surrounded by many who will both serve and love you as I do."

"I know, my dear cousin, but the lesson I have learned that allows me to endure, is that each of us is really stronger than we believe." José sadly shook his head and continued, "But, since the loss of my beloved Rosalita, I am attempting to live without having a purpose. This must change, for I owe it to those who remain alive and depend upon me."

"I had the perfect life and didn't take full advantage of it. We can all have a perfect love if we realize that we must learn to view our mates as perfection in our own eyes," José said wistfully, with a clap on León's knee. "Rosalita was perfect in my eyes. I will not let my wrath toward Spain steal the memories of my complete marriage."

Because of the unusually long time the journey from Madrid to Seville had taken the small entourage, Godoy's henchman had already searched the estate of María Gonzalez prior to the group's arrival. María Gonzalez,

213

unaware that José was intending to come to Seville, was convincing in her denial of any knowledge as to his whereabouts when she talked to the troops and Major Emmanuel Ortíz, the commander.

Ortíz and his group had the estate under surveillance for the next week. Nothing unusual occurred and, just one hour before José's carriage approached the estate, Ortíz ordered his troops to return to their barracks in Seville. Luck was now on the side of the former Spanish admiral.

After arriving and discovering that he was being hunted by the crown's finest troops, José made arrangements for José Pedro, Carlos, and Lucky to stay at María's estate with one of the servant families. José sent León to visit with the Gaspar family's longtime priest. The monsignor was now in charge of the famous monastery of Las Cuevas, across the river from downtown Seville.

How ironic it would be if José Gaspar were a fugitive of Spain in the same monastery that held Christopher Columbus a prisoner for six months in 1499. Ah, history surely has a way of repeating itself, José thought to himself, *at least in the way distinguished Admirals are treated.*

Because of the intense manhunt, José could not stay with his child and the others. He would be forced to use the Las Cuevas monastery as his hideout as he went about the process of recruiting those who would want to join him in a rebellious adventure.

León asked where he expected to find men who would want to follow him, as he doubted they would find anyone of quality in Seville who would want to leave.

"I tell you, cousin, everyone who lives life to the fullest is a potential adventurer, José boomed as if from a pulpit, "Thanks to our repressive government bureaucracy and the unforgiving rich upper-class, our prisons are full of such adventurers. I like men and women of substance who have nothing to lose and everything to gain by following me!"

"José, you don't mean you are going to recruit your followers from prison?" León stammered.

"Yes, while you arrange for us to stay in the monastery, I will pack my trunk full of disguises, which will allow me access into and out of the naval prison in Seville," José replied. "I plan to select for our Confederation those who hate Spain as much as I do."

When León went to town to make the arrangements, José took his son in one arm, and put his other arm around Carlos' shoulders. With Lucky following closely behind, they walked to the patio where María had taught José all about love, insight, and understanding. María followed, knowing this would be José's last words with with his son for a long while.

As they sat in the shade with José holding his son in his lap, the dog romped around them, joyfully playing with anyone who would give him recognition. José smiled sadly, and stroked the little child's head.

"You know, there are three things we can learn from a dog that can make our lives worthwhile," José said so all could hear. "I want each of you to learn these lessons. The first thing is to be loyal to those you love. Next, never pretend to be something that you are not. The third thing is to always practice obedience when it is in your best interest."

"Is that all?" Carlos inquired.

"No, you should always welcome fresh air, feel the ecstasy of the wind in your face, and enjoy every moment of what nature gives you." José smiled, looking directly into Carlos's eyes. Then he looked at his young son, "And, whenever loved ones come home, even from a short journey, always run to greet them."

Later that afternoon, León returned with the news that he and José could stay at the monastery. As the sun was setting, they were seved a dish of chicken, beans and rice. After dinner, Carlos took José Pedro by the hand and, with a gray mist rising from the ground, disappeared into the field with Lucky running alongside.

José gave María most of the money he had and embraced her with both arms. He detested good-byes and profoundly regretted leaving his son and the others. As the sun disappeared below the horizon, a blue-gray twilight still illuminated the way. José looked longingly back as he and León rode toward the city of Seville.

"This way is better," José said as they rumbled off. "It is always easier to live through your child then it is to rejuvenate your own life once again. In my heart, I want to stay and watch young José grow, but my mind tells me that I need to be responsible for myself and that I can only be complete again when I grow independent of his needs. You and I must go and make something of our lives, while young José does the same here under the expert guidancc of María."

For the next three weeks, José indeed became a man of many disguises as he made three separate visits to the heavily-guarded Seville Naval Prison in the older part of this riverfront port city.

In order to determine when the guard changed and to learn visiting procedures, the slight, former admiral dressed alternately as a nun, a whore, and an old mother. As he questioned the officers and guards of the prison, he was obviously convincing. Dressed in the nun's habit, José was able to discover information about the shift changes and the personalities of the officers in charge.

While dressed as a whore, José felt disgust towards the soldiers as they attempted to grope him, though he understood why. He was more angered by their condescending attitude toward a working woman, in spite of the profession. While he was wearing his black wig and a riding outfit, he flirted with the officer of the day, who worked Monday, Wednesday, and Thursday afternoons. This officer, puffed up with his own self-importance, told many secrets to "the whore" simply for the privilege of caressing her back and hips. This fat, ugly, mustached major would be the key person to unwittingly aid José in getting a crew of men from the prison.

In his motherly role, José was able to attract the attention of one of the enlisted jailers. The female-garbed José created a distraction by deliberately spilling a basket of fresh-baked rolls that "she" was was bringing to her imprisoned cousin. While the young jailer was helping pick up the rolls from under the desk, José quickly slipped one of the main gate keys from the large key ring on the desk, and slid the key into the pocket of his apron. Now, if he became trapped in the jail, he would be able to escape.

That same afternoon, he needed to use the key when Manuel Godoy and a troop of Asturias Cavalry entered the prison. José, still disguised as a matron, was looking over the list of prisoners on the desk of the absent prison guard. Since no women were permitted in that area, José was forced to quickly shed his dress and escape down a corridor to the outer door. This would be the first of three close calls with the vengeful Godoy in the Seville prison.

The following morning, a Tuesday, José appeared at the prison very early dressed in his admiral's uniform. Dressed in his finest, Cousin León, who was not at that point in time a fugitive, accompanied José on these dangerous visits. Before appearing at the prison gate, José had questioned his friendly guard as to why Manuel Godoy had appeared at the prison. The guard could tell him nothing.

Because of Godoy personally assuming leadership in the hunt for Gaspar, it was necessary for José to select a crew, effect an escape, capture a ship, and leave Seville in as short a time as possible. Since no one at the prison knew why Godoy and his henchmen had visited the prison, José took the bold step of assuming that Godoy did not want anyone to know of the massacre of innocents at Gaspar's estate.

"We must doubt everyone we meet; but we must never doubt ourselves," José whispered to León. "Selecting our crew will now be limited to those officers and men with the longest sentences and the most to gain by joining us."

"Recruiting talented people, capable of doing many jobs, is the first task," he continued. "They will be able to fill the gaps in our knowledge and capabilities. We need to recruit able and ambitious seamen. Truly gifted people can learn any task. We want and need people who are excited not only with our vision but excited about learning as well."

"José, are you really hoping to find perfect candidates in a prison?" León asked skeptically. "Shouldn't we simply find men we can use to fill the slots needed to steal a ship and sail from here?

"I want only exceptional people for my crew, not mediocre ones," José shot back angrily, "I prefer having someone who is inexperienced but capable and willing to learn. I would rather have a position vacant than to have one who is merely ordinary fill the slot. If we sail with average people, we are in danger. We cannot fulfill our ultimate dream with average people."

"José, as long as I have known you, you have been biased toward intelligence over experience." León shook his head. "I can't argue with your philosophy, but I do worry about finding such men in a prison!"

"Prisons have always been filled with talented people, some of whom can work together and others who are individual problem solvers. When nations have too many laws and rigid bureaucracies, there are even more creative people in prison," José laughed as the pair boldly marched into the prison.

All afternoon on Tuesday and late into the evening, José and León met with prisoners at the naval prison. The prison officials brought prisoners with leadership experience and the longest sentences to "Adm. José Rodriquez" and his aide de camp.

These officials were satisfied that the admiral was officially sanctioned to interview prisoners for a potential "suicide mission" for Spain. José had forged documents, including one with the signature of Navy Minister FloridaBlanca, by taking orders from FloridaBlanca's personal items and copying them onto official stationary. He even took the signature and wax seal from the documents that had appointed him an admiral years before.

At the end of the first day, José and León had picked twenty prisoners, including two American shipbuilders from Mystic, Connecticut, who had been arrested by Spain on board a British frigate. They had been impressed into service on the British naval vessel during the American Revolution. Gaspar chose them because he felt their shipbuilding skills would be important. José also believed that, upon the Confederation's arrival in North America, these two Americans might help him design and build the ships he envisioned. His ships would be constructed of American lumber instead of the damn teak used to construct the Spanish ships.

Each time that José encountered a prisoner who was hesitant about joining their adventure, he would first describe the warm subtropical islands with white sand and azure waters to gain their interest. If the man still refused, José would appeal to his survival instinct stating, "You have to fight for freedom, otherwise you will die. You need to be a survivor in order to have a life worth living."

Before they left the prison late on Wednesday evening, José notified the same major he had first met when dressed as a whore, that he and León would return on Thursday night, after the evening mess, to assemble his men and march to the Navy quay.

"But, Sir, ships never sail from a port on Friday," the major said.

"Exactly, Major," José retorted, "but since this is a secret mission for the crown, we must sail when no other ships will be leaving the Port of Seville and quickly make our way out to open sea."

Fortunately, the major didn't question the point, and José quickly left the prison office to go back to the Las Cuevas monastery and his last night on Spanish soil.

Late on Thursday afternoon, as the sun was beginning its descent, José appeared at the prison to sign the orders that would release the selected men to his custody. He carried with him the forged signature of FloridaBlanca.

A select group of forty-one prisoners were fed, given dress uniforms, and marched into the exercise yard to be turned over to José and León.

As darkness enveloped Seville, Adm. José Gonsalvo Rodriquez marched three columns of "naval officers" dressed in Spanish uniforms down the narrow streets. The forty-one men passed within fifteen feet of a beautiful carriage and attendants parked in front of the prison commandant's residence. The warden was hosting a dinner party for Manuel Godoy and Minister FloridaBlanca.

José hid his entourage in one of the many empty warehouses across the street from the docks while he searched the waterfront for the vessel. In minutes, José found the ship that would signal to Spain his intentions to become the archenemy of the monarchy.

Dominating the surrounding buildings, the *FloridaBlanca* stood proudly at the wharf. This handsome flagship weighing 2,550 tons, had three decks and carried one hundred cannon with long-range twenty-four pounders composing the main gun battery. She was higher and broader than most ships, which made her somewhat slower and less maneuervable.

The *FloridaBlanca* was steered by a tiller, fifteen feet long, operated by a rope and tackle from the wheel on the quarterdeck.

She was the pride of the Spanish Navy—179 feet long, twenty-four feet wide and with a draft of fourteen feet. Her three masts contained 13,000 square feet of canvas sail.

José returned to his men and informed them that shortly after midnight they would march quietly to the *FloridaBlanca* and board the ship. He would present the officer of the watch with counterfeit orders and, since the ship would have only a skeleton crew on board at that early hour, the men would be able to quickly spread through the ship and capture all hands. José would take care of the officer of the deck and any others with him. The sailors on board the *FloridaBlanca* would then have the option to either join them or be bound and left in the vacant warehouse on shore. The ship's officers also would have a choice: to join the Confederation or meet their death.

The plan worked perfectly, as the watch officer and his two seamen were sound asleep when José strode in to loudly slam the fake orders on the table. While still half-asleep, the officer looked over the papers and nodded. By this time, the prisoners had taken control of the others on board the *FloridaBlanca*.

When José broke into the captain's quarters, he was shocked to find his old friend and mentor, Capt. Pedro Sanibel, asleep in bed. After waking him, José gave him a big hug. Sanibel smiled, returned the embrace, and asked in a husky voice, "My son, what in God's name are you doing in my cabin at this time of night?"

"My good friend and captain, I have come to liberate your ship and those members of your crew who wish to join us, as we sail to form a new confederation, throwing off the cloak of foolish nationalism," José boasted as he rose from the captain's bed and put a hand out to help the senior captain rise.

"You are hijacking my ship!" Sanibel exploded, "No one can commandeer a ship which I captain. I cannot allow you to do this!"

"The choice is not yours to make, my friend," Gaspar calmly replied. "Your ship is already in the good hands of my crew."

"Then you must kill me, José, for I am a loyal patriot of Spain." Sanibel continued, "for me patriotism is not an emotional moment but a lifetime of dedication to serving my country."

"The crown has done me a great disservice. Through it I have lost those people dearest to my heart and have become a hunted fugitive. My ideals, dedication, and allegiance are now to a higher organization," José emphatically answered, "but I will respect your wishes to shed your blood for Spain, even if I don't understand it."

After Captain Sanibel realized the futility of trying to dissuade José, he looked directly into José's eyes and said deliberately, "You, of all people, know that I will never surrender my ship. I have no respect for captains who do not go down with their vessel. You know that you must kill me. I trust that your cause is just."

The two men shared a glass of rum. Sanibel went to his wardrobe and got dressed in his finest uniform. José hugged Sanibel with tears in his eyes. The old man smiled sadly and quietly stated, "If you want to be successful in stealing my ship, then we best get up on deck and get the unpleasantness over with."

"Before we go, is there anything I can do?" José whispered.

"Give this letter to one of my men so it can get to my daughters and grandchildren." Captain Sanibel answered, handing a brown envelope to José.

On deck, Gaspar walked the gallant old veteran to the gangway and announced that any officers and men who wished to join the new adventure could stay on board and receive one share in the new Confederation. Those officers who did not would meet a death similar to the one they were about to witness.

With that, José turned, and one last time asked Captain Sanibel to surrender his ship and to join the new Confederation. José's admiration and respect for his old friend was boundless as Sanibel proved his duty, honor, and loyalty to Spain by standing erectly and steadfastly refusing to surrender.

With tears in his eyes, José then pulled his sword from its scabbard and ran it through the heart of his former mentor. Sanibel stared at his protégé and smiled peacefully before his eyes went blank in a mask of death. He had given José a final lesson in the dignity of death for one's ideals, a lesson that José would not forget.

Gaspar ordered the old captain and the other dead officers to be placed carefully on the dock. He then covered the body of his hero with a Spanish flag.

As the sky began to lighten in the east, wind filled the sails of the pirated warship as she headed out of the harbor. At Gaspar's direction a sign painter was preparing to replace the name *FloridaBlanca* with *Doña Rosalita*.

CHAPTER 37

Forming the True Democracy

"We go forth with the expectation of forming a true democracy,
one that provides for the common defense and the wealth, health, safety,
and welfare of all members of this Confederation."
—José Gaspar, also known as Gasparilla, March 1784

Three days out from Seville, following morning mass, José strolled to the stern on the quarterdeck and leaned back to watch approvingly as the finishing touches were being placed upon the ship's name plate. The gold leaf of the plate shone in the sunlight above the windows of his cabin.

The two Americans from Connecticut joined him for coffee as he sat in his chair behind the helmsman. They gazed into the clouds of bulging canvas matching the puffy white clouds in the bright blue sky. The *Doña Rosalita* was heading west and had picked up a good wind, which moved it effortlessly over the sparkling whitecaps.

"We wanted to thank you for rescuing us," the younger American spoke first. "We had just gone to sea in our whaler when the British captured us. They took only four of us off the ship, the youngest and strongest. We were treated worse on the British ship than we were treated in the Spanish prison after our capture."

"Tell me about yourselves. I am a fan of the American sailor and shipbuilder," José said leaning back in his chair with his arms over his head. "It is a damn shame that your Continental Navy is in the process of selling off the warships and merchant ships that were instrumental in winning your independence."

"I didn't know the Continental Congress was selling our Navy," the older American, Thomas Green, angrily replied. "How can a nation with so much dependence upon the sea not possess a strong navy?"

"I cannot answer why you Americans do many of the things you do," José laughed. "I do know that your country has an abundance of natural resources and talented citizens. Tell me about your Mystic seaport."

"Aye, Captain, the village is located on the Mystic River. It is a small fishing and whaling community. Many of the farmers who have settled in our area are also excellent shipwrights."

"That is of great interest to me. Are either of you shipwrights?" José inquired, leaning forward in the chair.

Both nodded assent. The three men moved closer as José explained his "plan" about how the citizens of Mystic could serve the new proposed Confederation and increase their village's income at the same time.

"You see, in the summer your accomplished shipwrights could tend their farms. Then, in the fall, after the crops have been picked, you could build ships of my design with your famous oak woods. During the cold winter, you could sail them down to either the Caribbean Islands or Florida. We will pay you cash for the sloops and you will be back in Connecticut in time for spring planting. During the harshest part of your winters, you and your Mystic citizens could be enjoying blue skies, warm breezes and beautiful beaches." José smiled with a great deal of satisfaction at his impromptu proposal to these Americans.

"It does sound like a workable plan," the younger American stated. "I wonder if it is legal to deal with such a Confederation?"

"I intend to build a better democracy than the one you Americans claim to have," José answered. "As to dealing with us, it is my sincere desire that the Americans will want to do business with us. We will be taking no aggressive action toward American shipping and, in fact, will be protective of them. No, I see no problems with your country working with the Confederacy. Besides, they are selling their Navy so they may well need us more than we need them."

With that, further discussion was held and José's proposal was firmly incorporated.

"Where are we heading, Captain?" Thomas Green asked.

"To see the Fat Virgin," José slapped the back of the Yankee. "Actually, Christopher Columbus must get the credit for that name. We are sailing to the English islands in the area of Virgin Gorda."

"Will the British accept us?" Green questioned.

"Without a doubt. The British are above all else, good businessmen," José replied. "They have always permitted piracy so long as they saw the financial benefit. Besides, we will be attacking Spanish shipping, which makes us allies against the worst enemy of the English.

"When I was in Paris, I had the distinct honor and privilege to read many of the letters and writings of your Thomas Jefferson, whom I admire greatly" José said. "I want to pattern the articles of our Confederation after his writings in the American Declaration of Independence. The only difference is that our people will believe it and live it, not simply mouth it. Yes, our Confederation will include the second paragraph of your Declaration. I will write in our Confederation preamble the following ideals, 'All men are created equal and endowed by God with inalienable rights.' Our Confederation will exist to secure these rights for all men and women, regardless of color or country of origin. The only just authority of any government, including our Confederation, is the consent of the governed. We shall vote on every issue with each person having a vote."

"This seems a little idealistic, doesn't it?" Green replied sarcastically.

"It may be. It may be. But, I tell you that if an idealistic vision is not a part of any type of organization, that organization will certainly not become anything of importance," José thoughtfully replied. "Besides, we shall write into our Confederation preamble that when it fails to protect our individual rights or fails to recognize our consent to be governed, the members shall have the right to alter or abolish it. Yes, an organization of any democratic base must allow for revolution, either actual or through the democratic ballot procedure. When any form of government becomes oppressive to the people, those governed have a natural right to revolt against that government."

"Isn't the United States a democracy?" the younger American inquired.

"Not really, my friend. Your country is a republic, well organized and well founded, but, still a republic," José said emphatically. "Nowhere in your Declaration of Independence, your Constitution, or your Bill of Rights is the word 'democracy' even written. I have personally met Benjamin Franklin, John Jay, and Thomas Jefferson and they are noble men and great statesman. However, they have crafted a true republic, not a democracy. My Confederation will be the only true democracy in North America. This may cause the Americans to either envy or hate us."

"I don't think Americans will be threatened or envious of *your* enterprise," Green replied caustically. "We have a great country."

"I would hope the Americans would follow the Bible's teaching and love their neighbors," José laughed, "for our Confederation intends on geographically becoming their neighbor. What concerns me is that the Bible also tells us to love our enemies. I wonder whether this is an example of God's understanding that oftentimes our neighbors and enemies are the same."

After a long silence, his eyes became melancholy as he predicted, "The Americans will not like us because we will treat every man and woman, regardless of color or creed as equals within our Confederation. They profess many things but often do not believe in what they say. In the end, I fear they will not tolerate us as a close neighbor."

The following week, on a sunny Tuesday morning, José gathered all the men on the main deck of the *Doña Rosalita*. He stood, in a full dress uniform devoid of Spanish trappings, to read the Articles of Confederation that he had drafted using many of the words of Thomas Jefferson.

Before introducing the articles to the officers and crew, José spoke of his personal choice in this manner to all on the deck. "The story of Spanish Admiral José Gaspar's life began the day Princess Doña Rosalita came into his life. José Gaspar's life ended the day Spain took her precious life from him. From this day forward I shall be known by only two names. To the people of the world, I will known as Gasparilla. To the monarchies and nations of the world, I will be recognized as the king of all privateers. I will give all members in good standing of this Confederation a Letter of Marque, which will insure that your lives will not be taken, without due process, for your actions on behalf of this Confederation. With those who shall join us, we will become the largest democratic force in the world.

"One day I will be compared with my hero, Richard the Lionhearted, called Richard Coeur de Lion by the French. He was a great king whose tragic life I am re-living. I will also be called a lion king—the King Lion."

"Although I would like everyone to agree with me, the problem with complete agreement is that only a few people are actually thinking. Honest human nature does not permit true consensus. If you cannot live with these Articles and Laws, than we shall understand and drop you off at our first port of call on Virgin Gorda," Gasparilla continued.

"I shall now read the preamble and our Articles of Confederation. By noon tomorrow, I expect those of you who wish to join to make your mark or sign this document."

Articles of Confederation and Declaration of Independence

When in the Course of human events, it becomes necessary for one people to dissolve the political bonds which have connected them with any nation, and to assume among the powers of the earth, the separate and equal station which the Laws of Nature and of Nature's God entitle them, a decent respect to the opinions of mankind requires that they should declare the causes which impel them to the separation.

We hold these truths to be self-evident, that all men are created equal, that they are endowed by their Creator with certain unalienable Rights, which among these are Life, Liberty, and the pursuit of Happiness. That to secure these rights, a system of government is instituted among men and women, deriving their just powers from the consent of the governed. That whenever any Form of Government becomes destructive of these ends, it is the Right of the People to alter or to abolish it, and to institute new Government, laying its foundation on such principles and organizing its powers in such form, as to them shall seem most likely to effect their Safety and Happiness.

Prudence, indeed, will dictate that Governments long established should not be changed for light and transient causes.

But, it remains the right of the citizens of this Confederation; it is their duty, to throw off such Government, and to provide new Guards for their future security.

Confederation Code of Honor

1. Every man and woman who is a member of this Confederation or subdivision will have an equal vote on any and all matters brought to a vote.
2. All members of the Confederation are expected to attend and vote when a vote has been called.
3. Independence and Freedom require that income be gained by the Confederation. Therefore, if no prey or plunder is taken, no one shall be paid.
4. All merchandise, money, jewelry, valuables, or other sources of income acquired from a prize is to be turned over immediately upon capture, in good condition, to the Confederation for sharing.
5. Shares. The Confederation will receive ten shares for the common good and the defense, health, safety, and welfare of all members of the Confederation or subdivision.
   · The Captain of each ship will receive two shares, the Quartermaster two shares.
   · The boatswain and master gunner, one and one-half shares.
   · All other officers of the ship will receive one and one-quarter shares.
   · All other members, including musicians, shall receive one share of the total.

6. All men and women of the Confederation will follow orders, obey the laws, and shall learn to read and write.
7. Each man shall keep his personal weapons clean, sharpened, and ready for action.
8. All men and women shall be responsible for weapons and supplies assigned to their mess to include cleanliness, maintenance, and replacement when necessary.
9. All lanterns, candles, and fires will be extinguished at dusk.
10. No smoking on board ship.
11. No gambling with cards or dice for money or valuables while at sea.
12. No fighting among members of the Confederation at any time.
13. Women or men who are not members of the Confederation are not permitted on board ship or in restricted areas on land.
14. Musicians are expected to play every day except Sunday.
15. Each member of the Confederation shall eat only his daily allotment of food and drink while at sea. This applies to food allotments provided by the Confederation. Food, drink, and other consumables from a prize shall be distributed at the discretion of the captain and in accordance with shares established by the Confederation.
16. Members of the Confederation who marry shall live in an area separate from unmarried members while on land. No single members of the Confederation are permitted into married areas unless invited by the head of the household.

Rules and Penalties for Infractions

1. Desertion from the Confederation in time of battle will result in death.
2. Desertion or abandoning one's post may result in offender being marooned.
3. Fighting or causing a fight or disruption will result in forty lashes upon the bare back.
4. Stealing from another Confederation member will be punished according to trial by his mates, and punishment will range from a simple fine to marooning or death.
5. Laziness or lack of performing of responsibilities will result in possible loss of membership and banishment/marooning.

Confederation Responsibility to Members

1. Any member of the Confederation who loses an arm, leg, or

sight in battle shall receive a cash settlement of not less than $1,000.00 and shall be given on shore responsibilities that will earn him an annual income.

2. The Confederation will match any money saved by active members up to $500.00 per twelve-month period.

3. The Confederation guarantees the income of older citizens by providing new occupations as they grow older. For example, from gunner to cook onboard ship to warehouse worker on shore. All income will remain at a full share to the citizen.

"Always remember, my comrades, one of the greatest joys in the world is to begin a new adventure," Gasparilla shouted to his men. "Absolute power corrupts men. Our democracy will limit us to the will of the majority at all times."

"But, who is to say that a majority of our rank will not take from each of us some of our personal liberty," Marcos Carbonel, a former lieutenant on a man-of-war, yelled back.

"We have taken care to insure that our democracy is not simply marked by free elections," Gasparilla answered slowly so all could understand his words, "but by a rule of law as well. We shall also have an impartial judicial system that will protect the basic liberties of speech, property, and even religion. I can tell you that if a democracy does not preserve individual liberty, the fact that it is a democracy is of little consequence."

"And, we will be equals with former slaves and women as well?" Carbonel continued his hard questioning.

"Our Confederation emphasizes utilizing the strengths of each individual," Gasparilla responded emphatically. He then boomed with emotion, "When we utilize everyone's strengths we are all operating as equals. We will rise to excellence if that is what we demand of ourselves. If we expect the best from people and they respond by giving their best, then we will view them as equals. Remember, no man can govern another man without his consent."

"But, even the slaves?" Carbonel protested.

"Brotherhood is a matter about character, not color!" Gasparilla angrily shouted back.

"What about this learning to read and write?" Umberto Moreno, master gunner asked in a serious voice. "You expect everyone in the Confederation to read, write, and think?"

"Everything good that happens comes from thinking," Gasparilla replied. "Success in any endeavor is the result of positive, not negative, thinking. We must educate everyone to think if we want them and our Confederation to be successful. There can be no doubt that the principle of free thought is most important, not only for those who agree with us but also for those who disagree with us. This is what will ultimately make us as strong as we can be."

"Can we command those who think for themselves?" Moreno asked.

"Don't give commands you can't enforce," Gasparilla answered, "Jean Martinet, one of the most innovative officers in all history, believed that you must have discipline and a mission which all understand. It is far wiser to have intelligent, thinking officers and men. It is not wise for us to try to keep the advantages of an education only for ourselves."

The men asked additional questions for several hours and by the time the evening mess was served, most appeared satisfied.

Gasparilla called a meeting in his quarters later that night with Jesús Herrera who had served as both a quartermaster on a ship as well as a staff commander of the supply warehouses in Seville.

They decided that Confederation ships would offer a menu of food and drink that would cost the Confederation about thirty cents per person per day. More important, the men would be healthy and ready for battle if they were fed well. The following menu was designed for ships at sea:

Monday: One pound of salt pork, ½ pint of peas or beans, and ½ pound of cheese

Tuesday: One and ½ pounds of salt beef and one pound of potatoes

Wednesday: One pint of rice, ½ pound of cheese or beans

Thursday: One and ½ pounds of salt pork and potatoes

Friday: One and ½ pound of salt fish, one pound of potatoes and molasses

Saturday: One and ½ pounds of salt pork, one pint of peas or beans, and ½ pound of cheese

Sunday: Two pounds of salt beef, one pint of rice or potatoes, and dessert

In addition, men would get one pound of hard bread and one quart of beer or spirits, including rum or whiskey every day.

"This should provide our crews with enough sustenance to be in sailing and fighting trim," Herrera declared.

With the Articles of Governance and organizational items approved before the week's end, the *Doña Rosalita* entered the harbor on Virgin Gorda and was given a warm welcome by the British governor.

As Gasparilla pondered where to obtain a crew of approximately four hundred men for the *Doña Rosalita*, he began calculating the provisions that would be needed for the menu they had prepared, and the expense of equipping a large vessel for any length of time at sea.

As he had done on many other voyages, he based his calculations on keeping the ship at sea for a year, then asked Lieutenant Herrera to verify his figures. They agreed that feeding the *Doña Rosalita*'s crew would take: 325 barrels of salt beef, 325 barrels of salt pork, 16,000 pounds of rice, 2,000 pounds of butter, 1,500 pounds of cheese, 1,200 gallons of molasses, 1,800 gallons of vinegar, 250 bushels of dried beans, 55 barrels of flour, 50 barrels of Indian meal, 60 tons of hard bread, 20,000 pounds of salt fish, 750 bushels of potatoes, 9,000 gallons of rum, and 8,000 gallons of beer.

"Very few people realize what it takes to keep a ship at sea. I tell you, Lieutenant Herrera, the real money to be made on the sea is in the outfitting and supplying of a ship!" Gasparilla exclaimed. "If one owned a provision company, some taverns, a clothier, and a bordello, he would have it all."

"Gasparilla, if this Confederation becomes what you say it will, it would be wise to operate Confederation businesses to supply not only our needs but also those of other seaman who might visit our ports," Herrera suggested quite seriously.

"You are right!" Gasparilla agreed. "Besides, it would provide a productive outlet for those members of the Confederation who are too young or too old for the sea. We could also grow our own vegetables, raise our own cattle, and provide our own fishing craft. Would you be interested in overseeing such an operation, Lieutenant?"

"Yes, sir. I'm tired of being at sea. I'd like to bring my wife and son to a place where we could live together," Herrera replied enthusiastically.

"Then, by damned, we shall organize a program to provide our own sources of supply and entertainment. If we find it is not economical, then we can simply form a partnership with those who currently provide services or supplies and offer them protection in return for selling us what we need at a lower cost," Gasparilla said.

"Yes, Captain, then when either the Spanish or British are harassing local fishermen or merchants, we could simply move in and provide a defense against such actions," Herrera suggested.

"Exactly! The strength of our Confederation shall be in providing a common defense to all who participate in our elective democracy," Gasparilla stated emphatically.

CHAPTER 38

First Revenge, the Sinking of a Spanish Troopship

"Revenge is like experiencing the joy of killing a bull that has gored you."
—Gasparilla, June 5, 1784

As the morning winds picked up and the *Doña Rosalita* began moving effortlessly through the waves, Gasparilla found that a number of his men were upset and angry. The day was turning unusually hot and the sweating men were arguing with one another.

"What seems to be the problem?" Gasparilla asked.

"Sir, we are officers and educated men, and we are forced to work like slaves on this ship. Some of us were better off in prison in Seville!" Francisco Sosa, a tall, well-built former marine captain argued.

"Then you are learning a good lesson," Gasparilla began, to the astonishment of the irate men surrounding him. "The key to being a leader is to have empathy for those you lead. One can only learn empathy by doing their job. In this case, you are doing hot, dirty, distasteful work that you never imagined yourself attempting and now we all know what it is like. When we have a crew for you to lead, you will understand why the men react as they do to your commands. You will have emotional identification!"

Gasparilla continued while the tension lessened, "We toss about words by the thousands to the winds with little thought to their meanings. Very few of you have ever given thought to what all those words and phrases actually mean to those forced to listen to them day after day. When you use the phrase 'between the devil and the deep blue sea' or 'the devil to pay' do you really know what the deckhand feels? You know that the devil is the longest seam in a ship but now, since you have had to caulk or pay it yourselves, you know why it was named that by the poor souls who caulked it before. You are experiencing one of the hottest and most unpleasant jobs on the ship and learning how uncomfortable and nearly impossible it is to squat or stoop to try to get this job done."

At that moment, one of the lookouts shouted that a ship was off the starboard bow, and the men raced to the gunwales. On the horizon, where the endless blue water joined the matching sky, the silhouette of the ship appeared.

Gasparilla dashed to the binnacle, got his glass, and began yelling commands to the helmsman and the officer of the deck, Lt. Antonio Hernández, to bring the ship around to a more direct course with the potential prize. As he looked through the telescope, he quickly estimated the ship to be less than one hundred feet long, probably twenty feet wide with a deck of approximately seventy-five feet. The sail area looked about two thousand square feet and she was fully under sail. Gasparilla shouted that he estimated her tonnage at around one hundred tons and to record the information in the ship's log.

As the *Doña Rosalita* edged ever closer to the ship, Gasparilla further noted she was black-hulled, square-rigged and flying the flag of England. The ship appeared heavy-laden and showed much sign of wear and tear. He had seen these ships before and his heart grew heavy as he realized it was another slave ship. His mind pictured the hold full of chained black bodies stinking with sweat and their own waste in this heat. He recalled the slavers he was forced to escort earlier, and the agonizing torment and tragedy caused to these innocent souls.

"Sir, you were describing sea phrases," said Francisco Sosa as he ran up to Gasparilla. "On board that slaver are as many shelves as possible to haul the slaves. Because the hull is packed with humanity as its cargo, the captain and crew build themselves small man-size hutches on the upper deck as sleeping places. Staying in those hot, stinking boxes is called 'being in the dog house.'"

"Very good, Sosa," Gasparilla nodded, "Now, prepare our 'officer-slaves' for battle and we can capture a crew for this ship so you'll not find yourself 'between the devil and the deep blue sea.'"

The crew of the *Doña Rosalita* sprang into action and proved again that Gasparilla was a genius in selecting able seamen, as some of the former officers and gentlemen scrambled up the ropes and others manned the gun decks. In order to give the appearance of a full crew, the gunners moved from cannon to cannon, loading all with powder charges but only the swivel cannon and the long-range twenty-four pounders with actual shot. Gasparilla's plan was to create terror among the crew on board the slaver by apparently unleashing a full barrage of artillery when, in fact, no shots would initially land upon the prize. If it did not strike its colors, cannon balls would be loaded, the pirates' red flag would be run up the mid-mast giving notice of no quarter, and the slaver would be sunk.

"If we cannot save the unfortunate slaves without injury, they are better off drowned at sea than inhumanely sold at the slave market!" Gasparilla shouted.

Just before he gave the order to commence all firepower, Gasparilla was astonished to see through his glasses the red hair of the slaver's captain. It had to be a woman, for even though men wore their hair in ponytails or beribboned queues, this was no man. This captain had a bosom and José recognized the defiant stance in an instant.

"Hold your fire!" Gasparilla commanded. "I know this captain and her ship. Stand ready at your stations and be ready to commence fire if we are fired upon. She will either submit or go down fighting. Raise the white flag of truce."

Within the hour, the two ships gently rocked within yards of each other. By now both ship's captains had recognized each other. The slaver was the *Irish Lady II* and her captain was Brutal Betsy. Both captains were relieved that a flag of truce had brought them reluctantly but peacefully together, but each knew the other was willing to die on the spot rather than be taken captive.

Gasparilla and his officers lowered the longboat and began rowing towards the *Irish Lady II*. To those of Gasparilla's men who had not previously dealt with slavers, the smell was the first sense to be assailed. The sickening odor seemed to combine the smell of rotting fish and vegetables with that of human excrement as they rowed closer. Their ears were then subjected to plaintive moaning, crying, and screaming from the throats of those lying chained in the hull of this decrepit ship. But the impact on the boarding party's senses of smell and hearing was nothing compared to what they would see on board this sad ship of imprisoned Africans.

Gasparilla boarded first and greeted the *Irish Lady II's* quartermaster, a swarthy ugly man in high-buckled shoes, knee britches, and long black hair. The muscular sailor wore his tricorn hat in such a manner to shield his eyes from the afternoon sun.

Within minutes, Brutal Betsy emerged from her cabin where she apparently had gone to comb her red hair and primp a bit for Gasparilla. She looked out of place with the dismal and stark background of her ship. She ran up to José and gave him a big hug. After one look, Gasparilla was once again filled with desire for her as he took in her excessive cleavage and enjoyed having her robust breasts pressed against him.

José whispered, "Ah, Betsy, when I am with you, I cannot think of the other men who have known you, including my friend, Miguel. When I last saw you, you were with him in the slave market in Cuba, but we have all sailed many miles since then. And one more thing, you need to know that I am no longer José Gaspar to the world. I am now called Gasparilla. We have formed a Confederation and I urge you to abandon this ugly business and join us in the sweet trade." He ran his fingers through her thick hair.

"I would love to do it," Betsy responded enthusiastically, "but what of my present ship and its condition?" She hugged him tightly and pressed her hips to his.

"If you decide to join us, you will help me pick men capable of becoming both crew members and Confederation citizens from your crew, as well as from the Africans you have on board," Gasparilla stated. "Remember, I want only men or women who are bright, talented and able to learn, regardless of their color!"

"And, the remainder?" she asked quietly.

"You will put the remaining captives ashore on Hispañiola and allow the members of your crew not selected for the Confederation to continue on with an empty hold to Havana," Gasparilla stated. "They will then be able to make their own decisions. We will have our American friends from Mystic build you a new, faster *Irish Lady III*."

"From Mystic?" Betsy asked.

"Yes, the American shipbuilders are working with our designs," Gasparilla exclaimed proudly.

"And, just what kind of ships are these?" she asked.

"They will be built for speed and power. These Mystic shipbuilders will build them of flush-deck configuration with no tall quarterdeck or poop deck to impede their speed," José continued with excitement creeping again into his voice. "We will keep these ships low since we will not be at sea for great lengths of time and need not be overly concerned with hurricanes or severe seas. Because I intend to operate around the Keys of La Florida, we will keep their draft at no more than twelve feet fully loaded. Their rigging and sails will resemble a schooner with forward jib sails and lateen mizzen. With their shallow draft and high rigging, they'll be able to sail over shallow areas and shoals with great speed. And, in combat, they will be very maneuverable. And, you, Brutal Betsy shall captain the very first one built!"

"That seems a good deal!" Brutal Betsy answered, touching José's beard with her finger.

"I may also call on you to introduce me to some key naval figures, such as Commodore John Barry, the father of the American Navy. I understand you are both from Ireland."

"Tis true," said Betsy, "I will arrange a meeting."

At that point, a smiling Francisco Sosa, who was accompanying Cousin León said, "We have learned this day how many of our sea phrases become commonplace. In the timber trade a cut wooden plank is called 'a deal' and when you are lucky enough to get a good plank of usable quality, it is called a 'good deal.' Now we use that phrase not only when playing cards but in our everyday replies as well."

"Maybe I can accompany the fearless Captain Gasparilla back to his ship and tonight, by the light of the blue moon, have him take me down to the gun deck," Brutal Betsy said with a seductive smile.

"Yes, my dear cousin Gasparilla," León began with a wink, "and if what then transpired might produce a son, we could rightfully call the child, 'a son of a gun.' Another sea phrase we use loosely on land."

The boarding party from the *Doña Rosalita* left the *Irish Lady II* without Brutal Betsy, who stayed to help León and Sosa select a crew for Gasparilla.

The moon that night was full and as Gasparilla looked up at it, his thoughts turned from despair and sorrow at having lost Rosalita, to more prurient, earthly thoughts of women like Brutal Betsy. He shook his head and tried to focus on the needs of the new Confederation.

By the end of the third day riding at anchor near the *Irish Lady II*, a crew had been selected and brought on board the *Doña Rosalita*. Gasparilla had each of those chosen swim from one ship to the other. This served two purposes; to cleanse their filth and to see if they could swim.

After twenty-five days of intensive training, the men were becoming a disciplined crew. With only a few exceptions, it appeared that Gasparilla and the *Doña Rosalita* had a competent sailing, if not battle-tested, team.

Only one incident tested the new Confederation's rules. One of the *Irish Lady II's* former sailors, Humberto Hernández, allegedly stole a knife and coin from Anthony Perez, one of the officers that Gasparilla had selected from Seville's prison. In retaliation, Perez attacked Hernández and a fight ensued on the main deck.

Confederation rules prohibited stealing and carried a possible punishment for marooning. The Confederation rules also provided for up to forty lashes upon the back for fighting or starting a fight. As a result, two juries of the crew's peers were chosen and a trial was scheduled for the following morning.

The Hernández trial was held first and it took very little time for the newcomer to be found guilty as charged. The jury left the punishment to the discretion of Captain Gasparilla. Since Gasparilla felt that a democracy was only as good as the judiciary that enforces its laws, he knew he must enact the most severe of the punishment alternatives.

Speaking first to Hernández, he emphatically stated, "Humberto Hernández, your peers have found you guilty of stealing from another citizen of this Confederation. I hereby sentence you to be marooned on the island of Anegada. I can assure you that the treacherous reef surrounding Anegada will keep any ships from attempting your rescue. However, with the abundance of exotic fish near the island, you may well be able to survive. Since you have violated both our Confederation law as well as God's, we will allow God to judge whether or not you survive. For our part we will deliver you to Anegada Island with one gallon of water, a knife, and a pistol with one shot."

After Hernández was led below in chains, Anthony Perez was brought to the deck where again a jury decided that Perez was guilty of inciting a fight, even though the reason was understandable. The penalty was forty lashes upon his bare back in full view of all the crew.

Francisco Sosa whispered to Cousin León, "Captain Gasparilla is about to 'let the cat out of the bag.'" León nodded sadly, knowing how this punishment upset Gasparilla. As they knew, "Letting the cat out of the bag" meant a flogging with the cat-o'-nine tails. The "cat" was a whip with nine tails that was kept in a red cloth bag.

According to Confederation rules, the boatswain's mate, upon Gasparilla's order, performed the flogging in front of the whole crew. The beating this particular day was both brutal and bloody. Perez survived and was taken below deck for days of recovery in the sick bay.

The point had been made regarding fighting among the confederates. The punishment was not worth the crime. Better to save one's fighting for the enemy.

After the crew of the *Doña Rosalita* marooned Hernández, they lifted sail for the Florida coast along the tradewinds route. The westbound ship was sailing by and large, which meant it had a strong wind blowing steadily from the proper direction and was sailing with all canvas aloft.

It was now June, and a time when shipping was actively involved in delivering goods before the onset of the summer hurricane season. The *Doña Rosalita* was in position to acquire its first real prize.

It was a hot and humid morning with little breeze and few clouds, typical of Florida in summer. The rainy season had not yet taken charge of the turbulent summer storm season in that area of the globe. Gasparilla woke from a sound sleep and took his morning coffee on deck next to the helmsman, where he was the first to spot a large Spanish naval vessel off the starboard side. It was the type often used in carrying cavalry and infantry troops and resupplying land-based army activities.

"Yo, brothers, I see the first trophy since we have left the detested monarchy to pursue our own freedom, "Gasparilla shouted, "Assemble immediately on the deck so we may decide whether to claim this trophy so naturally handed to us."

Nearly one hundred officers and sailors gathered on the deck of the ship. Since many were still in a vengeful mood after their recent conversion to piratehood and escape from Spain, the vote was nearly unanimous to attack the solo Spanish vessel.

In what would become a Gasparilla trademark, the helmsman guided the ship towards the stern of the victim. Gaspar, the Spanish admiral, had effectively used this tactic many times, having learned that the stern of any ship is the part least protected by its cannon and therefore the most vulnerable, with the rudder often being a prime target.

As the enthusiastic pirates scurried about increasing the sail and preparing the ship for battle, the Spanish troop ship that had left Havana bound for the fort, Castillo de San Marcos, at St. Augustine, apparently spotted the intruders and began to take action.

A fully loaded ship, fresh from port and riding low in the water, is seldom, if ever, a match for a sleek vessel of war. León Gaspar later said it best, "It was like an overweight fish, fresh from another meal, encountering a hungry shark, and this shark was in a vengeful mood."

To his credit, the captain of the naval vessel steered a course directly for the shoreline in an attempt to beach his craft and allow the army cavalry to escape and defend themselves. Gasparilla, noting this, encouraged his crew, "we may not enjoy any fruit from this tree, but I say to you, this day will end with the Spanish Navy having one less tree! We will chase her to the breakers and cause her destruction."

As mid-afternoon approached, the *Doña Rosalita* scored her first victim as the huge Spanish ship was caught up in the breakers, ran aground and tipped on its side. There was a cracking sound—louder than the summer thunder—that echoed over the waves as the old galleon's back broke.

The soldiers of the Asturias Infantry Regiment, who had been en route to secure duty behind the bastion walls of Castillo de San Marcos, the oldest masonry fort in what is now the United States, scurried over the broken sides to wade and swim ashore. Meanwhile, Gasparilla ran to his quarters in the stern of his ship, rummaged through his trunk, and found the bright-red *joli rouge* flag—the forerunner of the more familiar black and white, skull-and-cross-bones flag—that he had captured in the Mediterranean campaigns earlier. As he raced past the sail locker below deck with the flag, he called out, "My brothers, our flag will be the only red flag, as the French call it, that shall fly proudly in this area of the Spanish Main so no one can ever confuse our ships with other pirates or privateers," Gasparilla continued, "but to allow them to understand our intentions, we shall keep the skull and crossbones beneath the foot of a lion—to remind them of my hero, Richard the Lionhearted—and to show them that now, Gasparilla is the king lion of the seas."

As the wet and beleaguered Spanish infantry and naval veterans watched helplessly from the shore, some of Gasparilla's sailors launched a longboat from the *Doña Rosalita* and rowed to the stricken ship, now broken in three pieces. From the bobbing stern section, they secured the Spanish flag and the captain's flag as the only trophies of this first successful engagement in what would become nearly four decades of revenge on Spain by the pirate Gasparilla.

Although many of his crew urged the killing of the beached and helpless Spaniard soldiers, Gasparilla argued, "a goodly part of our success depends upon the terror we invoke by our presence. Since dead men can tell no tales, let them go and speak terrible things of the Confederation pirates who fly the Confederation red flag of terror."

Later, as the triumphant pirate brotherhood set sail toward Cape Florida to the south, José leaned over and spoke to his cousin León Gaspar, "I wonder whether the Spanish will admit that we had a part in this sinking. After all, neither the English nor the French gave us credit for sinking their ships during our service to Spain. Although, to be honest, I wonder whether the French admit to anything that they do not control."

León reminded José of the furor that the release of a new French history had caused during the previous year in Madrid. Both men laughed as they recalled the incident in their minds.

The first copies of the new French encyclopedia, written by Nicolas Masson de Morvilliers, were distributed in Madrid in the summer of 1783 while Gasparilla, then Adm. José Gaspar, was in residence in the King's Court. Every Spaniard in the entire city, including King Charles, was incensed by Masson's writings. In his encyclopedia Masson asked, "To what do we owe Spain? What has Spain done for Europe in the past ten decades?" To Gasparilla and Cousin León, Masson was simply stereotyping the prejudice all of Europe felt toward Spain.

"I say to you León, and I will say to our brothers: as long as we attack only ships bearing the Spanish flag, we will be supported and cheered by the European powers," Gasparilla exclaimed. "The English and the French will allow us to sell our booty in their cities."

CHAPTER 39

Formative Years of Confederation

*"My brothers, it is always better to have your eyes open to new ideas
rather than have your memory stuffed with useless trivia.
This Confederation will always be on the lookout for new ideas
and ways of doing things, not relying upon past practices of our memories."*
—Gasparilla, July 4, 1784

For his initial base of operations Gasparilla chose the British Virgin Islands. This chain of sixty islands where the Caribbean meets the Atlantic Ocean has hundreds of secret bays and hidden coves and has provided a haven for seafarers for centuries. Gasparilla and his men chose one of the many forgotten cays that offered privacy and a safe place to careen the *Doña Rosalita*.

In May of 1784, they moved to Tortola, the largest of all the islands. Tortola offered green mountains that fell to palm-lined, white, sandy beaches below and dropped anchor in Brandywine Bay. Operating from Tortola, Gasparilla was able to embark on training missions to bring his crew up to fighting trim.

In late June, the *Doña Rosalita* was sailing near the Upper Keys of Florida when the men spotted a Spanish frigate en route from Philadelphia to Havana. Gasparilla decided to test the training of his new crewmen and ordered his ship to chase the frigate.

The Spanish ship, obviously outgunned by the former man-of-war, *Doña Rosalita*, took the only appropriate action and tried to outrun the larger ship. Gasparilla, knowing what would happen, saw this as a fitting trial for his sailors. As the afternoon progressed and the sea breeze intensified, the Confederation captain was pleased with the discipline and the talent of his predominately black sailors. The former slaves worked tirelessly and were quick climbing the rigging, allowing the *Doña Rosalita* to slowly gain on the sleeker frigate.

As the last rays of sunlight streaked across the Western sky, illuminating the surface of the sea to a golden yellow, Gasparilla talked at length with his officers. "Lieutenant Herrera, this chasing of ships, with the possibility of running them aground, makes a good deal of sense to me. If we can herd our prize into these shallow reefs around Florida, then we can pillage them without having to engage in a battle which could bring death to members of our Confederation and damage to our ships."

"Yes, sir," Herrera replied, "and if we moved our Confederation to the Keys we could spend most of our time in port, saving a great deal of expense, rather than outfit a ship for a long duration at sea."

"Also, we could attack more prizes since we would not be weighted down with booty," Francisco Sosa observed.

"We could use smaller ships, as you suggested to the Americans from Mystic," Cousin León added. "These ships would require fewer men and would increase the shares of each member of our brotherhood."

"Yes, my brothers," Gasparilla stated enthusiastically, "we can protect our smaller attack vessels with larger ships like the *Doña Rosalita*. We will need larger ships only to haul our booty to ports where we can convert it to either cash or supplies."

"Also, Captain, operating in this manner would allow us to selectively attack merchant ships for our supply needs, thereby eliminating the need to purchase supplies and allowing us to divide a greater amount of the money from our prizes," Lieutenant Herrera said.

"That is true," Gasparilla answered. "We will move our base of operations from Tortola and Virgin Gorda to La Florida."

Darkness fell and the *Doña Rosalita* continued to show full sail, forcing the rabbit frigate to maintain a dangerous speed for the conditions. To add terror to the quiet night, Gasparilla ordered his crew to break out the drums and pipes and play as loudly as possible. In addition, although the frigate was well out of range, Gasparilla ordered that one twenty-four pound cannon commence firing every fifteen minutes. "If nothing else, we'll keep our prize from going to sleep," Gasparilla laughed as he slapped the back of his helmsman.

At 3:00 A.M. on June 29, 1784, the frigate ran aground on the coral reef off the larger key and capsized, breaking the masts. The hull broke apart by 4:00 A.M. and the Spanish naval crew scrambled into lifeboats. As they attempted to row to shore, Gasparilla ordered his cannon to fire ahead of the survivors.

"What are you doing?" Cousin León screamed at Gasparilla.

"I am keeping them from landing on the islands that will someday become our home," Gasparilla shouted back, "We will give them directions, drinking water, and put them on their way to Havana at daybreak."

On the afternoon of June 29, 1784, the crew of the *Doña Rosalita* began salvaging the cannon, shot, and ammunition from the wreckage of the frigate. They also brought a great deal of rum from the wreck as well as other supplies. Late in the afternoon, a smiling Robert A., one of the ex-slaves, who had been schooled as a free man in England and was well spoken in the King's English, with the help of six men, brought out a chest from the captain's quarters. Opening it, they found over 100,000 Spanish silver dollars, apparently minted for Spain in Philadelphia, and intended to pay the Spanish naval garrison in Havana.

"Robert, you have found the first real treasure for our brotherhood," Gasparilla exclaimed. "We will all have a handsome income from this adventure."

Then, turning to his crew, he shouted, "We may well have established a new method of piracy. I think, instead of pirates, they will simply call us 'wreckers'!"

The men erupted in a cheer. A vote was then taken to distribute the food and rum from the wrecked prize and to move the *Doña Rosalita* to a safe harborage behind the island. "If we run out of rum, I hope there will be a tavern near," Robert said to no one in particular. Ironically, this first victory and prize was recorded in this ship's log as "Victory at Tavernier."

In July, as the *Doña Rosalita* continued training operations between the Keys and Cuba, a severe afternoon thunderstorm blew the ship off course. As the storm cleared, the lookout on the *Doña Rosalita* saw the Spanish frigate, *Santa Anna*, off the starboard side. "Yo, a Spanish warship, a frigate, that appears to be in some trouble," the lookout yelled to those below.

Gasparilla called for a vote of the brotherhood on whether to attack the stricken vessel. The only unanimous vote ever taken by the Confederation ensued and the *Santa Anna* was to be the next prize.

Gasparilla was impressed with the crew and the actions of the *Santa Anna*. In spite of a broken main mast, the Spanish ship made a valiant effort to escape. With the *Doña Rosalita* giving chase, the *Santa Anna* was soon run aground on a reef near Aroquito Key and broke up on impact. Many of the crew were drowned, but two lifeboats cleared the sinking ship and surviving crew members scrambled aboard. Gasparilla ordered the Spaniards be brought on board the *Doña Rosalita*.

To his surprise, the captain of the *Santa Anna* was Captain Miguel Ysnardy, a classmate of Gasparilla's from the Naval Academy in Cadiz. Also, among the survivors was a priest, Thomas Hasset, the parish priest of St. Augustine, Florida.

After a night of drinking and reminiscing, Gasparilla risked capture by ordering his crew to take the *Santa Anna* survivors dangerously close to Havana and deposit them in lifeboats. In appreciation, Ysnardy admitted to his old friend that one might find a good deal of money in the wreck of the *Santa Anna*. The "wreckers" of the *Doña Rosalita* made sure that the money was on board before the survivors were delivered to Cuba.

The *Doña Rosalita* returned to the British Virgin Islands and, instead of going to Tortola, went to Virgin Gorda. The large man-of-war anchored in the area near the Virgin Gorda Baths. The Baths, where huge boulders are arranged haphazardly, providing myriad rock pools, secret beaches and trails, proved to be a good site to hide the booty obtained from the two Spanish frigates.

Dramatic slopes that plunge from Gorda Peak to the turquoise waters around the Baths characterize Virgin Gorda, the third largest of the Virgin Islands. The Baths underneath made a perfect place to hide treasure and for the crew to enjoy the gentle breezes of late summer.

"Although I love these islands, if we are going to employ the tactics we learned on our voyage, then we must move to Florida," Gasparilla said sadly. "But, you must love a place that honors a pirate by naming an island after him. Jost Van Dyke, a Dutchman, with a neighboring island named after him. I wonder if anyone will name an island after me?

"My dear cousin José, you must remember that you adopted your new name from an island in West Florida, so in a unique way, there already is an island that bears your name," Cousin León ventured.

In the fall of 1785, Gasparilla moved his Confederation headquarters to Amelia Island near the state of Georgia. 1785 was a seminal year for Gasparilla and the Confederation operations off Florida's east coast. It was in 1785 that his former friend and now archenemy, United States Secretary John Jay wrote and proposed anti-piracy ordinances, which became law. These laws would be instrumental in the eventual decline of piracy around the United States and Gasparilla was convinced Jay wrote them specifically against him. "If not for his intense personal hatred of me, the only pirate he ever has known, Jay wouldn't give a damn about piracy," Gasparilla told Cousin León, "in fact, John Jay cares so little about the sea that he is one of those politicians responsible for selling all the ships of his own American Navy."

In October of 1785, with ample money in the Confederation treasury to purchase additional ships, Gasparilla met Commodore John Barry.

As she had promised, Brutal Betsy was the liaison between the pirate king and the commodore. She met Commodore Barry outside of Charleston, South Carolina and guided him to Amelia Island on one of the last United States Navy schooners, the *Alliance*. The *Alliance* was also one of the most famous ships of the American Navy in the Revolutionary War and the last officially commissioned American naval ship afloat in 1785.

The purpose of the meeting was to discuss the purchase by Gasparilla's Confederation of at least two of the swift schooners that had served the Americans so well during their Revolutionary War. These sleek craft had a valiant history of amphibious assaults during the war. This was the style of battle Gasparilla had envisioned only months earlier for the Confederation to wage. Barry was dealing with Gasparilla because no other nation had the need or saw the value of these small ships for their own navies.

As the five-foot, three-inch-tall, Brutal Betsy walked up the dock with the six-foot, four-inch-tall American commodore, Gasparilla couldn't help but laugh at the sight. John Barry was one of the tallest men he ever met. *No wonder his crews and enemies referred to him as Big John,* he thought.

Betsy told Gasparilla how both she and Barry were born in the same county in Ireland and that, when she turned forty, Barry's age, she expected to be his height. Gasparilla was glad for the opportunity to have a hearty laugh—the first in a long time.

The afternoon was productive for the Confederation and enjoyable for Gasparilla, Brutal Betsy, and Commodore Barry. After resolving the issues of price and delivery of two of America's finest remaining naval schooners, the trio of notable sea veterans enjoyed the warm, sunny afternoon on Amelia Island under the shade of one of the many live oaks covering the island paradise.

Betsy elicited from the American commodore the story of how he had set an amazing and unparalleled record of traveling two hundred and thirty-seven miles in a twenty-four-hour period by dead reckoning while commanding the two-hundred-ton ship, *Black Prince*. This adventure marked the fastest day of sailing recorded in the eighteenth century.

"Dead reckoning, my American friend?" Gasparilla asked. "Even as tall as you are, sir, I still question whether you are tall enough to see a hundred miles over the ocean."

"Gasparilla, like you, I sometimes feel as if my service and record in our Navy has been overlooked, as much publicity went to a friend of yours, John Paul Jones." Barry said in a friendly, tempered voice.

"Yes, my friend, we are often victims of those who write history," Gasparilla intoned, "we have each scored many victories which have been overshadowed or ignored while those who accomplish less instead receive the praise."

"Aye, Gasparilla; but the most tragic story is when a courageous man gives not only himself, but his possessions as well, and attains the true status of hero and then is branded a traitor," Commodore Barry said quietly, almost reverently. "Such a man was Benedict Arnold, formerly of Connecticut, who was one of our country's greatest heroes. Benedict's genius in having fifteen gunboats constructed to delay the British Army from splitting our colonial confederation of states was one of the turning points of our war against England. Benedict Arnold created the United States' first Navy! A veteran land soldier, captaining this naval fleet on Lake Champlain against an overwhelming British fleet. What courage this must have taken. As I have heard you propose, Gasparilla, Arnold designed ships with a specific purpose in mind. The next year, back on land, as an Army leader, Arnold led the American forces to victory at nearby Saratoga. This victory was crucial in turning the tide of our revolutionary war with England."

"But, I thought the United States considers him a traitor?" Gasparilla questioned.

"I think Benedict felt as you and I sometimes feel. He fought bravely and brilliantly for the American cause for more than six years. He was wounded and nearly killed twice. He invested all of his fortune and money into our cause and was never reimbursed. Worse yet, our Congress never thanked him once for his many victories over the British."

Commodore Barry paused and wiped a tear from his cheek, then continued, "Benedict was then approached by a glib British spy and he made the worst decision of his life—he switched sides."

Gasparilla reached out to the American and whispered, "Although those who are on the victorious side often wonder about their treatment, regardless of how brave one might be, if your side loses . . . . " Gasparilla's voice trailed off into silence.

After dining on wild turkey, rice and squash, and a walk on the beach overlooking the Atlantic Ocean, the meeting ended between the father of the American Navy and the head of the Confederation. As the three friends approached the temporary home of Gasparilla, Commodore Barry excused himself and stated that he would sleep on board his ship at anchor. "I am no friend of the unseen gnats that take particular joy in feasting upon my body," Barry laughed. "I shall join you for breakfast."

Betsy excused herself from accompanying Barry to his ship and stated she would stay ashore for the night. As he walked away, she turned, smiling at Gasparilla, and dropped her handkerchief. Before he could retrieve it, she stooped to pick it up, exposing her ample cleavage to José.

Gasparilla felt his manhood harden and throb imperatives to his brain as he stared at her breasts pressing against the cotton peasant dress. Betsy brazenly returned his stare without a smile and stood rubbing her hands on the insides of the shapely legs clearly silhouetted by the light shining through her skirt. Betsy's face was now bathed with perspiration that she licked off her upper lip with her long tongue. Her breathing had quickened and her commanding green eyes communicated desire. Gasparilla knew this was a woman who enjoyed sex and his own breathing became labored as he felt her heat.

Betsy's white dress was now soaked with sweat droplets. She unconcernedly slipped the dress off her shoulders and let it drop into the dirt at her feet as she continued to wantonly stare into José's eyes. José's surprise at her nude body sent another jolt through his own. The pointed nipples of her breasts quivered as Gasparilla silently leaned forward and licked each one, tasting the salt of her perspiration as he explored their firmness. As he continued to move his tongue over her bare breasts, his right hand slipped across the smoothness of her stomach and found her pubic hair damp with expectation. He gently stroked and caressed her as Betsy gasped in ecstasy and stepped back against the trunk of a tree. She reached forward, firmly grabbed José, and drew him against her naked body.

As she removed his trousers she whispered in his ear, "My little Spanish matador, I want you to fuck me like a bull!" Gasparilla drew back looking at her quizzically. "You know," she panted, "I want you take me from behind like an animal. Grab the cheeks of my ass and ride me!"

Though Betsy's frankness once again surprised Gasparilla, his body demanded gratification. He began by entering her slowly, but she cried out, "Give it to me! Pump me, my little matador . . . all of it. Give it to me!" She moaned with pleasure as José pumped her.

Gasparilla reached around her writhing body and firmly grasped both her breasts as they bounced opposite of the movement of her torso. Both wished this frenzy would last forever.

During the period of timelessness, when lovemaking knows no boundary, their final mutual orgasm caused both to shudder in spasmodic joy. Their cries of rapture shattered the quiet of the night before both crumbled to the ground in exhaustion.

Gasparilla finally rose, left the sleeping, limp body of Betsy, and walked to the deserted beach. As he looked out on the moonlight rippling on the waves, the memories of those infidelities of moments earlier, followed by feelings of guilt, caused a rush of anguish to cascade over him. He knelt to his knees, speaking in a whisper as if in prayer. When he arose, a sense of peace shown upon his face. Doña Rosalita would always be the love of his life; however, he now felt that she would understand his need to be a vital man.

The next morning Commodore Barry joined Gasparilla, Brutal Betsy, Robert A., and Cousin León for breakfast and to finalize details in turning the schooners over to the Confederation. It was a bright sunlit morning and Gasparilla felt more relaxed and at ease with himself than at anytime since the death of Rosalita. Brutal Betsy sat near Gasparilla and gave him a knowing smile. As they ate, a great deal of discussion centered on the problems of operating any type of government from an island base.

Commodore Barry and Gasparilla argued the ease of defense issue, while Robert A., Lieutenant Herrera, and Cousin León expressed concerns about the large amount of supplies that would need to be imported. Throughout the discussion, Brutal Betsy sat quiet and aloof from the animated conversation.

"The ability to defend one's self on an island is obvious," Barry asserted, "if you have stored enough supplies and built proper fortifications, it would take an overwhelming force to threaten you."

"Yes, but, it also would require a smaller force to lay siege to your fortress if you did not have enough supplies," Robert A. stated thoughtfully.

"There is considerable validity in what you both say," Gasparilla reasoned. "I personally prefer an island because I can see who is coming, either friend or foe."

"Normally, all of our supplies come over the water," Cousin León blurted out without thinking and immediately recognized that he had stated the obvious.

"Of course. We are on an island!" Gasparilla shouted with a laugh, then winked to the others at the table.

Commodore Barry then asked if the Confederation needed to borrow money from friends and supporters in order to purchase the schooners.

"We will pay cash!" Gasparilla exclaimed, then stated earnestly, "Before you borrow money from a friend, decide which you need most."

Barry left with the cash and Gasparilla's Confederation had now grown to four ships. Gasparilla took Commodore Barry's advice, moving the

Confederation operation further down the coast of Florida to take advantage of the shipping lanes around St. Augustine.

Gasparilla assigned Robert A. to captain the former *Effingham*, a quick schooner with thirty-two cannon. Robert A. requested that the ship's name be changed to *Freedom* to recognize the circumstances in which he and his black crew of ex-slaves now found themselves.

"And what will you call your ship, Betsy?" Gasparilla inquired.

"Well, my leader, since you have bought me this fine ship, what do you think? Betsy replied with a seductive tone.

"Let's name it after you," Gasparilla smiled, "your ship will hereafter be known as the *Lusty Lady*."

With that, Brutal Betsy assumed command of the former American naval vessel, the *Raleigh*, another thirty-two gunner. Former captains had remarked in the ship's log that it had "a mind of its own." It was fitting that the most independent captain to ever serve the Confederation would command such a ship.

The period between 1785 and 1788 were good years for the Confederation as they dominated the other independent pirates flying the black flag. The Confederation grew as many of these independent pirates, former privateers, and independent wreckers allied themselves with Gasparilla's Confederation.

At times the black flag pirates chose to fight and in those instances, Gasparilla's Confederation destroyed the enemy ship and sold the survivors to various slave camps throughout Florida. Although Gasparilla personally abhorred slave camps, the members of the Confederation outvoted him and enjoyed the money that these prisoners brought them.

A personal triumph for Gasparilla came when his ship captured a pirate schooner, *Queen of Death*, in a battle near the northern coast of Cuba. Gasparilla saved the Princess María López of Spain who had been taken captive from the *Francesca* years earlier near Pensacola in the panhandle of La Florida.

María López was grateful not only for Gasparilla's courage in rescuing her but for his patience and understanding in trying to help her. As the days went on, María López spent a great deal of time with Gasparilla, and their nights became full of lovemaking before he regretfully placed the princess on a Spanish Brigantine headed back to Spain.

One welcome addition to the Confederation occurred on May 3, 1786, near St. Augustine, when *La Esclavitud*, the Spanish brigantine *Jesús María*, and a schooner disappeared during a thunderstorm. The small fleet was carrying $40,000 in silver pesos as it neared its destination of St. Augustine. The schooner arrived there late and reported that it had lost sight of the other two ships. Fortunately, the lingering clouds had given cover to Capt. Miguel Rodriquez as he added two ships to Gasparilla's Confederation, along with nearly $50,000 in silver and other valuables.

Robert A.'s ship, *Freedom*, scored the first of many victories when it captured the British merchantman, *Caroline*, in May of 1786. The *Caroline*, bound for Charleston and then London, was captured in the Gulf of Florida.

As the men on the *Doña Rosalita* observed the first kill of the *Freedom*, Gasparilla commented to his staff, "I know not whether Robert A. is a genius or simply cannot sail in a straight line, but he confuses the enemy as well as me."

The *Lusty Lady* had many successes in 1786 as she forced "prizes" to sail into a number of traps set by Gasparilla. She was forced into a pitched battle with the Spanish naval schooner, *San José*, as it left St. Augustine bound for Havana. Skillful sailing by her crew allowed the *Lusty Lady* to land many salvos of cannon fire into the rigging and masts of the *San José*, forcing it to strike its colors.

When Betsy boarded the defeated schooner, she discovered that the ship carried three officers and forty enlisted men of the Inmemorial del Rey Regiment. The naval officers and men of the *San José* who surrendered were permitted to board lifeboats and leave the ship. There were those officers of the regiment who refused to surrender to a woman. "Bring us a man and we will consider surrendering our swords," the Spanish major stated sarcastically.

Angered by this sexist attitude, Brutal Betsy drew her sword and without a word or change of facial expression, ran the sword through the heart of the shocked major.

Her action caused the Spaniards to pull their swords with the intention of fighting the pirates on the deck of the *San José*.

A roar of cannonade and musket fire rained down upon the men of the Inmemorial del Rey Regiment and most were killed instantly. Betsy ordered yet another salvo to be fired into the dead and dying men on the bloody deck.

Calmly, she then replaced her sword, walked to her first mate, and stated evenly, "I'm not really a bad person, sometimes I just get irritated."

The *Lusty Lady's* victory over the Spaniards coupled with the death of Spain's King Charles III in December of 1787 caused great pressure to be placed upon the Confederation along the east coast of Florida.

The death of Charles III meant that the Prince of Austurias and his spiteful wife, María Louisa, came to power. The prince was now known as Charles IV and Manuel Godoy was the most powerful man in all of Madrid, since he was sleeping with the wife of the new king.

Godoy and María Louisa still harbored a smoldering hatred toward Gasparilla. This had been compounded when one of Godoy's cousins, a Spanish Army officer assigned to Inmemorial del Ray regiment was killed by Gasparilla's Confederation. That, coupled with Gasparilla's triumphs over other Spanish naval ships for three years, led Spain to launch a fleet of ships to search out and destroy Gasparilla in early 1788.

Another problem for the Confederation was the uncooperative attitude of the independent pirates, flying the black flag with the skull-and-crossbones, who refused to join Gasparilla's Confederation or at least sign a mutual defense agreement. The pirates and plunderers from the Carolinas and other islands off the east coast of the United States operated independently and held to the philosophy: "Burned ships and dead crews leave no evidence."

Gasparilla attempted to persuade them that this was a waste of potential income. He believed that living crews could be ransomed for additional income or at least sold to slave camps for cash. Gasparilla also believed that many of these sailors would agree to join a democratic Confederation if given the chance and that could enlarge the number of ships owned by Confederation.

The ships would be valuable either as replacements or additions to the Confederation's fleet or they could be sold. In fact, Gasparilla's Confederation often sold the ships they had captured or ransomed back to their original owners.

Many of the black flag pirates, however, were too independent to listen and this, along with the invasion of the deep draft Spanish men-of-wars, caused the Confederation to move to the two-hundred mile stretch of the Florida Keys from Biscayne Bay to the Dry Tortugas.

"This area encompasses many islands, reefs, lakes, bays, beaches, and shallow water not suitable for the Spanish ships," Gasparilla exclaimed. "I firmly believe that whoever controls the Keys, the islands of the Dry Tortugas, and the area between will control all the navigation in the Gulf of Mexico. We will establish the Tortugas as our western point and will settle primarily on the island of Cayo Hueso, the Isle of Bones. The Spanish Indians have shown me a freshwater well unknown to anyone else."

"I believe these twisted, torturous strips of land will provide us the cover to operate as we prefer," he continued, "wrecking ships and capturing their crews and cargo without endangering our crews. Then we will sell the plunder to benefit the Confederation and line our pockets."

"Cousin León, order the men to man the ships and prepare to sail to Cayo Hueso. Our Confederation will grow in shallower, but far less stormy waters, than on this coast."

CHAPTER 40

Golden Years of Success

"The goal of ships of the Confederation is to avoid fighting if it is honorably possible to avoid such action. But if we must fight, then we shall fight with all we have and demand unconditional surrender from our foe."
—Gasparilla, September 4, 1789

The growing Confederation fleet sailed to Biscayne Bay where Brutal Betsy and the *Lusty Lady's* crew chose to remain. There were many springs of fresh water in the limestone rocks and Betsy loved the clear blue-green water of the bay. She felt her ship could effectively carry out raids from a base of operations there.

"Gasparilla, although I understand and approve of your wrecker tactics to avoid a battle unless it is forced upon you, my Irish temperament is more geared to action than patience," Betsy confessed as the two embraced on board the *Doña Rosalita*. "I enjoy the thrill of a pitched battle on the high seas, man to man." Betsy laughed.

The remaining ships headed out of Biscayne Bay and went directly to Black Caesar's Rock, a tiny island between Rhodes Key and Elliott Key in the island chain separating the Atlantic Ocean and Biscayne Bay. Black Caesar's Rock was once the headquarters of the legendary pirate, Black Caesar, a black man who had escaped from a slave ship and become a one-man wrecker. Later Black Caesar became a favored lieutenant of the notorious pirate, Blackbeard. Now, sixty years after Black Caesar's hanging in Virginia, Black Caesar's Rock was considered haunted and caused fear in the mariners who plied these trade routes.

Robert A. decided to occupy Black Caesar's Rock as his base of operations for the *Freedom* and her crew. Robert would promote the myth that Black Caesar had been reincarnated and had returned to plunder those who would challenge him off the upper Keys. He was enthused with the designing of his campaign and in using the name of the old pirate as well as employing many of the terror tactics of Black Caesar.

Gasparilla and the crew of the *Doña Rosalita,* along with the now-recruited Miquel Rodriquez's *La Esclavitud* and *Jesus María*, sailed south, southwest towards Cayo Hueso, later to be known as Key West, where Gasparilla was to establish the new headquarters for the Confederation.

At Cayo Largo, or Long Island, the longest of all the islands in the Florida Keys, Miguel decided that rather than go all the way to Cayo Hueso, he would prefer to establish his operations here on the island surrounded by coral reefs, clear water, seagrass beds, and mangroves. "It is perfect José. There is plenty of land to farm—my contribution to the Confederation," Miguel announced. "Also, I will be able to visit Betsy often and protect her, if you know what I mean."

"Aye, that I do," Gasparilla replied with greater knowledge than his friend suspected. "A vital man such as you needs to be with a vigorous woman whenever possible so that your needs are met."

Gasparilla, León, Lieutenant Herrera, and the crew of the *Doña Rosalita* set sail for Cayo Hueso as one of the vividly colored sunsets, for which the region was known, illuminated their departure.

Arriving at Cayo Hueso from the Atlantic side of the island, everyone on the deck marveled at the raw tropical beauty of the island.

"The Spanish explorers called this 'bone island,'" Gasparilla told Cousin León and Lieutenant Herrera. "The Calusa Indians knew how important this island is, as are others in the area. Whoever controls this island controls navigation in all the Gulf of Mexico. The Calusas knew that and were willing to, and did, fight and die for this island."

"So, you are making a decision based on the history of long-dead Indians?" León asked with a look of incredulity.

"Those who do not learn from the past often commit the same mistakes," Gasparilla curtly offered. "With the French and Spanish needing to pass this place as well as the Americans, British, and others, I believe the Calusas are telling us the importance of this island. Cayo Hueso and the Dry Tortugas offer the Confederation two points of power in controlling shipping in the Gulf. This island will be the rock upon which our Confederation shall be built."

Gasparilla continued, "Archimedes insisted he could move the world with a lever and a place to stand. I believe we, too, can move the world and Cayo Hueso is the rock upon which we will stand."

"From St. Augustine to Cayo Hueso, the Confederation will have control of the shipping lanes," Gasparilla convinced his followers. "In fact, from the Rock, we will be able to safely trade with the dishonest merchants in Havana. Cuba is only ninety miles south, closer as a trading partner than any other point in our Confederation. All bounty seized by Betsy, Miguel, and Robert shall be brought to Cayo Hueso and we will either trade with the merchants in Cuba or the French in New Orleans."

In the fall of 1788, the *Doña Rosalita* rounded the western end of the two- by four-mile coral island rising from the shimmering Atlantic Ocean. Gasparilla's tropical island would serve as the Confederation's capital city for the next twelve years. These dozen years were to become known as the "Golden Years of the Confederation."

"The best thing about Cayo Hueso is that it is free of mosquitoes," Cousin León joked, "Now if you actually can find the Indian's freshwaters well, then we will have more water than Betsy has back at Biscayne Bay. Otherwise, we will have to buy water from her, two hundred miles away. No one would ever be foolish enough to do that."

"Never discount what some governments might do," José cautioned, "That is why our Confederation will always remain a democracy."

By the end of the first week, the Confederation had established its new headquarters and built a wharf from the timber washed on shore from shipwrecks. Gasparilla and Cousin León argued their way through the Indian map of Cayo Hueso and finally found the freshwater well that the Calusas had dug years earlier. This well would provide drinking and cooking water for the Confederation but, in addition, Gasparilla ordered his men to build cisterns to catch rainwater. "We must build these quickly so that we can take advantage of the last month or two of the afternoon rainy season," Gasparilla added, "With luck, we might have a tropical storm to give us enough water for all our needs during the winter dry season."

By the end of December 1788, Gasparilla's crew had built three dormitories and one warehouse with more of the planking from the wrecks. In January, Gasparilla ordered a church built across from the Indian well and, by the middle of February, the rough-hewed log church was constructed. A vote of the Confederation named the Catholic church, St. Mary's, in honor of the Blessed Virgin. Gasparilla remarked to Cousin León that it surprised him how these rugged pirates, capable of almost any atrocity, were so religious and had such affection for their mothers.

Gasparilla's men were friendly with Spanish fisherman and Spanish Indians who lived on the cays and islands making up the chain of the Florida Keys. Gasparilla was in awe of the size of these Indians remarking, "The American commodore, John Barry, was the tallest man I ever knew, but he would have to look up to look into the eyes of some of these Spanish Indians. I wonder how tall their Calusa ancestors must have been!"

The *Doña Rosalita* made several successful forays in the spring of 1789, capturing four ships, sinking five, and converting many of the captured crew as members of the Confederation. Sunk or wrecked during this time was the British merchantman, *Evenly*, which yielded many items necessary to make the headquarters at Cayo Hueso livable, including fine furnishings and even a harpsichord for the Church of St. Mary's. The pirate also took out his vengeance against the Spanish crown at every opportunity, wrecking and seizing ships attempting to do business with Spanish outposts in Cuba and La Florida.

Another victim of Gasparilla was the British merchantman, *Hazard*, whose crew was saved and then served the Confederation for some years. Upon their return to London, they were welcomed as heroes and were able to live well on the money that they had been given by the Confederation as their shares.

Two other ships were seized and served the Confederation ably. The *Apollo* and the *Edmund & George* were captured on the same afternoon, as the *Doña Rosalita's* crew caught a favorable wind in one spirited battle.

This marked one of the more remarkable days in Confederation history, for not only did Gasparilla capture two major vessels, but before sunset that evening, the two new schooner-type warships built by the Americans in Mystic, met Gasparilla and his battle weary crews off Cape Florida. Fortunately, the crews of the two prizes had chosen to serve the Confederation, so Gasparilla was able to divide his sailors in order to return the five ships to Cayo Hueso.

It took little time for Gasparilla's navy to grow in number in excess of twenty ships sailing to and from the deep water of the protected port on Cayo Hueso. The village at Cayo Hueso now numbered over 2,550 men, women and children. By the late 1790s, the number of ships in Gasparilla's Confederation throughout the Caribbean was more than 100 with nearly 7,500 sailors.

The Confederation generally adhered to the policy established in the rules of engagement. Ships that raised the white flag of surrender voluntarily were to only have one half of their cargoes seized for the Confederation. After unloading the cargo, the captain of the prize was given a Letter of Passage that guaranteed them further safe passage. It was signed by Gasparilla, under the name of King Lion of the Seas.

Ships that refused to recognize the red flag of the Confederation ships were not treated so gently; their cargoes were confiscated. Additionally, the personal effects, crew members, and passengers of resisting vessels became fair game. This often led to violence and the rape of women found on board enemy ships. In fact, most women were either captured or killed after these battles. Those captured were brought to Confederation compounds and became either whores or wives of Confederation sailors. In spite of the millions of dollars of merchandise, gold, and valuables acquired by the Confederation, Gasparilla became incensed because this treatment of the prisoners resulted in a lack of potential income for the organization. He met with all of the Confederation captains and introduced new rules for the capture of ships resisting the Confederation's red flags.

Illustrating man's double standard, Gasparilla began, "Men typically treat most women like whores, but they all want a virgin for a wife. When the woman is violated, he no longer wants her. So, from this day forward, women passengers shall be viewed as valuable bounty until such time as their husbands, lords, kings or whatever, refuse to pay ransom for them."

"What happens if we treat them well and no money comes for them," Robert A. questioned from the group meeting on Islamorada.

"Then they shall be brought to your compound or community and be given the right to become a member of the Confederation," Gasparilla replied. "Many of your men seek wives and these women will provide suitable candidates as well as engaging in productive work for the Confederation. Until such time as a ransom is offered, these women shall be held captive in a safe environment, given food, exercise, and appropriate medical attention. Tell each of your men that the penalty for violating any captive being held for ransom shall be death!"

Sensing tensions running high, Brutal Betsy asked, "Sir, does that apply to the current female citizens of the Confederation?"

"That applies to all the women," José laughed, "We want to insure that these ladies are anxious to return inviolate to their men."

The change in policy towards captives had a dramatic effect on the Confederation and, indeed, ransom in the hundreds of thousands of dollars was paid for the repatriation of prisoners, particularly women.

One of the other major decisions affecting the Confederation came shortly after this change in policy towards captives. Many of the captains felt that the beer, rum, grog, and other alcoholic concoctions mixed by pirates were hurting the discipline on board ships of the Confederation.

Gasparilla met with a number of the ship's doctors and various other men of the Confederation at Cayo Hueso. They decided to mandate that only fruit juices or sarsaparilla would be consumed by sailors while they were at sea or on patrol. Considered by the doctors as an excellent blood purifier and used as a treatment for skin disorders, sarsaparilla was known to others as a treatment for liver disorders, jaundice, hepatitis, and gout.

"In addition, I have been told sarsaparilla is also used to alleviate flatulence and increase urine flow," one elderly doctor added with a wry smile.

"That would have untold benefits to crews gathered together on board our ships," Gasparilla remarked, with a laugh.

After two weeks of experimenting with the beverage, Gasparilla established processing centers on Cayo Largo and on Cayo Hueso. A mixture affectionately known as Gasparilla Sarsaparilla—made with sarsaparilla, sassafras, burdock root, dandelion root, and red clover—was concocted from ingredients confiscated, traded or grown on Cayo Largo.

The men actually enjoyed the refreshing drink, which tasted better than the warm beer, grog, and other drinks that had been on board the ships, and the captains were enthusiastic in their reports of how much better the crews performed.

During September 1796, Gasparilla, in command of one of his Mystic-built "keys schooners" was challenged by a British naval brig-sloop, built in 1795 to counter and protect British shipping from Gasparilla's pirate Confederation ships.

The one-hundred-seventy-ton brigantine schooner, the *Bermuda*, was armed with fourteen twelve-pound carronades and was built to match the Confederation schooners in speed and handling.

The *Bermuda* surprised Gasparilla's flagship, the *Intrepido II*, in the shallow waters of the Gulf of Florida. Because of the shallow draft of the key schooners, designed by Gasparilla himself, the typically deeper-draft European vessels in the area had never challenged them.

The ensuing chase and battle lasted for two days and nights with the ships exchanging cannon salvos each day. Both days they were close enough for grappling hooks to be tossed with each hoping to entangle the other and resolve the issue in hand to hand combat.

By noon of the second day, the riflemen on the *Intrepido II*, using breech-loading muskets, acquired in large numbers by Gasparilla, were able to fire three times as many rounds as those on the deck of the *Bermuda* could return. The result was that many sailors of the *Bermuda* were killed and the others cowered below the deck, leaving the British ship foundering before running aground and breaking up. All hands were lost.

"No form of government should stop acquiring or developing the latest in technology when it comes to defense or armament." Gasparilla told his captains later. "The temptation is always there to give more money to individuals and cut funds allotted to the Confederation, but our victory over the *Bermuda* should convince all of us that those with the latest technology will prevail."

As the Confederation continued to grow through the decade of the nineties, Gasparilla was forced to spend less time at sea and more of his time administering the growing empire. For a man convinced that saltwater flowed freely through his veins, the last five years of the century were miserable. This confinement made him increasingly morose. People who knew him when he was a young man with a sunny disposition would not have recognized him now.

During the last two years of the profitable decade, one of Gasparilla's only voyages from Cayo Hueso was to Cayo Largo to resolve a heated dispute between Robert A. and Captain Thompson, a volatile but highly organized Confederation pirate, who generally operated south of Cayo Largo. Captain Thompson had confronted and run off a group of friendly Conchs who periodically occupied Cayo Tabona, or Horsefly Key, on the seaward side of Cayo Largo. The Conchs were Bahamians who anchored in the summer off the key and rescued passengers from shipwrecks. The grateful passengers rewarded them and thus provided an income for them.

Captain Thompson thought they were taking money that could be going to the Confederation and gave that as his reason for wanting to destroy them or run them off the Cayo Tabona.

Gasparilla sailed to the anchorage off Tavernier and met with Captain Thompson, Robert A., and the head of the Conchs. After each had made his position clear on the issue, Gasparilla indicated that he felt the Conchs provided a necessary service to the Confederation. "I compare the Conchs to the sucker fish who swim with the sharks. The shark fills his belly and the suckerfish feeds on what the shark leaves them. We sink or wreck ships and take the cargoes and crew that want to join us. The Conchs come along and take the other survivors either to Havana or some other safe port. This relieves us and frees our ships to seek additional prey, instead of dealing with leftovers."

With that, the Conchs spent their time in peaceful coexistence with the Confederation. Gasparilla had again used his wisdom to prevent a cancer that could have grown within the Confederation.

The other time Gasparilla left Cayo Hueso was to sail to Cuba and Mexico to establish an understanding and a working relationship with the Spanish *intendencia,* established in 1787 as the new local unit of Spanish colonial administration. This trip proved fruitful in purchasing the support of Spanish *intendencia,* which allowed the Confederation to exchange captured booty for money and supplies from the unscrupulous merchants in these two countries.

"Our Confederation depends heavily upon those corrupt officials who make up the bureaucracy of the *intendencia,*" Gasparilla wisely told Cousin León. "If only they look the other way while we bring goods to their lands and sell them to the equally corrupt merchants, then they are of great value to us."

Arriving home after the long meeting, Gasparilla penned a letter to Thomas Paine, one of his favorite authors and the person whom he felt inspired the American Revolution. By this time, Paine was living in France after having been expelled from England, jailed and subsequently released, in France, and finally recognized for his work, *The Rights of Man.*

Gasparilla felt that the church that he had started on Cayo Hueso, as well as the Catholic church which he had always supported, might now turn against him, much in the same way the Christians had branded Paine an atheist for his writings and analysis.

Cayo Hueso and the Confederation were growing at such a rate that Gasparilla was forced to relocate many newcomers to other cays along the chain where more fresh water was available. Walking with Cousin León along the wharves that now covered nearly the entire north side of Cayo Hueso, Gasparilla unloaded his frustrations with church and government to his patient cousin. "The biggest problem is our growing population. Inevitably, when you have problems or challenges to individual freedoms, it stems from too damn many people trying to occupy a small area."

"What do you mean, Gasparilla?" León questioned as they walked in the shadows of the many warehouses, active with men unloading or loading ships of the Confederation.

"When we first arrived here on Cayo Hueso, we all thought it was paradise, did we not? Then, as the fortunes of our Confederation prospered and more people wanted the freedoms and lifestyle it offered, we grew too fast. Too many people! I tell you, León, the true genius is the person who can recognize utopia at the moment it happens. Too often, we only know utopia after we have gone beyond those elements that made it that in the first place." Gasparilla continued, "I do know that human nature and organized religions work against the establishment of a perfect system, a true democracy if you will."

"How can people and the church be against a utopian society?" León asked in earnest disbelief.

"Simple, my dear cousin. People will propagate themselves without regard to their impact on the natural environment. That is why I say it is human nature for man to destroy the slices of heaven he finds here on earth. Then, they want government bodies like the Confederation to enact restrictive laws which in fact limit the freedoms they sought in the first place," Gasparilla reasoned. He pondered a moment and then continued, "Organized religion has everything to gain from encouraging its members to have as many children as possible. Members beget more members who tithe and enrich the coffers of the church. The more people, the more income for the church, hence the paradox."

"You have not told this philosophy to Father Mendez, have you, cousin? León asked haltingly.

"No, writing to my worldly friend, Thomas Paine, allowed me to vent my feelings to one who would both understand and empathize," Gasparilla smiled warmly.

"Good. It bothers me to see you this frustrated," León replied.

"Well, this island has grown too small for me. The time has come for one of us to go!" Gasparilla laughed as he picked up a piece of coral rock and threw it into the crystal-clear water.

Before the weekend, the *Doña Rosalita*, heavy with barnacles from sitting at the wharf so long, the *Intrepido II*, and two brigantines left Cayo Hueso heading northwest in the Gulf of Mexico for Gasparilla Island.

CHAPTER 41

The Glorious Period

"Leadership is not determined by position, either rank or geography.
Leadership is action, not location. We can lead the Confederation
effectively from Gasparilla Island."
—Gasparilla, on moving his capital to the West Coast of Florida

A light breeze, turquoise skies, and matching water escorted the *Doña Rosalita* and the other ships across the Gulf of Mexico past Marco Island as they headed north. A pod of dolphins jumped and played in the waves, coming so close to the ships that some of the crew feared they would damage the craft.

As the bright afternoon sun, shimmering on the gentle Gulf, warmed those on the ship, Gasparilla, with the enthusiasm of a new venture, was in a jovial mood. Playfully, he yelled down from the quarterdeck to his cousin, "León what lies at the bottom of the ocean and twitches?"

Barebacked and sweating profusely, León looked blankly back at him.

"A nervous wreck!" Gasparilla bellowed with a roar of laughter, which was echoed by the crew.

"Yo!" came a shout from the lookout, "Sir, we are approaching Lover's Key. Is this the island near which you want to anchor tonight?"

"Yes, Juan, the water is smooth enough for us to anchor just off shore tonight," Gasparilla shouted back. Then to those on the quarterdeck he explained, "This will allow the crew to go ashore, build fires, and be able to smoke. Also, tonight we shall break out a ration of beer for each member of the crew."

The sound of the gentle surf lapping on the beach added to the comfort that Gasparilla felt concerning his decision to move the capital north. At dinner, with his officers and Cousin León, Gasparilla further explained his reasoning.

260

"Do all of you realize that no part of the entire area of Florida is more than sixty-five miles from an ocean? If we were to expand upon the canal system built by our predecessors, the Calusas, we could build our capital even in the middle of the Florida peninsula."

"Do you ever think people other than Indians will live in the middle of Florida?" León asked inquisitively.

"I don't know," Gasparilla replied, "I think as long as men need to farm, the answer is yes, but I think most people will live near either coast-lines or navigable rivers. Mankind has a natural affinity for the water and desires to be near it."

"So, of what value are the inland areas to us? We are seafarers." León asked.

"We have amassed millions of dollars worth of gold and silver, have we not?" Gasparilla asked standing up from his chair. "We can use the canals and waterways built by the Calusas to transport our valuables safely inland where they can be hidden until we have need of them. The canal and river network they developed remains useful to us even today, especially since many people believe superstitions that the Calusa canal systems are haunted by long-dead Indians."

"Can our Confederation really survive without our capital being centralized?" asked Isidro Ruíz, a youthful Spanish Naval Academy graduate who had recently joined the Confederation. He had known Gasparilla's son, now a midshipman in Cadiz, Spain, and brought news of the young man.

Gaspar was overjoyed to learn of his son's successes. Once he had fled Spain, leaving the boy in the care of friends, it had been difficult to stay in touch. And both he and the child's caretakers feared further retribution and vengeance by Gasparilla's enemies when the boy was very young. Occasionally, Brutal Betsy was able to use her connections to smuggle a letter from father to son, but no letters had made it back to Gasparilla's hands. The pirate leader's heart was heavy; his only surviving family member appeared lost to him. Gaspar was surprised to learn from other seaman that his son had come out of hiding and had entered the academy to follow in the footsteps of his father and great-grandfather. He wondered if the Spanish crown and his enemies were allowing his son to train for a naval career in the hopes that he would lead them to the former admiral. *No*, he thought, *I must not think that my son would be used against me. After all, he is a Gaspar.*

He refocused his attention to answering Ruíz's questions. "While monarchies and nations have layers of staff and bureaucrats to slow down the decision making process, we have structured our Confederation as if we were two hundred and fifty individual ships," Gasparilla pointed out. "Each ship has to stand on its own. No prey, no pay! Each sailor has both a vote and a stake in its success. They feel they are crucial because they are one in one hundred or several hundred instead of one of hundreds of thousands as they would be in a typical nation. They realize that individually they are responsible for their own success as well as that of the Confederation. They understand that their contribution is of major importance."

"I know this vision is what caused me to join," Ruíz answered honestly.

"The Confederation sees its role as providing you and the others with anything that you would ever need in your lifetime," Gasparilla explained. "We not only clothe you and give you food, but you have your independence and the freedom to choose whatever course you envision for your lives. The freedom to choose, the freedom to be, and the chance to feel a part of an organization that values your talents and appreciates your strengths is what this Confederation is all about."

"Plus, all of us are becoming very rich, wealthy men," Ruíz added with a smile and a pat on a pouch of coins hung around his neck. "I do like your idea of burying some of our treasures along the Calusa canal system. It is a very ingenious idea."

After more discussion on the advantages of relocating the capital to Gasparilla Island, the officers adjourned to the deck of the *Doña Rosalita* for rum before going ashore where the men were singing loudly around driftwood fires on the white beach.

After his longboat arrived on shore, Gasparilla and the others were surprised to also hear women giggling. They found that some of the Spanish-Indian women had paddled over from Estero Island and Mound Key to join them. Gasparilla explained to Ruíz that many ancestors of the Calusa Indians had mated with the Spanish fishermen during the last hundred years or so. Before the night was over, Gasparilla and the others learned why even the Indians called the island Lovers Key.

When he departed at sunrise the next morning, Gasparilla smiled as he looked back to shore at the last wisps of smoke from the previous night's campfires.

"Señor Castro, prepare the capstan!" Gasparilla shouted as the crew began scurrying around the ship in preparation for departure and the day's journey to Gasparilla Island.

As the *Doña Rosalita* and other ships caught a warm breeze and moved gently along the waters off Estero Island, the lookouts kept their eyes on the shoreline in a vain effort to spot the infamous Black Caesar, part-time pirate and full-time slave camp owner. The mangroves kept the infamous slave camp well concealed.

Off Sanibel Island, Gasparilla went to the helm to talk with Moses St. George, one of the brightest men of the Confederation. Moses, who had become one of Gasparilla's most trusted advisors, was an ex-slave who had helped José design the shallow draft Mystic schooners during the formation of the Confederation. He was also one of the young slaves rescued from Brutal Betsy's *Irish Lady II* during the hurricane many years before.

Moses demonstrated his brilliant mind and a quick wit as he challenged Gasparilla.

"Moses, how goes it, my valued friend?" Gasparilla asked as he clapped his hand on the large muscular shoulder. "It is good to be going to Gasparilla Island for I was feeling crowded at Cayo Hueso. I tell you, Moses, there are simply too many people on this earth!"

"Aye, Gasparilla, what you say is true," Moses flashed a bright smile and chuckled. "It always surprises me that there are only *two* kinds of people."

"Two? I don't understand."

"Well, Captain, there are those people who say 'here I am' and then there are those who say, 'there you are.'" Pausing until Gasparilla grasped the difference, Moses broke into a belly laugh, having again confounded the man he most admired with his reference to those who are leaders and those who are followers.

"Moses, you got me again!" Gasparilla exclaimed. "I have never met a man who views things quite like you do, my friend!"

"José, I view you as one of the wisest men I have ever known. You are a true genius," Moses said with genuine praise and a broad smile.

"Always remember that the secret to any enterprise's success is the people involved," Gasparilla replied. "I try to find the best people and recruit them for our Confederation. I build upon their strengths and encourage them to excel with their talents. With the same goal, together we strive to bring out the best in everyone."

"But, Gasparilla, the people identify with you personally," Moses exclaimed.

"I found that if I began to use myself to promote the ideals of the Confederation, more brothers could identify with our causes. Now my pirate name, Gasparilla, and the Confederation have become one and the same," Gasparilla thoughtfully replied. "Since the death of my lovely

Rosalita and end of my prior life, I have decided to experience as much as I can. The battles, the adventures, have all added excitement to my life. I now try to take pleasure in everything!"

As they reached the mouth of Charlotte Harbor, Gasparilla meticulously laid out plans for the development of the Confederation capital. As called for in the original Confederation documents, he determined to set up separate living areas for the married members of the brotherhood and the single members. Since most of the brothers on board the first four ships were single, the small fleet sailed directly to Cara Padilla, an island just to the northeast. It was one-half mile wide and nearly one mile long off Jack's Point—a future favorite thinking-place for Gasparilla. Within three months, the brothers occupying the island had changed the name to Cayo Pelau. To the sailors' delight, they discovered a single deep channel to the island that may have been dredged by Indians through the shallow tidal flats surrounding it.

The first things to be built on Cayo Pelau were a wharf and three warehouses. In order to hide their existence from either harbor or gulf view, Gasparilla had them constructed on the northeast corner of the island. The pier was L-shaped and allowed for the simultaneous unloading of up to six shallow-draft ships. Another similar L-shaped pier was constructed near the southern tip of the island near the site of the general store and the town saloon. This pier provided dockage for visiting Confederation vessels and additional unloading sites during the busiest times of the year. Gasparilla ordered the channel to the island widened and deepened by his prisoners and ex-slaves. Sailors who were familiar with the channel passed through with ease. Others quickly went aground and were captured.

The men slept in the warehouses while they built the remainder of the village that would become Low Town. During the morning hours, they worked on building the general store, saloon, doctor's office, and other public buildings. Gasparilla and Moses St. George designed a system in which all rainwater was caught and transported to wooden tanks built on the island. St. George joked to Gasparilla that his black ancestors must have designed the famous Roman aqueducts since he had little trouble designing a trouble-free efficient system for collecting fresh water.

The waters on the west side teemed with fish, so José ordered a small wooden pier constructed near the tanks. The pier became instrumental in providing the older or infirm pirates, unfit for regular sea duty, a creative means of providing fish for the village. Within the Confederation, everyone was expected to be productive with his or her talents. Others too old for sailing farmed small gardens, tended the cattle and hogs, or worked in the warehouses or village.

Gasparilla's men discovered that shells made a solid road base allowing wagons to transport the heavy loads of gold and silver between the two piers and the warehouses. Construction of the roads also made it possible to roll the large copper casks, containing booty to the warehouses, piers and eventually to the longboats, which Gasparilla used to transport his treasures to hiding places.

On the northwest corner of Cayo Pelau, Gasparilla's men constructed one of the finest ship-repair yards in all of the Florida territory. Using a man-made deep-water channel and the soft, white sandy bottom, the men laid a pair of wooden rails with strap-iron tops at a forty-five-degree angle. These rails, spaced twelve feet apart, were constructed of twelve-inch-square cypress logs. They rested on timbers, supported by cross ties. A ship's winch, normally used to raise heavy anchors, was brought from a wreck in Tampa Bay and mounted at the head of the rails. This allowed ships to be completely brought out of the water for careening and repairs to their hulls. The shipyard allowed Gasparilla's navy to quickly and efficiently field-clean their vessels throughout the early 1800s. Two large buildings were constructed on the site of the shipyard and a shell road was laid from the shipyard to Low Town.

Cayo Pelau became the trading port for shipment of booty to the ready markets of New Orleans to the north, Havana to the south, and Charleston, on the East Coast of the United States. This trade allowed millions of dollars in gold and silver to come to Cayo Pelau. With all the millions brought to the islands, it became important for Gasparilla to devise a system of hiding and preserving the Confederation wealth, and to silence the indigenous peoples or Cuban fishermen who might be tempted to talk.

On Cayo Pelau and throughout the Confederation, Gasparilla devised a plan which he called *fool's treasure*. Gasparilla believed that anyone who would hide or bury treasure anywhere near the coast or near where they actually lived was simply a fool and deserved to lose what had been stashed away. Conversely, Gasparilla reasoned that men were naturally lazy and greedy and would take any treasure found easily. So, he designed copper-covered chests in which he placed some gold and silver ingots, jewelry, figurines, and coins. He then intentionally buried these "fool's chests" very close to the towns and coastal operations of the Confederation. This served two purposes: 1) through temptation, to test the honesty of members of the Confederation and; 2) if the islands were attacked and overrun, the plunderers would find and take these chests and depart, leaving behind much more treasure worth millions of dollars that was better hidden.

On Cayo Pelau, Gasparilla buried some of these fool's chests near an Indian mound northeast of the warehouses. Another pair of chests was buried just to the south of the warehouses, and one was buried at the base of a large oak tree near an Indian midden.

And he bought the silence of the Indians and fishermen with a combination of gold, mutually beneficially trading, and the threat of murder. As a result, none of the other residents, or their descendents, of the Charlotte Harbor area would admit to having seen Gasparilla or his island empire.

On the eastern peninsula, jutting into Bull Bay, Gasparilla's men under the direction of Bill Gallagher, a former officer on Brutal Betsy's *Lusty Lady II*, constructed a fort they called Little Fort Matanzas. Named after a similar Spanish fort constructed near St. Augustine, Little Fort Matanzas was constructed from ship timbers and coquina rock. There were three twenty-four-pound cannon mounted at the fortification, designed to prevent a surprise attack on the nearby warehouses.

But, by far the largest building on Cayo Pelau, was a three-story building, which housed a brothel on the top two stories and a saloon on the first floor. Women who were captured, when the ships they were on resisted Gasparilla's Confederation, and who had no value for ransom, were offered two choices. They could either become citizens of the Confederation or prostitutes. This policy was the same throughout the Confederation, making Gasparilla, according to a laughing Brutal Betsy, the world's largest pimp!

Sitting on top of the tall building, camouflaged as an Indian mound, was a combination lookout and signal tower. In fact, every island occupied by Confederation in Charlotte Harbor had a similar tower, which oversaw not only the islands but also all the surrounding waters for miles. Lookouts blew conch shells to alert each other of intruders.

With the construction of Little Fort Mantanzas on Cayo Pelau completed, the Confederation builders, under the direction of Bill Gallagher, then turned their attention toward the construction of a fort at the northern tip of La Costa. Despite the protests of the Spanish fisherman on La Costa, the construction of this fort was essential. The fort at La Costa, built to guard the entrance of the harbor, was made of coquina rock, cement, and ships' timbers. The walls were built at forty-five-degree angles so that they would not absorb direct impact of cannon fire, but deflect the shots. The site was chosen because at this point, the land was fifteen feet above sea level, having been elevated by the spoil of the dredged channel. This was very high for the Florida coastline. The fort had eight twenty-four pounders and six twelve-pound cannon in addition to carronades at each corner. Gasparilla also had rifle slits cut in the impregnable walls for the marines to fire their muskets from, adding to the fort's defense characteristics. An observation-signal tower, twenty feet tall, was constructed behind the La Costa fort and manned twenty-four hours a day.

The two forts insured the Confederation's safety from attack either from Charlotte Harbor to the east or the Gulf of Mexico to the west. Additional land-based forts, or "castles" as the Indians referred to them, were built south of Sarasota Bay along the coast, and another smaller wooden fort was constructed on Useppa Island to the south.

Gasparilla and Gallagher decided that no force could navigate the shallow channel between Pine Island and Sanibel that the small Useppa Island fort could not defend. Three twenty-four pounders and three carronades were assigned to it.

Gasparilla then asked Bill Gallagher and Moses St. George to help him design and supervise the construction of High Town, including his own spacious house, the largest house of those constructed. The house was filled with works of art, exquisite paintings, and fine furnishings brought by his ships. Gallagher and St. George constructed the house of coquina rock, cypress timbers, and, with input from two Cuban construction workers, applied an adobe-style plaster to both the interior and exterior walls. It had the appearance of a white castle. The main part of the structure measured more than one hundred feet in length and eighty feet in width. Attached to the main house were four patios, which added to the apparent size of this Boca Grande "castle." One patio faced southwest, with a view of the radiant sunsets over the Gulf and a private harbor. On it Gasparilla placed a replica of the peddler's cart, and a shrine to his beloved Rosalita. Servants often heard him carrying on animated conversations with his deceased wife.

The main house became the site of many lavish social occasions and Gasparilla was often seen with a beautiful woman on each arm, attended by two or three of the Brothers dressed in their finest clothes. Gasparilla used these women as showpieces and as a means of subconsciously flaunting his power. When they were of no further use to him, he had them taken to Cayo Pelau to become either prostitutes or workers of the Confederation. After Rosalita's tragic death, Gasparilla viewed women in a materialistic way to satisfy his desires. He chose not to fall in love, and when he truly liked a woman, he would send her away rather than to risk becoming involved.

Gasparilla rewarded Bill Gallagher and Moses St. George, for the fine design of his house by giving them title to some of small keys just off Cayo Pelau. Gallagher immediately named his two islands after himself and built a small coquina blockhouse on the easterly key. St. George obtained possession of the island just north of the first key. St. George who loved snakes, immediately began raising snakes and his island was referred to as Snake Key by the brothers. Understandably, Moses had few visitors.

Occasionally, there was strife among the members of the Confederation. The Bocilla brothers, who were valuable members of the Confederation in Charlotte Harbor, had a difficult time getting along with those living on Cayo Pelau. They were constantly fighting with other ship's crews, and this feud threatened to cause a revolt on the small island.

Gasparilla intervened and suggested that the Bocilla brothers move their schooners and crews to the long, narrow island at the northern end of Big Pine Island. At first they resisted, insisting the others go, but Gasparilla offered them ten whores, the services of Bill Gallagher, some brothers to help them build housing, and ships' timbers to build their house.

The unskilled seamen built simple houses from palm tree trunks with thatched roofs, woven by some of the native Indians on Big Pine Island. They also built similar houses for the ten wenches and a saloon facing north, looking over Charlotte Harbor.

The Bocilla brothers had a coquina-stone-and-ship's-timber house built for them with main-door entrances on either end of the structure. A common wall divided the house into two separate living areas. Gallagher's design of the house insured that the two fiery brothers were separated.

"The most difficult work of all is trying to maintain peace in your own community," Gasparilla told Cousin León as they headed northwest across a choppy Charlotte Harbor back to High Town.

* * *

As he approached his fiftieth birthday, Gasparilla's vision seemed to be working as he had dreamed. The Confederation ships from the Gulf of Mexico, around the Keys, and into the Caribbean continued to grow in number and everyone prospered. With the ten shares of each ship's captured bounty flowing into Charlotte Harbor, Gasparilla delighted in sailing to Cayo Pelau to inventory the gold and silver that came for the Confederation coffers. He also enjoyed the "artistic and classical tributes" that his Confederation often sent along as gifts to their illustrious leader. The furniture, artwork, books, and paintings that graced the walls of the saloons of the Confederation were often of greater value than those in museums worldwide. It was well known that Gasparilla had exquisite taste.

With the millions of dollars in gold and silver flowing into the ware-houses, it became Gasparilla's primary duty to supervise the placement of these ingots and coins into specially designed small oak chests with cop-per linings. Through Moses St. George, Gasparilla had ordered hundreds of these beautiful chests marked with the crest of Richard Coeur de Lion to be built by an old carpenter in St. George's native Madeira, off the West Coast of Africa.

Gasparilla confided to Cousin León, "As a man grows older, his power comes from the knowledge and wisdom he has accumulated."

León nodded, "Yes, José, that is why younger people often seek ad-vice from their elders."

Gasparilla smiled and told of an even deeper belief, "You are right in most circumstances, my dear cousin, but when you are the leader in a democracy such as ours, it is more vital that your subjects continue to support you because you have a knowledge greater than theirs."

"I don't understand," León replied honestly.

Gasparilla laughed deeply, giving his cousin a big hug, then whis-pered in his ear, "My dear cousin, have you not noticed that I alone take our Confederation's treasure and bury it safely for our futures? Since I am the only one who knows the location of the treasure, worth millions, it is in their best interest to keep me healthy, alive, happy, and, most impor-tantly, in power."

Gasparilla would have two or three of the small chests loaded onto a flat bottom skiff with a single sail and various long poles. He would then sail from Cayo Pelau in the middle of the night, all alone, and distribute these treasures inland or plant them as fool's treasures.

These journeys were sometimes quite lengthy as Gasparilla often trav-eled as far north as Tampa Bay. He used three methods to bury the trea-sures. The one he most favored was to dig caves or utilize animal or In-dian mounds in which to hide the chests. This often required higher ground, which Gasparilla often found in the backwaters of Tampa Bay. These all were ideal hiding places and Gasparilla spent the majority of his time building elaborate camouflage exteriors and traps to kill the possible plun-derers. He often transplanted entire landscapes, including mangrove trees, to hide the exteriors. "Mangroves are the carp of vegetation. The damn things grow anywhere along the shore and their root systems quickly hide any trace of my work," he once exclaimed to Cousin León after a success-ful mission. "Plus, they are good for raising fish to an edible size," he laughed.

Gasparilla kept a small book, with the locations of his treasure burial sites in an unknown location, and in a second book, recorded only the locations of the fool's treasure chests. He also kept a number of false copies of his records, which he sometimes did not conceal in order to check the honesty of his Confederation.

On August 7, 1804, a Confederation schooner, the *Arabella*, under the command of Pedro Valladares, left Cayo Pelau. The previous day, Valladares had taken three beautiful French women to Gasparilla to be ransomed. As was his custom, Gasparilla provided a lavish meal for the captain and they drank late into the night. After Gasparilla passed out from the excesses of rum and wine, Valladares tore a page from his treasure-map book. The next day, hoping to find gold, he sailed into Charlotte Harbor in the direction of the Peace and Myakka rivers.

As the *Arabella* neared Cotton Key, Valladares ordered his longboat over the side so that he could row it through the shallow waters to a small point of land. As the afternoon sun shown hot upon their backs, the men from board the *Arabella* learned a fatal lesson.

Back at his castle, Gasparilla was finishing the third of the ransom letters he had written for the three women, who sat quietly in the room.

"There now, ladies, these letters will be delivered to the first French ship we encounter and hopefully within a short period of time, your sponsors and husbands will come forth with the admittedly low price I have indicated for your release." Gasparilla leaned forward with kindness. "I still cannot understand how three sisters were on the same ship?"

"We hadn't planned on being captured by the likes of your kind," the tall, red-haired one shot back.

"You do understand that, had your captain surrendered quietly, you would not be here, do you not?" Gasparilla questioned.

"I believe your Captain Valladares was going to sink our ship regardless of what flag we raised," the smaller one stated bitterly.

"Did Captain Valladares not treat you with respect and as valued bounty?" Gasparilla asked.

"He did nothing to decrease our alleged value to you, but while his men held our arms behind us, he pulled our dresses down and bared our breasts. Then he and his officers groped us while the filthy sailors yelled and whistled at us."

At that instant, out of a perfectly blue sky the muffled sound of distant thunder rumbled from the east across Charlotte Harbor.

"It sounds as if I can guarantee you that he will not ever touch you again," Gasparilla quietly said in an even tone, almost to himself.

"You ladies will be taken to those three small islands over there where I hope you will find your accommodations adequate," he continued. "You are most beautiful women, so I hope you will not attract too much attention."

With that order, the three French women were escorted from the castle.

Gasparilla had learned a great deal from the Chinese pirates, including the manufacture of both land and sea mines, when, loaded with explosives, would blow up either man or ship. All the true treasure of the Confederation had similar protection. Only the fool's treasure was left to be easily discovered.

Gasparilla went out onto *Rosalita's* patio and leaned over the railing to witness plumes of black smoke in the southeast, reminiscent of the wild fires in the area caused by lightning. However, on this clear day, he knew that one of his mines had served its purpose well. Reports came in days later describing the burnt remains of the *Arabella* near the Cotton Key, with the large cannon and beam still visible.

As he stood, with mug of tea in his hand, he looked from north to south, and quietly told Rosalita of the places where he had buried treasure: "The Manatee River, Passage Key, Long Island, Longboat Key, Siesta Key, Sarasota, Venice, Point-O-Rocks, Blind Pass, Lemon Bay, Coral Creek, Placida, Catfish Mound, Sandfly Key, Cash Mound, Powderhorn Key, John Quiet Mound, Cape Haze, Bull Key, Alligator Creek, where I need to return and plant some more mines, Black Panther Key, Useppa Island, Cabbage Key, North Captiva, Black Island, Clam Pass, the Caloosahatchee River, Estero Island, Mound Key, Black Creek, Marco Island, Lostman's River, Clark and Harney rivers, Cape Sable, and many more. I tell you, my lovely Rosalita, I am near fifty years old, but I feel like I am one hundred. I would sacrifice all these treasures to simply hold you in my arms and have our little family together as one."

CHAPTER 42

Changes in Attitude

*"I believe that success often means succeeding over a long period of time.
I am beginning to believe that success is impossible beyond the period
it takes to become successful."*
—Gasparilla, speaking to Confederation on Cayo Pelau, October 17, 1804

The huge success that the Confederation was enjoying meant that the membership had grown explosively. Unfortunately, not all the new members were of the quality and character of the majority of the brothers who joined prior to 1800.

Many newcomers rebelled at being required to read and write. They were young, wild, and reckless and came to the Confederation seeking wealth and fame rather than the freedom and security that drew the original members to the brotherhood.

One of the pivotal instances in the history of the Confederation occurred on September 22, 1804, when the three female French captives were serving their ransom captivity.

Gasparilla alternately assigned crews of the Confederation to various shore duties when their vessels were in the shipyard on Cayo Pelau for repairs, careening, or maintenance. The men worked in warehouses or, when necessary, guarded prisoners or worked in the fields.

The captain and eleven crew members of the schooner, *San Pablo*, were assigned to guard the three French female prisoners during the second half of September. These men had not been citizens of the Confederation for quite a year.

On the evening of September 22, the twelve men sat around a large campfire, smoking, drinking, and telling tales. Shortly after a spectacular sunset, one of the female prisoners called out that she needed to relieve herself.

The captain, Miguel Molina, rose from the group, took the keys from his first mate, and went to the women's quarters. He unlocked the door and escorted the young woman down the path to the latrine.

A few moments later the men heard screams coming from the maiden. Fearing animals had attacked her and their captain, they grabbed rifles and swords and ran towards the direction of the screams.

As they reached the edge of the woods, the light from their campfire illuminated the naked figure of the young woman being dragged by her long red hair. The captain, his eyes wild, was dragging the terrified woman with his right hand and with his left was hitting her bare buttocks with the flat side of his sword.

The men stopped in unison, shocked at what they were witnessing. The angry captain, by now very drunk, carried her through the armed men to the side of the fire.

He threw her to the ground and while she lay sobbing in the wet muck, Molina took off his boots and trousers. He reached down and again grabbed her long, muddy, hair to pull her to her knees. In front of his men, he grabbed his hard penis and forced it into her mouth thereby muffling her cries and sobbing.

José Jiminez, a sixteen-year-old cabin boy, ran from the group to help the young woman. As he jumped upon the back of Molina, the captain turned sharply, throwing the boy to the ground. Before the boy had a chance to get up, Molina ran his sword through the boy's left thigh, just missing his genitals and pinning him to the ground. José cried out in pain, screaming for the others to help. The girl tried to crawl to him, but was kicked repeatedly in the stomach and buttocks by the wild and leering captain. She fainted and fell silent at which point Molina went over to the cabin boy and, with a backward kick, struck him in the mouth, knocking out his teeth and causing him to fall unconscious.

Molina, now clad only in a shirt, and with sword in hand, approached the remaining ten sailors. "You shall either be with me this night or damn well be against me!" he exclaimed. "We either do this together or you each will die!"

After assuring his control of the men, Molina ordered them to drink heavily, for this would be the most unforgettable night of their young lives. "You shall know what it is like to have a lady, not the whores you are used to."

Molina then returned to the unconscious girl, picked her up and placed her next to the fire for all to see. He savagely spread her legs apart and ravaged her while she lay motionless.

The men, originally fearful for their lives, now drank heavily and became aroused as they watched their captain repeatedly assault the limp young woman. Soon, one loosened his pants and joined the captain on top of the helpless girl.

Another, Roberto Viscaya, lurched to his feet, picked the keys off the ground, and stumbled to the other cells. Crying and cowering as they had witnessed the savage brutality, the two French women were dragged from their rooms and taken to the fireside.

Viscaya led the assault on the remaining two women. Their clothes were torn off their shaking bodies and throughout the night they were assaulted repeatedly.

As the sun rose upon the smoldering fire and the eleven male, dirty, naked bodies stirred to life, they looked upon the three battered and bleeding women, and the unconscious form of their cabin boy, and realization of what they had done began to set in.

Before they could wake everyone and make a plan, one of Gasparilla's patrols, which protected the waters by night, arrived. Horrified at what he saw, Carlos Alvarez, head of the marine unit, immediately arrested the naked men and marched them to his longboat.

Upon hearing the charges against the men and realizing the gravity of the situation, Gasparilla ordered the naked prisoners be taken to Cayo Pelau and "chained like the animals they are" in front of the saloon.

"They will be better off dying of heat stroke than what I plan for them!" Gasparilla shouted to those in High Town as he left in his longboat for Cayo Pelau.

Two days later, a Confederation trial was held. During the trial, Gasparilla served as both chief prosecutor and judge. A jury of twelve of the oldest, most loyal, captains of the Confederacy was selected, thus guaranteeing a guilty verdict before the trial began.

Still naked and dirty, now sunburned and scruffy, the eleven accused remained chained to palm logs planted in front of the saloon. Gasparilla and the jury sat in the shade of the porch. The three women, wearing fine dresses, but visibly bruised on their faces and arms, sat quietly behind Cousin León and four guards.

The trial lasted less than ten minutes. Gasparilla simply walked from the shade of the porch to the sundrenched hot sand and read from a scroll: "Captain Molina, Lieutenant Viscaya, and nine seaman. You are charged with breaking the Confederation Rules in regard to stealing from another brother. When you chose to violate these prisoners and render them worthless for ransom, you stole from the brothers in this Confederation an amount equal to $30,000. That is the same as stealing at least thirty dollars from each brother assembled here. What have you to say in your defense?"

In a hoarse, raspy voice, Molina whispered, "We simply had too much to drink and lost control. We didn't really mean for this to happen. . . ."

"You are an example of why the Confederation does not approve drinking alcohol or beer while on duty. We give you sarsaparilla, fruit juices, and water for this very reason," Gasparilla answered, turning to the jury.

As in the days of gladiators in the coliseum of Rome, the jury stood and gave the thumbs down signal, indicating the most severe punishment, death.

Gasparilla walked back to the porch and in an animated gentleman's gesture offered the red-haired French victim his arm. With the four armed marines at their side, they walked over to Molina. The guards, without command, grabbed the guilty sea captain and threw him on the ground. Each guard held an arm or leg and forced the naked Molina to lie on his back, squinting into the sun.

Gasparilla reached to his waist and pulled the famous Chinese sword from its scabbard. He handed it to the silent woman.

Without saying a word, the young victim stooped down and cut off Molina's penis and threw it in his face, as his screams of pain echoed throughout the bay.

With a nod of the head, the marines then grabbed Viscaya and held him to the ground. Taking what seemed like an eternity, Gasparilla walked the first woman back to the porch and offered his arm to the next. She came forward and repeated the punishment upon Viscaya.

Gasparilla had choreographed the scene very well; it took most of the afternoon for the three women to surgically remove the genitalia of their rapists. They took their time to prolong the misery of their attackers.

As the guilty lay moaning in their own blood and in various stages of pain and consciousness, Gasparilla gave each man a knife with which to kill himself if he chose. He announced, "You may choose to end your own life, or you may be the cowards I think you to be. If you are still alive when we come out of the saloon, I shall gladly end your miserable lives for you."

At that point, Gasparilla called for a meeting of all voting members of the Confederation present and they retired inside the huge saloon hall for their meeting.

"Most of you realize that I love dogs," Gasparilla began, "so I don't want this taken in the wrong sense. However, I believe that men are like dogs. Most men who are drawn to women are constantly seeking a bitch.

Whether she is in heat or not doesn't matter to us. We only want to mount her and satisfy our desires. If she is also pleased that is simply a bonus."

"What is your point, Gasparilla?" Captain Gálvez asked of his old friend.

"The answer is simple," José replied in a loud, clear voice. "When we have women prisoners we shall guard them only with our brothers who seek other men. From this time forward, only brothers or other women who dislike women sexually shall guard females being held for ransom. That way we will not have another occurrence of what happened this week."

"Part of the problem is that the prison island is too close to Cayo Pelau," Gálvez protested.

"I agree. We shall build a prison on one of the islands south of La Costa. We will call it Captiva Island," Gasparilla stated. "No one shall be permitted upon that island except the selected guards and those carrying a letter of authorization from a leader of the Confederation. They will be full-time guards and will receive an equal share from the Confederation as they would have earned if at sea."

A majority of the Confederation members voted in favor of creating the prison island as described by Gasparilla.

"What about the current island?" Gálvez asked.

"I move that we give the island to the three sisters, and that we refer to this island as Three Sisters Key and that the story of their rape and what happened to their perpetrators is told throughout the Confederation. We can never have a repeat of what happened to them," Gasparilla answered.

The Confederation voted in large majority to accept the suggestion. A later vote also gave Molina's ship and remaining crew to the three sisters who now became members of the Confederation. Gasparilla agreed to personally teach the three to become good sea captains.

Only two of the eleven dying prisoners refused to take their own lives. So, true to his word, on his way back to High Town, Gasparilla quickly and coldly dispatched them to the hereafter.

José Jiminez was given the option of serving the women on board their ship or of being placed on a prize ship and given his freedom for his attempt at saving the women. He chose to serve as a helmsman and the ship was renamed, *The Three Sisters*.

It was during one of the shakedown cruises that Gasparilla, on board the *Doña Rosalita*, observed *The Three Sisters*. Both ships converged on a French ship, *La Belle*, just off Sanibel Island. The *La Belle* was bound from New Orleans to Le Havre.

For some unknown reason, the French ship decided to stand and fight. This suited Gasparilla as he had determined the French vessel only mounted twenty cannon and would be a good challenge for *The Three Sisters* schooner with her twelve cannon and four carronades.

Believing in baptism under fire, Gasparilla ordered the *Doña Rosalita* to full-battle stations, while at the same time ordering the huge ship to hold fire and stay downwind of the other two vessels. This maneuver insured that *La Belle* could not escape the man-of-war regardless of the outcome of the battle with *The Three Sisters.*

Gasparilla then signaled *The Three Sisters* to attack and destroy *La Belle*. In a hit-and-run battle lasting nearly four hours, Gasparilla was impressed at how *The Three Sisters* darted in and out, delivering punishing blows each time. "They attack like a mongoose. Go in and bite, then retreat before the snake can strike back, all the while wearing out the enemy," Gasparilla described the action to those on the helm of the *Doña Rosalita.*

Gasparilla was getting hungry as evening approached and felt the battle had proven the worth of *The Three Sisters* to the Confederation, so he ordered the twenty-four pounders on the *Doña Rosalita* filled with grapeshot and chain.

Within an hour, the *Doña Rosalita* came alongside *La Belle*, towering over the smaller vessel. Gasparilla bellowed to the gun crews and a salvo of fire and steel as if straight from hell tore through the rigging, sails, and upper decks of the French ship. The impact caused *La Belle* to nearly capsize. When the smoke cleared, only the broken sides of the hull of *La Belle* were visible—the masts and upper decks had been blown away and were now splinters bobbing in the Gulf of Mexico.

Peering into the carnage, the lookouts reported that only a few survivors could be seen moving on the second deck of the fatally wounded ship. An hour later, eleven beautiful Spanish women and a ten-year-old boy were rescued and brought on board the *Doña Rosalita.*

Gasparilla ordered the crew of *The Three Sisters* to thoroughly search *La Belle* and retrieve any cargo of value, then to burn her so that she would sink. The crew unloaded a large amount of gold and silver, which explained to Gasparilla why she chose to fight. Also taken were coffee, tea, and tobacco.

On board the *Doña Rosalita*, Gasparilla insured that the young women and the boy were well cared for. The ship's doctor checked them over and the quartermaster found some clothing, albeit ill-fitting, to replace the women's wet and bloodstained dresses.

While the two ships quietly moved towards Charlotte Harbor, Gasparilla had the captives brought to his quarters. Offering them coffee, tea, or sarsaparilla, and bread, he interviewed all as a group.

The women were daughters of Spanish officials and noblemen stationed in Mexico. Their parents had put them on the French ship headed for Spain where they were to attend school.

"It feels as if we have spent our whole summer on a ship," cried a tearful, brown-eyed sixteen-year-old girl plaintively. "First we were on a ship from Mexico and suffered through two terrible storms. Then, in New Orleans, our French ship ran aground because of the weight of our cargo. It took two days for us to get out of the Mississippi mud."

"And who might you be?" Gasparilla questioned, observing that this was one of the most beautiful girls he had ever seen.

"I am Princess María Louisa of Spain and I demand you give us our freedom." She haughtily insisted, as she stood defiantly before him.

"Sit down," Gasparilla ordered as he stood to confront her, wondering briefly if she might be the daughter of a former consort during his younger days in the Florida Keys. *No, the woman he knew was not fiery like this young one.*

She refused, and ran, sobbing angrily, out the door. The others sat in silence and cried quietly.

"And you, lad, you don't look like a girl," Gasparilla smiled while returning to his chair. "What brings you?"

"I am Juan Gomez and my hateful mother was sending me back to Spain," he answered, near tears himself. "Can I join your pirate ship?

Gasparilla liked this young boy and admired his spunk. "We'll think about that. I don't know whether we are in need of cabin boys or just boys to serve as chum for sharks," Gasparilla joked.

Gasparilla agreed to write letters of ransom for the ten remaining girls and to consider Juan Gomez's request to join the Confederation.

The following afternoon, the women were taken by schooner to Captiva Island where they would wait until their parents paid ransom. The muscular guards welcomed the prisoners to Captiva and helped each make up her quarters for the stay that could last a year.

Juan Gomez was made Gasparilla's private cabin boy and served with the house staff at the Boca Grande castle. Gasparilla also agreed to take him to sea when the occasion called for it.

The disrespectful Princess María Louisa was also kept at Boca Grande Castle until Gasparilla could decide what to do with her. He felt uncomfortable with the strong sexual desire he felt towards this unruly teen. He hadn't been so strongly sexually attracted to another woman since the death of Doña Rosalita. Every time he saw María or talked with her he became aroused and wanted to possess.

María Louisa sensed his desire for her and quickly turned away when she realized that her peasant blouse exposed her small, but firm, breasts. When she saw him looking at them, she would quickly back away.

At other times, when she carelessly pulled her skirt up, briefly exposing her shapely legs and smooth thighs, or appeared, scantily clad in the castle, she became angry when she noticed the old captain gazing at her with lust in his eyes.

In spite of his sense of misgiving, the infatuated Gasparilla refused to send the tempting little princess over to Captiva Island where she might be safely held for ransom.

He became obsessed with thoughts of having this young virgin for himself and began to actively pursue her, following her anytime she left her room. He then tried to walk beside her, but she ignored him and hastened her stride. Her arrogant aloofness began to enrage him.

Becoming more and more infatuated by the day, Gasparilla began calling her Josalin because she reminded him of the first girl to sexually excite him. However, María Louisa never acknowledged the name he called her.

At the urging of Cousin León and others, who were concerned with Gasparilla's increasing moodiness, he finally moved María Louisa off Gasparilla Island and gave her an island, most of which was an Indian mound. The small island, which Gasparilla named "Josalin's Mound," was almost three miles down the coast from Bokeelia, the village the Bocilla brothers had built.

Josalin, or María Louisa, lived quite well in her new surroundings. A house had been constructed for her by Gasparilla and was outfitted with fine furnishings. She lived an opulent life complete with servants. The men of the Brotherhood often derided her position and referred to her as the "virgin bitch child queen."

Gasparilla visited Josalin about once every two weeks. During his visits she would sarcastically belittle his thoughts and ideas. However, the elderly José's fixation continued to mount as he consistently pursued his out-of-reach prey.

A year after the capture of the eleven princesses, a French naval frigate, *La Reunion* from Marseilles, arrived at Gasparilla Island. The ship carried ransom to claim the Spanish princesses as called for in the letters Gasparilla had sent.

Gasparilla invited *La Reunion's* Capt. André Chenot and officers join him at the Boca Grande White Castle while arrangements were made to retrieve the princesses from Captiva Island. Captain Chenot, a highly decorated French Navy officer, enjoyed Gasparilla and suggested that the two of them go for a walk around the island. Gasparilla hesitated until Chenot said that he wanted to tell about the courage of José Pedro, now a captain.

"Hero? My José?" Gasparilla asked incredulously, "You say my son is a hero?"

"Yes, Gasparilla, that is the good news," Chenot continued. "I was one of the few French captains who escaped from the Battle of Trafalgar, thanks to him."

"Go on, please tell me the story," Gasparilla pleaded.

"On Sunday, October 20, 1805, after the French fleet fled to Cadiz, your son and his commanders agreed to join forces with our ships and break out of the blockade the British fleet had established months earlier. That afternoon, after we attended mass on shore in Cadiz, we returned to our ships. We had six frigates and thirty-four ships of the line. Your son, who had risked his life earlier that week to sneak out and determine the strength of the British fleet, found that they had twenty-seven ships and that the blockade could be broken. The Spanish Navy in Cadiz believed that if they did not attempt to break out immediately, a larger British fleet would be assembled and a land invasion might be launched. Neither of these options pleased the Spanish who had become reluctant allies of our French forces.

We set sail in the rain and had a good wind as we sailed out the narrows from Cadiz. By Monday, the 21st, we confronted the British fleet. Your son was in command of one of the Spanish frigates, *Santa Clara*, as we sailed alongside one another into battle.

José Pedro Gonzalvo Gaspar, a slight, muscular man like you, stood next to the wheelman and seemed overjoyed when he spotted the flagship of the British fleet. With a grin, he drew his sword and pointed to the British ship and waved as if we were cavalrymen instead of navy ships.

"To kill a snake, it is vital to strike its head," your son yelled as he ordered his ship to attack. "I have studied Admiral Nelson, and I believe in his quest for glory, he will be somewhere on the deck of that ship! I hope to end his illustrious career!"

All around us, the British ships were having their way with us. No matter where we looked, one of our ships was either on fire or being fired upon. Every ship except your son's ship. God, he was daring and skillful in his command, so we stayed close to him.

Rather than simply running when we reached clear water, the way we did, your son turned his ship for another pass at the English ship. I saw José Pedro Gonzalvo Gaspar climbing the rigging with a rifle and wondered what he was doing. As the ships each threw grappling hooks toward one another, a shot rang from your son's rifle striking the British Adm. Horatio Nelson. I could see immediately that he had been mortally wounded.

The ships were locked in battle and the last we heard your son and his crew were captured by the British and were being taken back to England for interrogation. We have heard that although the British may claim the Battle of Trafalgar as a victory, twenty of our ships escaped that day. We have also heard that your son is being hailed as a hero back in Cadiz," Captain Chenot concluded.

"My son—is he still alive?" Gasparilla asked, almost pleading.

"I am not sure," Chenot slowly answered, "but, there is a rumor that he is being held a prisoner for trial back in England."

Gasparilla was both pleased and stunned at the news the French captain shared. The idea that his son was brave and a hero pleased him, while the uncertainty about his fate upset Gasparilla greatly.

"I must prepare a ship to go and rescue my son!" Gasparilla exclaimed in frustration. "I cannot allow my only son to remain a prisoner and be judged by the English!"

"You know that is impossible!" Captain Chenot shouted, "Hell, man, no one is even sure your son is alive, much less where he might be held captive. We do not know his present circumstances, nor whether he is alive or not."

Tears streamed down the weathered cheeks of the pirate Confederation leader as he ran from the room. "Life can be so damned frustrating! It is an emotional battle we must fight within ourselves when we know we cannot accomplish what we would like to."

He suddenly felt an overwhelming need to be comforted and reassured and to hold someone he loved. He ordered that not only should the ten ransomed captives be returned to Gasparilla Island, but also that young Josalin be brought to him from her island.

About noon the following day, the women arrived at Boca Grande and were immediately taken on board the *La Reunion*. Captain Chenot questioned Gasparilla as to the status of the young woman at his side. "Captain, unless you brought extra money with you to pay her ransom, you must return another time to claim her," Gasparilla stated in a businesslike manner.

His attitude visibly upset Josalin, who turned and ran into the house while Gasparilla bid the French captain and his ship good-bye and a safe journey.

That evening Gasparilla drank heavily during dinner and, then he summoned Josalin to the front porch of the great house. As he spoke to her at length about his concerns for his son, she sat in stony silence. Then, without a word, she rose and, with tears in her eyes, rapidly walked into the darkness.

Gasparilla staggered after her and was gasping for breath when he finally caught up to her as she walked on the south beach facing the Gulf of Mexico. He grabbed her long hair and turned her around, pressing her supple young body firmly against his. Crying out, "How can you care so much for your son and not recognize me or care how I feel!" she allowed her body to go limp and fell to the soft, sandy beach.

"Get up, you damn whore," Gasparilla yelled angrily, his voice echoing over the water. "I do not know what has become of my only son and I am upset and tired of your games. I will make love to you this night, whether you like it or not!"

Josalin clawed a handful of sand and threw it up into Gasparilla's face. As he cried out in pain and surprise, she sprang to her feet and began to run down the beach. Clearing his eyes, Gasparilla gave chase, caught up to her and tackled her. With the release of pent-up emotions, he savagely tore the blouse from her shoulders and began to roughly suck her nipples. Josalin squeezed her eyes shut and again let herself go completely limp, with no visible reaction to his advances. This familiar passive resistance only further infuriated the inebriated Gasparilla. He rose to his feet and commanded her to do the same.

When she remained motionless on the wet sand, Gasparilla reached down and grabbed the capricious seventeen-year-old by the hair, trying to pull her to her feet. However, her dead weight slipped from his grasp.

Gasparilla reached down for her hair again and this time pulled her to her knees. Thoroughly enraged by this time, he screamed, "For over a year I have tried to show you love. You have teased me with your body and then rejected me. You have humiliated me in front of my men. I am a man and I will tolerate no more of your childish ways. I need a woman tonight!"

While Gasparilla ranted, Josalin slowly raised her head and stared into his eyes. She then carefully and deliberately spat into his face. In a fit of rage, he instantly jerked the Toledo from its scabbard. As the sword swung up, it glistened and flashed briefly in the moonlight. As Gasparilla slashed wildly, he heard her scream, "But I am the daughter of María López. You are my father."

Gasparilla was unable to stop his downswing, severing the girl's head without a sound. It flew into the high surf, disappearing under the water of the Gulf of Mexico in the outgoing tide. Blood still spurted from the headless body, running down between the cleavage of its naked breasts while the arms and legs jerked in death spasms.

Suddenly sobered by the enormity of his actions, Gasparilla's knees buckled and he collapsed on the corpse. Unconscious of the passage of time, he finally stumbled to his feet and, in a daze, with his stomach revolting, he vomited again and again. He finally carried the limp body to his longboat. After a fruitless search in the surf for the head, he cast off the longboat and quietly paddled south toward Josalin's Mound.

Tears streamed down his feverish face as he anguished not only over how he could slaughter a girl, but also one who claimed to be his daughter. He remembered the wonderful starlit nights after he had rescued Princess María López from a black flag pirate ship. She had been captured after the pirates sank the Spanish *Francesca* years earlier near Pensacola. Gasparilla had been kind to her after the rescue and, as María López needed the understanding he gave, she had given herself in return. Many nights of lovemaking must have resulted in the lovely young lady whose body Gasparilla was now taking to her grave.

Arriving at sunrise, Gasparilla carried the lifeless body up the steep mound. He stripped off the remainder of Josalin's clothing and used it to gently wash the dried blood off of her body. When he had finished, the realization of his depravity once again made him physically ill. It took all his strength to dig a grave and bury the headless body of the girl he loved so strongly.

Enraged at his hideous act, Gaspar became increasingly cruel and sullen. He was constantly haunted by what he had done to the young girl and vivid nightmares became a constant part of his life. Often he would wake up screaming and, in a cold sweat, swear that he had seen the headless body of the girl walking along the South Beach, seeking her head and crying his name.

Many sailors also claimed to hear the cries and sobbing of a woman far off shore from Gasparilla Island, particularly on nights of the full moon. Many more swore they saw the headless woman's body roaming naked on the south shore in the moonlight.

CHAPTER 43

A Turn for the Worse

*"What happens within a man is much more important than
what happens to him on the outside."*
—Gasparilla, discussing his depression en route to New Orleans, 1805

Following the slaying of Princess María Louisa, Gasparilla was often drunk for days on end and often became argumentative—without the benefit of his past quick wit and wisdom.

He was unkempt, profane, and became overweight and given to bursts of temper. Brothers stopped coming to White Castle, and the formerly dashing and charismatic pirate found himself lonely and bitter.

The Confederation, on the other hand, continued generating millions of dollars and grew at a record rate. Unfortunately, without Gasparilla's personal influence, the new members of the Confederation continued to be of lesser and lesser quality. Gasparilla, who during the early days of the Confederation had sought only men of character, was now uninterested and allowed Confederation captains to staff their ships with the criminal elements.

However, a letter to Gasparilla from a captain stationed at one of the Confederation's most northern points, temporarily rekindled his enthusiasm and leadership. When he had moved the Confederation headquarters from Cayo Hueso to Gasparilla Island, Capt. John Wilson of the Confederation schooner *Saluda* decided to sail to New Orleans. Wilson had decided to take advantage of those persons plying the Ohio and Mississippi Rivers on defenseless flatboats. His adventuresome crew included Americans from Kentucky.

Things had gone well for Wilson and his river pirates. They had established themselves along the Kentucky side of the shore near the mouth of the Cumberland River at a place called Cave-In-Rock. As its name implied, there was a huge cavern extending into the solid rock wall of the river's edge. The river in this area was quite treacherous and offered the river pirates numerous opportunities to attack lightly armed civilians trying to use the western trade route to get to the lands of the western frontier. It was near this spot that, years later, descendents of these same river pirates would attack Abraham Lincoln as he traveled.

Wilson's men were able to trade and sell most of their plunder to unscrupulous merchants and river captains in the local area. For the more expensive plunder, Wilson and his men used the Confederation merchants in New Orleans. The business became so lucrative that Wilson even advertised his cave and ran gambling, a saloon, and a brothel out of the Cave-In-Wall. He called the establishment, Wilson's Liquor Vault and Place of Entertainment.

In his letter, Captain Wilson explained how millions of settlers, merchants, and supplies traveled down the river on flatboats and how "these flat boats are designed to only go one way and are not very maneuverable. They float with the river's current right into our waiting hands. They are unarmed and it is like picking corks out of a pan of water."

"Another unique advantage to this river pirating," Wilson went on, "is that more often than not, storms and Indians are blamed for the losses. The outfitters upstream do not want to discourage people from buying their boats and supplies. We simply have one of our women dress in pioneer clothing and wade into the river, waving for help. When one of these honest flatboaters comes along and poles over to help, we attack and rob them. Depending on how attractive the women are, and how uncooperative the men might be, we kill the men and place the women in our brothel, or simply let the ugly and poor ones go on. Unlike your captives, our captives have no ransom value. It has worked out very well for us, as you no doubt have noted in our payments to the Confederation," Wilson added.

"The party continued for us at Cave-In-Rock until recently when the Harp brothers showed up. I now need the Confederation's help in dealing with this crisis. The Harps are cruel beyond anyone we have ever known," Wilson concluded.

So Gasparilla assembled a fleet of three ships and two platoons of marines under Carlos Alvarez to accompany him to New Orleans and from there on to Cave-In-Rock. Cousin León, John Gomez, and Samuel Mason, an American with a fine education who had served in the Revolutionary War, also joined the group. Mason had indicated a desire to return to the area and become involved in the river piracy on a higher plateau.

Arriving in New Orleans, Gasparilla set out to find the merchants who often bought his bounty for cash. The plan was to outfit the troops with food supplies and more weapons in New Orleans, and then, to book passage for all on the steamship *New Orleans*, which had just gone into service and offered the only easy transportation north out of New Orleans.

By evening, Gasparilla had contacted his friend, Jean Lafitte, and after dinner, they walked along the wooden sidewalks to Madame John's, 632 Dumaine Street. It was a large two-story structure that had survived the raging fire of 1789 that nearly had destroyed New Orleans.

"It surprises me not that New Orleans has been nearly burned down twice by fire," Gasparilla said. "These wooden sidewalks, for example, appear to be very flammable."

"Yes, my friend, but very cheap," Lafitte replied, "you see, when these flatboats come down the river, at least those the upstream pirates see fit to let through, they arrive here and are worthless since they cannot return upstream. So, rather than sink them or burn them, both rather dangerous choices, we simply disassemble them and make them into sidewalks and other buildings throughout town."

"It makes sense, especially with the mud and muck," Gasparilla frowned. "I wonder why anyone would build a city below sea level?"

"For the money, my friend," Lafitte laughed. "New Orleans is a city that makes money for everyone who wants to make money. It is the largest shipping port of the western trade route. The food and merchandise shipped from here make all of us rich."

"I tell you, Jean, we must make money quickly. This steam power that is being used now will bring civilization and laws to our territory," Gasparilla warned as he sipped another glass of bourbon. "These steamships can go in any direction at any time. They are fast and, believe me, someday will be able to carry many people and materials. Technology will be the downfall of our way of life."

"I don't understand," Lafitte questioned, looking Gasparilla in the eye.

"We are successful because we live in a permissive environment. The Spanish don't give a damn about law and order so long as we pay them a tribute," Gasparilla ranted. "As long as Spain and the French control the lands around which we operate, we shall be fine. But, the United States is likely to extend its law and order to the territories and will then eliminate the likes of you and me."

"What can we do?" asked the French pirate.

"The only thing we can do is to move our operations to those countries that have not won their independence from Spain or France. For me,

South America has a great deal of interest," Gasparilla stated, looking longingly up in the sky.

"The frightening part is that the Americans and other revolutionaries believe they are fighting for freedom and then they form governments that restrict those freedoms," Lafitte mused.

"Only those who defend an individual's rights first shall truly possess freedom," Gasparilla sighed, clasping a hand on his counterpart's shoulder. "The problem is that as governments become corrupt, as they all eventually will, they will enact more laws to limit the individual citizen's freedom."

"I fear you are correct, my friend," Lafitte replied sadly. "Nations tend to have diminishing ideals as they seek to control their citizenry."

"They say history repeats itself because nobody listens to the likes of us," Gasparilla quietly replied. "History will always repeat itself until we learn by studying it."

"Reality is simply the accommodations we make to make our lives livable," Lafitte added. "This often means that we accept restrictions on our freedom simply so we can all live together."

"I tell you, Jean, that it is easier to please hundreds of people you don't know than to please only one person who knows you," Gasparilla said. "Well, I will see you after my return from Cave-In-Rock."

"Believe me, Gasparilla, I shall await your return," Lafitte smiled. "Enjoy yourself in the madam's care this night. I am told some of these French whores are taken with the Spanish reputation as great lovers. I hope you can fulfill their expectations!"

"Rest assured, I shall try," Gasparilla laughed, "but remember, exactly one hundred years ago on this spot nothing happened. Why should I change history?"

The next day, the Confederation entourage, armed to the teeth, boarded the smoking, noisy, New Orleans steamboat. Many of the men were openly afraid of this noisy contraption which was to take them north on the mighty Mississippi.

Riding with Cousin León and Juan Gomez, Gasparilla again stated his belief that a combination of technology and growing populations would cause the end of pirate Confederations. With more people, the demand for laws and enforcement would result in limitation on individual freedoms for everyone.

"How can technology hurt us?" young Gomez asked.

"We have used this body of knowledge to grow our Confederation; however, as with this steamboat, when everyone adopts the latest technol ogy, the advantage to one side over the other diminishes," Gasparilla answered. "Within a few years, Fulton will invent a steam-powered submarine like this boat. The business of making money through enterprises such as ours will continue to cost more and more because of these technology advancements."

Their conversation was interrupted when just south of Cave-In-Rock, five men dressed as Indians fired old flintlocks at the steamship from shore. The Confederation marines returned fire with their new rifles, killing three of the outlaws on shore and wounding another "Indian," who was screaming profanities that sounded very English.

Arriving at Cave-In-Rock, Gasparilla and his party were saddened to learn that Big Harp and Little Harp had driven off John Wilson and some of the loyal Confederation followers. After nearly six months, the remaining Confederation pirates had succeeded in driving off the two Harp brothers and their three pregnant women.

Efrain Marrero, one of Gasparilla's original pirates, who had come north with Wilson, described how vicious the Harp brothers were, "I tell you, Gasparilla, that Micajah Harp—Big Harp—and his brother, Little Harp, kill simply for the joy of it!"

"How do you mean?" Samuel Mason asked.

"They kill *all* of their victims, whether the victim cooperates or not. They first rape the women, often as their husbands and children are forced to watch. Then they kill the parents in front of their children, and finally kill the children." Marrero hesitated, wiped a tear from his eye, and continued, "Then they gut the bodies, disembowel them and fill them with rocks. Big or Little Harp then toss the bodies into the river where they sink."

"Brothers, I have heard enough," Gasparilla began, "the state of Kentucky is offering a large reward for these two cowards. We shall kill these two and claim the reward, which we shall share equally."

It took two months for Gasparilla, his marine posse and local citizens to locate the Harps and to creep up on them and the women. As the posse moved in, the two Harps jumped on horseback and began riding off—without the women.

Gasparilla grabbed a long rifle from a posse member named Thompson, aimed and fired, hitting Micajah Harp squarely between the shoulders, fatally wounding him. The younger Harp—Wiley—managed to escape into the nearby woods.

Carlos Alvarez and the marines captured the three women on foot and brought them forward.

Gasparilla looked at each of them, then drew his bright Toledo from his scabbard, grabbed Big Harp's head and in one swoop, decapitated the infamous murderer. The women screamed in anguish and fear at the sight.

"Now you know how your innocent victims feel," Gasparilla roared. "Sometimes the Old Testament lessons are the best learned. An eye for an eye, a life for a life."

Gasparilla ordered Carlos Alvarez and his men to take the three women and claim the reward for killing Big Harp. He then picked up the Harp's head and forced it into tree branches on the heavily traveled trail.

"Let this be a warning for those who would attack any Confederation member," Gasparilla said with conviction and hatred.

When the hunt for Wiley Harp proved fruitless, Gasparilla established a $25,000 reward for his head. Rumor had it that the fugitive had crossed the river and was hiding in the Illinois territory.

Gasparilla also appointed Samuel Mason to take over the operation of Cave-In Rock and to cooperate with James Ford and the other river pirates.

"Samuel, learn all you can from James Ford," Gasparilla cautioned. "He operates a ferry system and a tavern, and believes in covering up his acts by surrounding himself with honest people. He has men who patrol the roads and who, like Robin Hood, rob only the rich, while allowing the poor to go on their way. Ford has a good system. Learn from him."

"I will José. We will restrict our business to gambling, operating a bordello, and counterfeiting," Mason promised.

"And robbing?" Gasparilla asked.

"Only the rich, I promise," Mason laughed.

As Gasparilla and his men sailed south on the Mississippi towards New Orleans, thoughts of fine food, a good bed, and a soft woman filled their thoughts. "This land is changing. Like Cayo Hueso, there are too many people on this river," Gasparilla sighed. "All these people will demand laws and a government. This, I fear, will cause yet another war in the near future."

CHAPTER 44

Choosing Sides, War of 1812

"When you hear the word 'opportunity' come from the mouth of a politician or bureaucrat, it simply is another politically correct word for problems."
—Gasparilla, discussing allegiance with Jean Laffite, 1811

By the beginning of the 1800s, Spain's monopoly over the colonies of South and Central America and throughout the Caribbean was crumbling. The dishonest and corrupt leadership that Spain had offered, plus its refusal to properly invest either resources or industry into the New World, left the colonies in poverty. As the first decade of the 1800s unfolded, many South American countries had won their independence.

Gasparilla and the Lafitte brothers, Jean and Pierre, met at Barrataria, down river from New Orleans. The Lafittes had become the first privateers commissioned by the new country of Cartagena, a republic in South America.

The purpose of the meeting was to determine with which side Gasparilla's Confederation and Lafitte's sizeable fleet would ally in the impending war between the English and Americans. This decision was a crucial one since the British would certainly defeat the Americans if the Confederation supported the British or remained neutral. On the other hand, if the Americans could secure the support of Gasparilla and the Lafittes, they could concentrate on dealing with the English primarily in the North and Canada. The British would not dare open naval warfare with Confederation vessels, so the allegiance of Gasparilla, Lafittes, and other pirates to the American cause was essential.

The American Navy consisted of only twenty ships—eight frigates and twelve sloops—after it had sold its ships early in the 1790s, only seventeen American warships were available.

The British Navy, on the other hand, had five hundred and eighty-four ships at sea. There were one hundred and two line-of-battle ships, one hundred and twenty-four frigates, and elements of fleets at virtually all French ports. In addition, the English held in reserve eighteen battleships and fifteen frigates. England had not lost a battle at sea for over twenty-two years.

In fact, the Napoleonic wars were a constant source of conflict between the Americans and the British. The British were guilty of impressing American sailors into service on board English ships. Often English ships captured American merchant vessels and held them for up to one year or more.

As the pirate leaders met at Barrataria, their discussion of which side to support lasted many days. The weather was typical of the Delta region with rain, followed by more rain. It was unusually hot and humid and the combination of hot weather, high temperatures, and rain heightened tensions among those deliberating.

Jean and Pierre Lafitte hosted and ran most of the meetings. Gasparilla had brought Brutal Betsy, Robert A., Miguel Rodriquez, Cousin León, and Juan Gomez with him. William Augustus Bowles, a part-Creek Indian, was with Lafittes. Bowles had recently trained an Indian crew for his new ship.

In addition, a number of other black-flag pirates from the Caribbean attended the discussions, as did newer pirates from the new independent republics of South America.

"There is nothing worse than having a good understanding of both sides of an issue," Gasparilla remarked caustically. "No matter how things turn out, there will be someone to tell you, 'I told you so.'"

"All the troubles of man come from not making the right decisions," Bowles agreed with a big smile. Bowles had heard a great deal about the brilliance of Gasparilla and wanted to know him better. Bowles himself had been born in Maryland, but ran away and fought on the British side during the American Revolution. An officer and gentleman, Bowles often fraternized with English lords and ladies, and was equally at ease with Creek Indian tribes with whom he lived after deserting the British Army in Pensacola.

"The fact is that we can choose to align ourselves with the most powerful navy in the world or we can remain neutral," Lafitte stated. "But if we choose England, then we lose our markets in New Orleans for the balance of the war. Clearly, the French and Americans could not win a war against England unless we join their side. By remaining neutral, we can still attack the Spanish ships at will, but would have to limit our attacks on both the British and French ships. I'll be damned if I know what is right!"

"If you want to get hit from both sides try and straddle an issue such as this," Brutal Betsy shouted with a wry smile. "If you want things done, you should ask a woman."

"And, what are your thoughts, my English-sounding lady," Lafitte questioned.

"I'm Irish and I hate the English more than anyone here," she retorted with a red face to match her crimson hair. "However, I do believe that in order to understand an enemy, you must gain an insight into what made him what he is!"

"I know that the English have many ships and show them as a source of power," Pierre Lafitte replied.

"Yes, my friend," Gasparilla interrupted, "Thomas Hobbes, the English political philosopher observed more than one hundred years ago, 'The reputation of power is power.' The English are bullies and they get away with it!"

"What are you suggesting Gasparilla?" Bowles asked, looking around at the others in the group.

"I suggest that we meet with the Americans as well as the English," Gasparilla replied. "I suggest we consider whomever will grant us the best opportunity, but, I must tell you, no matter whom we chose, I fear that our days of operating as we have in the past are becoming shortened."

"What do you mean?" Lafitte asked.

"The Spanish were so corrupt that we were able to operate as we saw fit so long as we rewarded the proper Spanish official," Gasparilla said, while walking towards the still water of the bay. "The United States and France, for that matter, are becoming most intolerant of the sweet trade. The English, who originated privateering are now withdrawing their support for they have enough navy to enforce rules in all their colonies and possessions. No, regardless of who wins the coming conflict, I fear each of our days will be numbered."

"*Merde!*" Lafitte shouted, "I think that, as in the current situation, there will always be the need for the likes of us."

"My good friend, Jean, I normally like people who live in fantasy worlds," Gasparilla smiled while turning and walking towards him. "It allows us to see life from a different perspective. However, in this case we must face reality."

"Gasparilla, if monarchs can be corrupted, then it stands to reason that we should be able to bribe an elected official of a democratic republic like the United States," Jean Lafitte intoned angrily. "Hell, how can they expect to govern a country with such a variety of ethnic groups?"

"Yes, Gasparilla, not only cream rises to the top; more often, scum," Bowles added. "Nations inevitably are led by scum that rises to the top."

"I would generally agree," Gasparilla nodded. "But, as for my group, I believe our future to be in South America dealing with the dishonesty we have come to expect from Spanish bureaucracies. A good friend, Gen. Juan Monteverde, is leading an army sure to win independence in Venezuela."

"But, what about Mexico?" Lafitte questioned. "For me the islands off the Texas coast would be better."

"José Morelos, a priest I have known, is a leader in the revolt of Mexico against Spain," Gasparilla stated. "Perhaps he will have success. There is never one place or one thing that can make you successful. It takes the right combination of place and outside events."

That night, Gasparilla and Miguel Rodriquez rowed out to the *La Esclavitud* to further discuss the events of the evening.

As they sat drinking in the captain's cabin, the door swung open and Brutal Betsy stood naked in the dim light. Both men gasped at the sight of her in the doorway. The breeze caused her hair to gently blow in the perfect silhouette that she created.

"Betsy, my love, what are you doing?" Miguel asked, shocked.

"Since we are the guests of a Frenchman, I thought you two might be interested in something very French, a *ménage à trois*," Betsy purred. Miguel and José looked at each other in surprise, then broke into broad grins. The trio spent the night together in passionate lovemaking. The *La Esclavitud* rocked more on the still water than the surrounding ships.

The following day, Gasparilla, Miguel, Brutal Betsy, Bowles and Cousin León sailed for Florida Town, a trading post in the western panhandle, where they were to meet with American Gen. Andrew Jackson and Davy Crockett, the famous frontiersman.

The meeting was arranged by Zephaniah Kingsley, Florida's most prominent plantation owner and slave trader of the first decade of 1800. Kingsley imported slaves, then put them through a period of schooling and training before they were sold. Kingsley had come across Florida from his plantation on Fort George Island, overlooking the St. Johns River. This meeting and the preservation of the United States were important to him.

Gasparilla immediately took a liking to Zephaniah Kingsley, in spite of the fact he was a slave trader; Kingsley was a humanitarian in his handling of the slaves he purchased.

"I don't fully understand why you spend so much time in teaching your slaves to read and write. Then you train them to be efficient workers as well," Gasparilla asked shortly after meeting Kingsley.

"Very simple, Gasparilla," Kingsley smiled. "My slaves are well trained, are in excellent physical condition and, most importantly, have a positive mental condition. I ask a price fifty percent above the average market price of other slaves."

"And, you get it?" Gasparilla nodded.

"Yes, Captain, my slaves have a reputation of becoming successful," Kingsley smiled while grasping Gasparilla's shoulder. "My 'graduates,' if you will, soon rise to foreman's status. Our slaves have great value to those who buy from us. Gen. Andrew Jackson, whom you'll meet today, buys a great many of them for his plantation in the Tennessee country."

"Very smart. You are proving that education does have a value," Gasparilla agreed as he shook Zephaniah's hand.

"I'd like to introduce you to my wife, Anna Madegigine Jai." Zephaniah guided Gasparilla to the beautiful woman seated across the room. As they soon learned, she was the daughter of the famous Indian chief of the Senegal.

At mid-afternoon as a thunderstorm threatened, a large column of men approached Florida Town from the northwest. Kingsley and Gasparilla walked from the porch to greet the new arrivals. Gasparilla got a chill as he walked towards the riders, sensing that in the future, Andrew Jackson might well become his personal Judas.

Meeting in the saloon long into the night, the Americans and pirates argued as to the merits of working together against England. The discussion ranged from thoughtful to intense as the mosquitoes feasted upon Jackson's troops outside the building.

"General Jackson, I believe the English are far too confident to defeat your Americans," Gasparilla exclaimed. "The Royal Navy has not tasted defeat for nearly a quarter century. You tell your President Madison that I believe that the British will not move any additional ships against the American Navy. Stubborn British pride will work in your favor. The French have obligated a great many of the English ships in the Napoleonic War. If we choose to join with you, the English will never attack you in force."

"You seem confident, Gasparilla," Davy Crockett interrupted. "Why do you think the English will not attack us with everything they have?"

"You are a great hunter, I am told, so you know how important it is to understand the habits of the animal you stalk," Gasparilla replied. "The English tend to be reserved in all things. This gives you Americans the advantage in the short term."

"What do you mean?" Crockett asked.

"We all know that if the English reacted like the Americans or the Spanish, they would send a fleet and end your American dream in a matter of months!" Gasparilla responded, "but, instead they will be conservative which will allow your government the two-year's time it takes to build the fine ships you are noted for."

"Interesting possibility," Jackson said thoughtfully. "At the very least, worth the gamble."

"It is the only possible hope you upstart Americans have," Gasparilla exclaimed. "With time, the fine shipbuilders, like the ones we use in Mystic, can build you navy ships like ours—forty-six gun frigates that actually carry fifty-six to sixty cannon and are able to navigate shallow depths as well as heavy seas."

"We are indeed able to construct almost anything," Jackson boasted. "Our country has a wealth of raw materials. We can build the best of any thing in the world."

"From my current experiences, let me warn you Americans about materialism," Gasparilla said in a harsh whisper. "Materialism and greed are two things sure to destroy your democracy. How easy it is for us to forsake our principles for material things. I warn your new nation to take advantage of the ability to construct the finest of everything without allowing itself to be consumed by materialism."

He decided to offer Andrew Jackson, an incurable gambler, to a wager that could greatly benefit his Confederation with no risk to the pirates.

Gasparilla bet Jackson that he could beat him in a horse race down the only street in Florida Town. Besides the money wagered between Gasparilla's crew members and Jackson's militia, Gasparilla's bet included an unlimited number of Letters of Marque, enough for all the ships in his Confederation if he should win. Gasparilla knew the incorrigible Jackson could not refuse such a bet.

The race, at high noon the following day, proved exciting. The aging sea captain rode a strange horse to a narrow victory, proving that all the skills José Gaspar had learned from María Gonzalez had not been forgotten over the years.

Two days later the Americans, and Gasparilla's entourage agreed to work together. Gasparilla's Confederation and the other pirates would serve as American Privateers under nearly one hundred Letters of Marque. Gasparilla's gamble would mean literally millions of dollars in privateer booty for the Confederation.

"When one has the gambling disease, he often lets his emotions cloud his rational thinking," Gasparilla told Juan Gomez and Cousin León as they sailed away from Florida Town. "We had everything to gain. Jackson had nothing to gain, but, he also wasn't losing anything personally."

A month later, the group reassembled at Dog Island—listed on maps as Isles aux Chiens—at the entrance to St. Georges sound off Carrabelle. The small island—seven miles long and uninhabited—offered both privacy and a quick escape.

"Whoever named this island?" Juan Gomez asked as the two ships silently approached it.

"The French," Gasparilla grunted. "If the English had named it, it would have a fancier-sounding name. Remember, Juan, the English give significance to everything by the way they name it. In the sixteenth century, the Tudors had a private island specially for their dog kennels."

"What was it called?" Gomez asked

"The Isle of Dogs, of course," Gasparilla laughed.

That afternoon General Andrew Jackson distributed official Letters of Marque to Gasparilla to be distributed and carried by every Confederation Captain who agreed to become a privateer to the United States of America in their war with England.

Gasparilla took one of the Letters of Marque and read it aloud to everyone on Dog Island:

> James Madison,
> President of the United States of America
> To all who shall see these presents, Greetings:
>
> BE IT KNOWN, That in pursuance of an act of Congress, passed on the 26th day of June one thousand eight hundred and twelve, I have Commissioned, and by these present do commission, the private, armed ships owned or controlled by José Gaspar, King Lion of the Seas, and Allies or Confederates of same, officers and crew, to subdue, seize, and take any armed or unarmed British vessel, public or private, which shall be found in the jurisdictional limits of the United States, or elsewhere on the high seas, or within the waters of the British dominions, and such captured vessel, with her apparel, guns, and appurtenances, and the goods

or effects which shall be found on board the same, together with all the British persons and others who shall be found acting on board, to bring within some port of the United States; and also to retake any vessel, goods, and effects of the people of the United States, which may have been captured by any British armed vessel, in order that proceedings may be had concerning such capture or recapture in due form of law, and as to right and justice shall appertain.

The said Gaspar, King Lion of the Seas, and allies or confederates of same is further authorized to detain, seize, and take all vessels and effects, to whomsoever belonging, which shall be liable thereto according to the law of nations and the rights of the United States as a power at war, and to bring the same within some port of the United States, in order that due proceedings may be had thereon.

This commission to continue in force during the pleasure of the president of the United States for the time being.

GIVEN under my hand and seal of the United States of America, at the City of Washington, the Twelfth Day of July in the year of our Lord, one thousand eight hundred and twelve and of the independence of the said states the thirty-seventh.

BY THE PRESIDENT, *James Madison*
James Monroe, Secretary of State

"My dear General Jackson, I note that my name has been replaced by my pseudonym King Lion of the Seas?" Gasparilla looked at Adams quizzically.

"Yes, Gasparilla, President Madison felt that politically it would be better to recognize you as a 'monarch' instead of the notorious pirate you have become," Adams answered diplomatically.

"Or is it that your president and politicians do not like a true democracy so close to them?" Gasparilla asked. "I can understand why some people choose not to look into a mirror unless absolutely necessary."

As Adams winced, Gasparilla smiled, knowing he had made his point, then said, "It matters not what lies behind us and what lies before us matters little compared to what lies within us."

Gasparilla then turned to the brothers. He walked slowly towards them, before looking into the blue sky and saying, "I remember what the explorer, Ferdinand Magellan, is alleged to have said in 1520, which I believe applies to our alliance with the Americans. Magellan said that the sea is dangerous and its storms terrible, but these obstacles have never been sufficient reason to remain ashore. . . . Unlike the mediocre, intrepid spirits seek victory over those things that seem impossible . . . it is with an iron will that they embark on the most daring of all endeavors . . . to meet the shadowy future without fear and conquer the unknown."

"Are we not putting our ships at risk?" Jean Lafitte questioned.

"If we do not join the United States and instead keep our ships in the harbor, then the ships will be safe, but I don't believe that warships were made for that," Gasparilla said with determination in his voice.

General Jackson passed some letters to Gasparilla, which he took on board the *Intrepido II* for the sail back to Charlotte Harbor. On the voyage back Gasparilla read them to Cousin León and Juan Gomez.

The letter from Napoleon Bonaparte was one that urged Gasparilla to join with the United States against England. In addition, Napoleon stated that "history is the version of past events that people decide to agree upon. By joining the Americans in this fight, you will have the opportunity to regain your name." He then closed with the line, "I ask you again, what is history but a fable agreed upon?"

"I must answer Napoleon and ask him under which name I shall be remembered?" Gasparilla smiled. "President Madison would rather have me remembered as a king."

The other letter was from an old Spanish friend, Col. Vicente Folchy Juan, who served under the governor general of Louisiana and West Florida. This letter said that Ching Shih, the Chinese pirate Confederation leader, had surrendered to the Chinese government a year earlier. This marked the end of the largest pirate confederation and left Gasparilla's Confederation as the final independent world power.

During the years of the War of 1812, Gasparilla's Confederation, under the Letters of Marque granted to José Gaspar Coeur de Lion, controlled the Caribbean and Gulf of Mexico and captured or sank nearly one hundred vessels.

It was the disposition of the captured ships, cargoes, and crews of these British flagged ships that became a point of contention between the United States and the Confederation. The Letter of Marque clearly indicated that captured ships, cargo, and crews were to be brought directly to United States ports. A trial would be held and the assets would then be distributed after the hearing or trial.

Gasparilla felt that his Confederation was in fact saving the youthful United States from certain defeat at the hands of the English. Therefore, he continued to operate as he had for decades only with a greater emphasis on seeking out the British vessels. The Confederation made its usual offers to the captured crews.

However, an incident in 1814, just south of the mouth of Tampa Bay, caused the Americans to mistrust and despise Gasparilla. A British payroll ship sailing from Jamaica to New Orleans to pay British soldiers and civilians in that city encountered Gasparilla and his flagship, the *Intrepido II*. The heavily laden English ship was no match for the quick *Intrepido II*. Gasparilla ordered his flagship to circle the British vessel and fired broadsides into its starboard side. The British ship was badly damaged and limped into the Tampa Bay where she dropped anchor. Her crew fought bravely to save her from sinking until they were driven away by Gasparilla's marines. Before the ship sank, Gasparilla's men had acquired $50,000 in British gold and silver coins.

The crew of an American naval vessel later captured the British crew, who were by then near death from dehydration and starvation. This combination of cruelty and outright theft by Gasparilla enraged the Americans in Washington who vowed privately and publicly to get revenge on the renegade privateer.

An uneasy truce was reached, but no love would be lost between the Americans and members of the Confederation for the remainder of the war. A great naval victory by Gasparilla's Confederation over a fleet of British warships at the mouth of Charlotte Harbor in the fall of 1814 did not rally any new support from the Americans. But this naval victory, combined with Lafitte's buccaneers' alliance with Andrew Jackson the following year in the Battle of New Orleans, insured victory by the United States over England in the War of 1812.

Gasparilla learned during the summer of 1814 that the American ship *Wasp* had engaged British ships off the coast of England, capturing ten British ships, including one that had his son on board as a prisoner. The thirty-two-year-old José Pedro Gonzalvo Gaspar was free at last. The elder Gaspar longed that they would one day soon meet on the seas. But the pirates were about to become the hunted, instead of the hunters. Instead of honoring the privateers who insured victory over England, the Americans determined to rid their waters of these same heroes.

CHAPTER 45

1815–1821, Last Years of Florida Piracy

"Those who foresee the tragic future are often consumed by madness; their insane actions then bringing about the fruition of what they feared most."
—Gasparilla, November 2, 1821

After Gasparilla and Lafitte insured Andrew Jackson's American victory at the Battle of New Orleans in 1815, the War of 1812 came to a successful close. For the next two years, the Confederation, Lafitte's pirate band, and the United States lived peacefully with one another.

However, mutual distrust grew. It was obvious to all that the United States would not officially recognize these freedom-loving pirate groups. Andrew Jackson had developed strong alliances with Thomas Jefferson, who believed that the United States must have both Florida and Cuba.

For Spain, the second decade of the nineteenth century was more troublesome than the first. Madrid technically held title to both East Florida and West Florida, but had removed most Spanish troops from both provinces to fight the many rebellions erupting across Latin and South America. Losing more battles than they won, the Spanish continued to not only recall its soldiers and government officials, but also to take money away from the Florida provinces as well.

Without any semblance of government, or law and order, the provinces of La Florida became fertile grounds for Confederation pirates, renegade Indians, fugitive slaves, robbers, and black-flagged pirates. Many of these groups regularly crossed into the United States to rob, rape, pillage, and burn out citizens. Presidents Madison and Monroe were determined to put a stop to these atrocities.

Initially, Gen. Edmund P. Gaines had been authorized to chase Indians out of Georgia and back into Florida. General Gaines respected the

Spanish forts and possessions as well as Confederation communities. "These are Spanish forts and are entitled to their integrity," Gaines often stated. Gasparilla actually supported Gaines and had four Confederation ships escort the United States troops on the East Coast of Florida.

The incursions, smuggling, and lack of any allegiance to the United States were the reasons that Andrew Jackson stated publicly for invading Spanish Florida. However, one of the real issues was increased pressure by Americans who were envious of the tremendously profitable mullet fisheries operated by Cubans and Spanish Indians along Florida's west coast.

"The Americans are more materialistic than any pirate in our Confederation," Gasparilla exclaimed in exasperation. "They can't tolerate our Cuban allies who successfully operate 'fish ranchos' along with our Indian neighbors. They don't understand how much work it takes to fish and to farm. The Americans are greedy and want to own too many things!"

Andrew Jackson, encouraging raids throughout West Florida and around New Orleans and fanning dislike and hatred toward the Seminoles, was finally placed in charge of the Southern U.S. Command.

He was a spiteful man in combat, and as he began leading his troops south into Florida, he unofficially declared war on everyone in the Floridas who was not a citizen of the United States. Jackson's actions, independent of either presidential or congressional authority, began his punitive war.

After a number of successes in his first campaign, he wrote to President Monroe, "The whole of East Florida should be seized and this can be done without implicating the government."

"Andrew Jackson is the most cruel pirate ever to operate in Florida!" Gasparilla exclaimed as he exhorted his mates to vote to help the Indians fight against Jackson's barbaric army. "The man has no soul; he is a racist swine particularly in his dealings with our Indian allies," he added. "The Seminoles came south to Florida to escape conflict and Jackson brings nothing but killing and fear to them."

Gasparilla went ashore at Gonzalez, the estate of Don Manuel Gonzalez, fifteen miles from Pensacola. Don Manuel had come to Pensacola as a Spanish Army officer in 1784, about the same time Gasparilla was breaking his ties with Madrid. Gasparilla had met and saved the life of the current Spanish crown's Indian agent and commissary officer and, during the ensuing twenty years they had developed a profitable and honored relationship and friendship. Gonzalez, who had received a Spanish land-grant for raising cattle, now had a ranch so large that it nearly encircled Pensacola.

In 1814, with General Jackson's first attempted raid on Pensacola, General Jackson requested that either Don Manuel, or his son, guide the Americans into the settlement.

Gasparilla was in attendance when Don Manuel, with his son by his side, refused, saying, "Shoot him or both of us if you must, but do not ask me to be a traitor to my native Spain."

Without Gonzalez's help, Jackson could not directly attack the Spanish settlement at Pensacola and left with the warning, "You will be forever sorry that you failed to help me win this campaign."

The Seminoles were a hard-working and independent people. They lived in open, palm-thatched dwellings called chickees near the Everglades. Outstanding hunters and traders, the Seminoles had managed to escape capture by the United States army for nearly thirty years. They often boasted that they were the only "unconquered people."

During the last years of James Madison's presidency, Andrew Jackson managed to spread lies and half-truths against Gasparilla and the Lafitte brothers. No doubt, John Jay, archenemy of Gasparilla, used his position and influence to poison the thinking of President Madison. Madison, who had written the Federalist papers with Jay, was led to believe that Gasparilla and the Lafittes were serious threats to the American republic and although he would not authorize official action against Gasparilla and the Lafittes, he did little to stop Andrew Jackson until it was too late.

At the same time, West Florida was not profitable to Spain. Tobacco, indigo, and lumber were the top products, and all could be bought cheaper from Mexico and the new Latin American republics. This was but another reason that the Spanish government in Madrid was not willing to risk a war with the United States and did not actively defend West Florida against the advances of Jackson and his marauders.

Gasparilla's ships commanded the seas shortly after the War of 1812, but, because of his insistence before the war that the Americans build fleet warships to his design, the growing American Navy was now becoming the Confederation's equal.

Although there was no direct confrontation between the Confederation and American warships prior to 1816, such a showdown was inevitable. The presence of American warships not only inhibited the Confederation vessels but also eliminated many of the foreign-flagged merchant ships of Spain and England. Only thirty-seven ships were captured or sunk by the Confederation during this three-year span. The brothers were getting impatient with the lack of action and income from the limited number of prizes.

Henry Caesar, the Black pirate of Sanibel Island, was a giant ex-slave who had become a member of the Confederation near the end of the War of 1812. He was more famous for his size than his skill as a pirate ship's captain. What he lacked in skill, he more than made up in ruthlessness. Caesar le Grand as he often called himself, was the most vicious of all the Confederation sea captains.

Upon joining the Confederation, Henry Caesar and his men were ordered to set up a camp at the southern end of Sanibel Island, near the mouth of San Carlos Bay and the Caloosahatchee. It was at this site that, later in the century, the U.S. Lighthouse Service would place the Sanibel Island lighthouse. Gasparilla, with a well-fortified fort on Cayo Costa, was concerned about an attack from the south, perhaps up Pine Island Sound. Although the Spanish fishing rancho at Punta Rassa had six shore batteries, they were generally out of range of any intruder who would choose to sail up that waterway.

Caesar and his men built a village of palm-thatched huts on the bay side of Sanibel Island. With Henry Caesar at the end of the island, Gasparilla would be protected from an attack up Pine Island Sound.

Caesar fulfilled his role very well, capturing many ships and enlarging his village, which now included three twenty-four-pound artillery shore batteries. Caesar and his men, while not role models of the Confederation, did contribute a great deal to its economy.

But then, on January 21, 1818, some of Caesar's men, in a six-gun sloop, stopped at Captiva Island and drank heavily with the guards. By the end of the day, two women being held for ransom were dragged from the stockade and one of Gasparilla's special guards was killed.

On January 27, Gasparilla was told of the attack by Caesar's men and the kidnapping and killing that followed. Enraged, Gasparilla sailed south towards Henry Caesar's encampment with a fleet of eight ships.

On the morning of February 2nd, Gasparilla ordered a volley of cannon fire on the village. Over one hundred shells landed upon the sleeping community and within ten minutes Caesar's compound had struck their colors and surrendered.

With six longboats of heavily armed marines, Gasparilla landed on shore and marched up to the six-feet, five-inch-tall Henry Caesar. Nearly a foot shorter than the pirate captain, Gasparilla insisted that Caesar look him in the eye and listen.

"I want to know which of your men killed my guard and took two of our hostages from the stockade on Captiva," Gasparilla shouted at the shaking pirate.

Caesar regained his composure and declared with disdain, "The guard was not a man, but a woman in a man's body!"

Enraged Gasparilla, with a swift movement, drew his Chinese dagger and plunged it into the thigh of Black Caesar roaring, "Every person in this Confederation that does the job we ask of him or her is important to all of us. Remember, the power of this Confederation is that we recognize individual strengths, not focus on their weaknesses!"

On the ground and bleeding from the cut in his leg, Caesar painfully pointed to one of the palm huts at the northern edge of the village and gasped, "It was the three Cubans who took the women, they are over there."

Gasparilla had the marines surround the house and with three other men, burst into the small house. Inside, lying naked on the floor were the two women and three men. The women were beaten, bruised, and apparently had been raped many times.

Furious, Gasparilla had the Cubans taken outside the hut and then demanded that they tell him the reason that they had gone to Captiva Island.

"We have no women and you guard the virgins only with weak men," Adaro Mercado spat near Gasparilla's face.

"None of our citizens of our Confederation is weak; we depend upon each other," Gasparilla angrily shouted as he flashed his famous Toledo and decapitated Mercado.

Next to feel the cold steel of Gasparilla's sword was Manuel Gerena, who could not control his emotions and wept openly, pleading for his life. But Gasparilla showed no mercy, as he believed that punishment for violation of the laws had to be consistent.

The third man, César Rodriquez, implicated Henry Caesar in an attempt to spread the blame and save his own life.

According to Rodriquez, Caesar had told them that the women held on Captiva were often ransomed for $10,000 or more and that they were guarded by weak men who loved only other men. They had planned to go to Captiva and take the women to ransom on their own, but when one of the sober sentries caught them, they had to kill him. It was an accident, claimed Rodriquez, but the men drank heavily because of it and raped the women. When they later became sober, they found themselves in the woods with the two unconscious, bleeding women so they brought the women back to camp. Caesar then agreed to let them keep the women only with the condition that they make monthly visits to Sanibel and that he would have them for himself the first two nights they were there.

Gasparilla quickly disposed of Rodriquez and returned to where Henry Caesar was lying in his own blood while being attended to by other members of his crew.

Gasparilla then ordered Caesar and his ships to leave Sanibel before sunset the following day. "I never want to hear of you anywhere near Florida. If I do, then you will die as those three did."

After Caesar's fleet left, heading south, Gasparilla ordered the village to be burned except for the two larger houses and the battery of three twenty-four-pound cannon. He left Sergio García, forty-seven men, and two twelve-gun sloops to maintain the camp and the defense of Pine Island Sound.

"I am truly getting too old for this," Gasparilla sighed as he slumped down upon a small log. "I used to believe that age was often a question of mind over matter; but, what matters as you grow older is that there seem to be more aches and pains to overcome." Then, with a silence surrounding the group, Gasparilla added, "and too many changes and problems to deal with."

"Things will get better, Captain," Juan Gomez said hopefully.

"Being old, I know when we are suffering and I know when we are satisfied," Gasparilla said wearily. "Things in this part of the world will never get better for us. We had Utopia but, looking back, we were too busy chasing our goals to realize that we had it."

On July 17, 1816, an American Navy patrol on foot was attacked on the Apalachicola River during the reconnaissance of a former English fort, which was now occupied by three hundred free slaves. These ex-slaves were allies of Gasparilla's Confederation, with as many as two thirds owing their freedom to members of Gasparilla's navy. Four Americans were killed in the action. The fort's location in Spanish Florida meant little to General Jackson as he viewed it as a threat to the limited American commerce on the Apalachicola River.

In retaliation for the killing of the four American sailors, Lt. Colonel Duncan L. Clinch, with an American Army and one hundred and fifty Creek Indians opened fire on July 27, 1816 on the blacks in the fort. A "hot shot" cannon ball penetrated the fort's main ammunition magazine, and the initial explosion instantly killed the almost three hundred Confederation defenders. Only thirty people survived.

This battle marked the worst defeat and loss of life ever suffered by the Confederation. The battle had lasted less than two hours. Because it was a land-based army that had won the victory, the Confederation's navy could not retaliate.

"This is the ultimate in frustration. We cannot exact revenge. We cannot protect our citizens on land. I have never felt so powerless," Gasparilla wearily admitted with tears in his eyes.

Andrew Jackson continued his assault on East Florida for most of 1817. Then, in 1818, Jackson reported to John Calhoun, secretary of war, that he was going to begin an assault of the Panhandle and West Florida.

President Monroe sent Jackson a letter that was vague at best. In the letter, Monroe told Jackson that his move against the Seminoles would bring to Jackson a theatre, one that would have other interests to be dealt with as well. Jackson perceived this to be permission to attack Spanish forts and holdings.

In April 1818, Jackson's troops first captured St. Mark's, where Jackson personally tore down the Spanish flag and raised the stars and stripes. Following the battle, Jackson's troops captured Alexander Arbuthnot, a seventy-year-old Scottish citizen, who was a noted Indian sympathizer.

Days later, Old Town, inhabited primarily by members of the Upper Creek Indians, and one of the largest Indian villages in all of Spanish Florida, was attacked during a punishing assault by Jackson's army. The Indians offered little resistance and the battle was over quickly. Another Englishman, a former army officer, twenty-one-year-old Robert Armbrister, was captured during the attack.

Against the advice of his fellow officers, Andrew Jackson overruled a military court and had Armbrister shot dead. He then ordered the old man, Arbuthnot, to be hung from a tree near the center town and told his troops that these men were "unprincipled villains" whose executions should warn others of the revenge coming to "unchristian wretches" who would aid Indians.

Gasparilla felt that, finally, Jackson had gone too far and the English and Spanish would rise up in righteous indignation, forcing the Americans to withdraw from West Florida.

He called for a meeting with Jean Lafitte and others to discuss the future of operations in West Florida and Panhandle. Prior to the meeting, Gasparilla had met with his most trusted captains and discussed the Confederation's options in dealing with the upstart, aggressive Americans.

"I must tell you that I am a believer in luck. I also must tell you that I also once believed that the harder you worked, the luckier you became," Gasparilla began the meeting. "I think the Americans have added another dimension to what luck really is. How else can you explain their defeating of the greatest navy and army in the world not once, but twice in less than fifty years? And now they pillage and burn Spanish forts at will and hang and shoot British citizens without fear of reprisal."

"This will not be tolerated by the British, I can almost assure you," Robert A., the former slave, stated seriously with an exaggerated English accent.

"I pray you are right, Robert," Gasparilla answered hopefully. "If the English bring armies to deal with Jackson and his marauding scoundrels on the land, then we will join with their Royal Navy to defeat them on the seas."

"And, if the British do not?" Brutal Betsy asked in almost a whisper.

"Then we will have no choice. We cannot stay here and defeat the Americans," Gasparilla declared. "We will need to seek out a new home in South America. We have acquired millions and millions of dollars. Perhaps it is good that we become gentlemen farmers in a country like Venezuela where my cousin serves the governor of the Province of Caracas."

"We will stand with you no matter where, José, "Miguel Rodriquez confidently. "You have always made the right decisions for all of us."

"Previously, I always felt confident about the decisions we made, but now with the changes in our world, I am beginning to lose faith in myself," Gasparilla said quietly. "I believe that an organization can grow too large or try to govern too big a territory. If you become too large, then you lose the ability to make quick decisions and take immediate action."

The Confederation members agreed that if England and/or Spain did not declare war on the American invaders of Spanish Florida, they would leave the territory of Florida for the new republics in South America.

The Confederation members, a proud and brave lot, also decided to attack American flagged vessels and quoting Brutal Betsy, "give these Americans some bad memories." During the period of 1818 through 1821, Confederation vessels were involved in nearly 3,000 engagements with a variety of vessels in both the Gulf of Mexico and Atlantic Ocean. Some estimates indicate that the Confederation confiscated over six million dollars during this three-year period.

Gasparilla met with Jean Lafitte for the last time in the fall of 1818 and the two old friends agreed that there was no way to defeat the Americans without the English declaring war on the United States.

"Lord Castlereagh, the British foreign secretary, is too interested in the material and money that trade with the United States can bring the crown," Gasparilla argued. "Hell, he is so completely consumed with fixing the border of Canada and the United States that he will sacrifice a few British deaths to avoid another war with the United States."

"You are right, my friend," Lafitte agreed. "I am planning to bury a great amount of my wealth before I go to an island off Texas."

"How are you doing it?" Gasparilla smiled, not expecting an answer.

"Well, you know how often people are superstitious about gravesites," Lafitte began. "I bury my treasures near a false grave where I erect a tombstone. On the tombstone, beneath a fictitious name, I then inscribe information regarded as important in the deceased person's life. In reality this information tells me the latitude, longitude, and other information needed to find the exact spot where I buried the treasure. I then keep it in our burial book which has no apparent value and is seldom destroyed by our enemies if captured."

"Very interesting, I will need to consider your methods for some of my treasure," Gasparilla smiled while pondering the thought. "It makes a great deal of sense."

"Better sense than Luis Aury is making," Lafitte said sarcastically, regarding the former Frenchman who had left the French Navy in New Orleans in 1810. Aury then bought a Swedish schooner from Lafitte. Aury still owed Lafitte money when the Americans first seized the ship, claiming it was a privateer working for England.

"Aury has captained more ships than most men ever sail upon," Gasparilla chuckled.

"If it were only the money, I could laugh with you, but now the damn fool has captured Amelia Island and claimed it for Mexico," Lafitte said shaking his head in disbelief. "Then I heard that he was drafting a constitution declaring a Republic of the Floridas."

What happened?" Gasparilla asked inquisitively leaning forward.

"Obviously President Monroe had enough and sent a fleet of American ships against our ex-friend," Lafitte said and then, lowering his voice, he added reluctantly, "I hear tell that the American fleet was commanded by a handsome young captain of Spanish descent."

"What are you saying?" Gasparilla rose, grabbing Lafitte's shoulder.

"José, my friend, I must tell you that José Pedro Gonzalvo Gaspar is now a ship's captain in the United States Navy. I am told that, like you, he is a skillful and daring sailor. I have heard he will soon join the American 'mosquito fleet' in the Keys," Lafitte stated.

"Why? How can that be?" Gasparilla stammered. "I would have thought he would return to Spain at his first opportunity."

"After his capture by the British, he was rescued by the Americans. He was impressed with the Americans and sought to join their navy to continue his fight against the British." Lafitte paused and continued, "After the war ended, José was given the choice of either going back to Spain or staying in the United States Navy. Well, with the trouble Spain is currently in, he chose to stay an officer with the Americans."

"Well, I'll be. . . . " Gasparilla began to interrupt but Lafitte continued talking.

"Not only that but he was chosen to sea trial a swift, new twelve-gun schooner, which the Americans hope to use to stop the slave trade," Lafitte added breathlessly.

"My son is following in the family tradition," José stated proudly. "He detests the slave trade and loves swift ships. I only hope that they never use those schooners against us. I would give almost anything to see my son and to talk with him—to tell him of his beautiful mother and the life we had as a family before . . . ."

The two looked directly at one another, a long pause ensued, and then they changed topics, each man knowing what the other was thinking.

"Luis Aury brings the American Navy down on the Atlantic side with his crazy ideas and slave trader mentality. Henry Caesar and his men capture a shipload of innocent men, women, and children off Sanibel Island. I see no possibility that we can avoid future naval confrontations with the Americans," Gasparilla sighed as he slumped down in a chair.

"I agree, it won't be long until we have no markets for our booty," Lafitte replied mournfully.

"As I always say, too many people are the problem," Gasparilla answered, " Pirate confederations depend upon some isolation in order to operate efficiently. We must leave Florida before we are crowded out."

"It takes decades to develop a business and a reputation and a matter of days to see it destroyed," Lafitte lamented. "You are right, José, we are getting too old for this."

At that moment, Bowles rushed in breathlessly, "I have bad news. Do you remember Commodore David Porter of the American Navy?"

"Why, yes, we escorted him when he sailed to New Orleans on the *Enterprise*," Gasparilla answered. "Did something happen to him?"

"Not exactly," Bowles answered. "But, I have learned that he is taking command of newly built American schooners with orders to stop the slave trade and end the piracy in these waters."

"That is not good news," Gasparilla said sadly.

"It gets worse, José. Your son has been ordered to command one of the ships seeking to destroy us."

Gaspar felt the cold blade of dismay slice his heart. He knew that like his father, the young captain would loyally follow orders.

CHAPTER 46

The Dream Ends

"A mere madness, to live like a wretch and die rich."
—Robert Burton, English author, 1577-1640

"There is no turning back now, Captain," Moses shouted, awakening Gasparilla from his pleasant daydream."

Gasparilla squinted into the bright mid-afternoon sun, as the barnacled *Doña Rosalita* moved slowly with the outgoing tide, past the massive fortifications on Cayo Costa. Once outside the defensive protection of the two forts and the waters of Charlotte Harbor, the tiny crew and the creaking old ship were on their own against this unidentified intruder.

"This brigantine captain teases us like a flamenco dancer! It is strange, but I feel as if I know what he thinks," Gasparilla reflected as he stood next to Moses at the helm. "Damn, I don't like the feeling that I have for this. One should never be tentative and should give himself fully to any endeavor."

"I know, Captain, I have a wife, three kids, and more money than I ever dreamed of having," Moses answered, "I have my freedom, thanks to you. I must not have a sound mind, though, to be doing something as stupid as this."

"This ship is a hulk of what it used to be. The bottom is badly eaten with worms, the sails are tattered," Gasparilla sighed, "and the barnacles are so thick below the water line that I fear we are scraping bottom."

"Aye, Captain, and she is so heavy she is not responding well to my commands," Moses said in a strained voice. "We should not be pursuing any prey with this ship."

Most of the lower-deck cannon had been removed from the deck of the ship for use on Cayo Pelau, and Gasparilla had them replaced with trunks of palm trees painted black. Gasparilla told many of his followers that he could not bear to deflower his first flagship. But now, with a skeleton crew of only thirty-four sailors and only twelve working cannon, the *Doña Rosalita* was ill-prepared for a skirmish.

The merchant brigantine made a sharp turn west toward the open Gulf of Mexico. The maneuver seemed familiar to Gasparilla who, sensing a trick, ordered the *Doña Rosalita* to return to Gasparilla Island. The *Doña Rosalita* grabbed a gust of afternoon sea breeze and began turning back towards the safety of Charlotte Harbor.

Santos Veslasquez, the youthful leader of the younger sailors ran breathlessly up to Gasparilla, "Captain, what are you doing? The merchant ship escapes."

"I have many years of engaging merchant vessels," Gasparilla shouted, looking the younger man straight in the eyes, "and I can tell you that ship's captain and crew are not simple merchant seamen. The move they just made was brilliant seamanship. I fear we have been tricked, Veslasquez."

"But, she is a simple merchant vessel," Veslasquez protested.

"Maybe, but her captain and crew are too great a challenge for this ship and this crew at this time," Gasparilla replied. "We shall be lucky to get back to our island. Look, the merchant vessel is now pursuing us!"

Nearly everyone on the deck turned to stare at the intruder. They gasped almost in unison as the unidentified merchant ship dropped large false facades from the hull of the ship. Beneath the disguise, which fell into the foaming blue water beneath the prow of the ship, was a twelve-gun American schooner warship!

Unlike the legendary Trojan Horse that made it safely inside the walls of Troy, this American Trojan Horse had lured Gasparilla from the safety of the harbor. Two miles offshore, well beyond the range of the land fortifications of La Costa and Boca Grande, Gasparilla was vulnerable.

Gasparilla remembered how just months earlier, Commodore Daniel Patterson, the American hero with whom the Confederation ships had sailed during the War of 1812, had attempted to penetrate the defenses of the Confederation at Charlotte Harbor. His small squadron had been driven away by effective artillery shelling from the Cayo Costa fort.

Later, Patterson had attempted to sail into Tampa Bay but was repelled by more Confederation vessels that controlled the commerce and fishing of the great harbor. Patterson's small fleet, with three vessels damaged in the two actions, returned to New Orleans. Gasparilla now realized this had been a mission to probe his defenses.

Now he understood why just one month ago, the American Navy under David Prescott had sailed within easy eyesight of Gasparilla's forces up and down the west coast. No doubt, Prescott was sending a silent message that soon piracy would no longer be tolerated.

With the sale of Florida to the United States on July 17, 1821, Gasparilla decided that the Confederation should relocate to the new Spanish republics in South America. He was within twenty-four hours of leaving Florida as a rich man and yet here was an American warship pursuing him.

"The American is rigged at full sail and is gaining on us," Miguel shouted to his old friend. "We will never make it back to the harbor."

"We do not need to make it all the way back," Gasparilla yelled back. "If we can only make it within range of our shore batteries, our pursuer will need to break away. Order our stern cannon loaded and fired. This will send a message both to our American enemy and our shore battery as well."

The *Doña Rosalita* shook violently as the two twenty-four pounders fired. The shells splashed harmlessly in front of the intruder. The firing of the cannon actually propelled the ancient ship so Gasparilla ordered another salvo. The roar and smoke filled the clear air and roused the remaining Confederation sailors on shore to action.

Just a few days earlier, when the seven sleek Confederation schooners were in residence at Cayo Pelau, Gasparilla's tactics would have alerted his captains and, combined with the devastating shore batteries, this intruder would easily have been captured or destroyed. But this was November, not October, and the strategy was ineffective; he had sent the schooners to South America.

"That captain knows he must overtake us before we get to the mouth of the harbor. God, he is smart! Look. He turns port into the outgoing tide and unfurls a jib sail," Gasparilla shouted in obvious appreciation. "He is doing exactly what I would do. He is taking his ship out of range of the shore batteries while using the current and sea breeze to pass us. In fact, right now he is shadowing us, keeping us between our shore cannon and him. That captain is a genius!"

As Gasparilla turned to shout an order to the helmsman, a roar of thunder came from *Doña Rosalita's* port side. The American had fired six cannon and as Gasparilla turned back, he saw the shells explode on the deck of his beloved ship.

The shrapnel tore into the vessel and the men on her deck. Gasparilla's youngest warriors screamed in agony as they lay bleeding where they fell. The grapeshot, intended to disable the tattered sails, had instead landed directly upon them, tearing off their limbs and disemboweling them. The white sand, spread on the deck for traction, turned crimson with blood.

The gun crew on the second deck of the *Doña Rosalita* managed to fire a round at the American warship and landed two shells into its rigging. A muffled cheer came from below; however, the gunners below had no idea that half their comrades lay dead or dying just above them.

The intruding warship turned a hard tack to starboard in an attempt to ram the *Doña Rosalita* before it could get inside the umbrella of safety that the shore batteries would provide.

Gasparilla ordered the *Doña Rosalita* hard-to-port in an effort to avoid being rammed and to force the American ship to expose itself to the La Costa fortress guns.

The American craft turned even sharper to starboard to insure a collision with the pirate vessel. "Another brilliant move!" Gasparilla agonized out loud.

Within minutes the grinding, cracking collision took place. The American ship rode up on the smoking deck of the treasure-heavy *Doña Rosalita*. The name of the American ship was plainly visible—*Alligator*.

Gasparilla pulled his sword and pistol from his waist. He yelled for the crew to grab muskets and swords to prepare for hand-to-hand combat, and anxiously watched to see if the American sailors would scramble on board from their ship.

A loud crack and shudder from within the innards of the *Doña Rosalita* signaled to Gasparilla that his wonderful old ship was seriously damaged. Men crowded up from below and shouted that the pumps could no longer be worked. Water was rushing into the treasure-filled hold. A shift in the cargo caused the *Alligator* to slip off her deck.

As Gasparilla raced to the port side of his stricken vessel, he looked just twenty-feet across the water into the eyes of the American ship's captain. It was his son.

Instinctively, and without speaking, the younger man solemnly saluted the elderly pirate captain. Time was suspended and seconds seemed like hours. The old man nodded, saluted back, and pointed to his broken ship. The son broke the silence. "Father, please surrender to me. Your old friend Stephen Decatur, who died in a duel last year, signed a pardon for you for your service in the War of 1812—if you will only surrender and leave Florida and the Caribbean. The pardon expires at the end of this year, which is why I came to ask your surrender," the younger Gaspar pleaded.

"That may be fine for me, but what about the thousands who have faithfully followed me all these years?" Gasparilla shouted back. "No, my son, I have an obligation and a responsibility to all the loyal citizens of our Confederation. You can understand that, can't you? Some people are born with leadership and others achieve it. In this instance I have had it thrust upon me but it doesn't lessen my responsibilities."

"But, father, I love you. You are a brilliant captain and I have tried to emulate your seamanship. I graduated from the academy in Cadiz, served Spain bravely and well, fought the British, but became their prisoner. Then the Americans rescued me and offered me a position in their navy. They pay twice as much as any navy in the world," José volunteered. "Please father, there is so much I need to learn from you about our family and about your experiences."

"The family from which you come has a fine and proud heritage," Gasparilla sadly smiled. "But the family you come from is not nearly as important as the family you will have in the future. I always hoped to be a grandfather." Gasparilla ripped the purse from around his neck and tossed it the short distance to his son. The younger Gaspar grabbed the pouch and opened it.

"The glove you will find was the one your mother was wearing the first day I met her. The handkerchief was from our wedding day," Gasparilla shouted. "The lock of hair I took from your mother after Spain killed her. The map is for you to find my personal share of treasure and share it with the family I shall never see."

"But, father, please . . .," the young Gaspar began.

Gasparilla, with sword and pistol still in hand ran to his friend, Miguel Rodriquez and whispered, "I shall force the Americans to deal with me. While they are distracted, escape into the harbor. It will be your only chance. Take care of yourself, my friend, and give my regards to the others in our brotherhood."

Miguel took the wheel to try to maneuver the damaged vessel.

Gasparilla then leaped to the charred and smoking main deck and went to the main mast. Removing the red Confederation flag, he wrapped it around his body, then crawled up on the railing so the Americans could see him plainly.

Fearing what his father might do, the younger Gaspar ran to the bow of the *Alligator* shouting, "No, Father, no, please!"

Gasparilla yelled back across the water, "Gasparilla dies by his own hand only, not the enemy's." That said, still wrapped in the heavy red flag, he dove head first into the blue waters of the gulf.

As Gasparilla had predicted, the *Alligator* immediately went to the spot where he had entered the water and a desperate young Gaspar ordered his crew to search until dark for his father. As expected, the search allowed Miguel Rodriquez and surviving crew members escape with the heavily listing *Doña Rosalita*. Skillful sailing allowed the ship to round the northern end of Cayo Costa and proceed into the shallow bay behind, where the *Doña Rosalita* slowly, gently, rolled on her side and partially sank as the men scrambled off. It was a peaceful, surreal scene as the late afternoon sun cast long shadows. The gold leaf name—*Doña Rosalita*—sparkled in the last rays of sun. As the crew swam to shore, many thought she was a stately ship, even in repose.

In the gulf, the American warship, *Alligator*, crisscrossed the spot where Gasparilla had vanished. As the lingering sunset subsided, hopes of finding the old pirate alive faded as well. A shaken José Pedro Gonzalvo Gaspar leaned over the railing for one last look at the darkening water. He pressed to his cheek a small leather pouch and choked out the order, "Sail on!"

About the Author

James F. Kaserman is an educator and businessman and has served in public office for more than ten years. Following graduation from Washington High School in Massillon, Ohio, he earned a bachelor's degree in business administration from Kent State University and a master's degree in educational administration from the University of Dayton. He was honorably discharged with the rank of staff sergeant from the United States Army.

Kaserman has been a newspaper columnist and currently serves as coordinator of the Business and Industry Services program for the Lee County School District. He became interested in the truth about pirates when doing research studies of government and business organizations, and concluded that pirate organizations had many similarities to the businesses of today.

Kaserman is married to Sarah Jane, is the father of two sons and a grandfather, and has lived in Fort Myers, Florida, since 1985.